D1604334

A GERMAN COMMUNITY
UNDER AMERICAN OCCUPATION

———

Stanford Studies in History, Economics,
and Political Science, XXI

JOHN GIMBEL

A German Community
under
American Occupation

Marburg, 1945-52

STANFORD UNIVERSITY PRESS
STANFORD, CALIFORNIA
1961

STANFORD UNIVERSITY PRESS
STANFORD, CALIFORNIA

LIBRARY OF CONGRESS CATALOG CARD NUMBER: 61-7798

PRINTED IN THE UNITED STATES OF AMERICA

PUBLISHED WITH THE ASSISTANCE OF
THE FORD FOUNDATION

Acknowledgments

There are many people to whom the author is deeply indebted for their direct and indirect contribution to this study. A special word of appreciation is due Oberbürgermeister Gassmann of Marburg for permitting me to study the files in the city hall and to Karl Seibel who guided me through the municipal files and provided office space for study; to Landrat Eckel for permitting me to study the files in the Landratsamt and to Richard Bromm who guided me through the Landkreis files; to Guy A. Lee, who did so much to help me gain access to the files in the U.S. High Commissioner's Office in Germany and who helped me in many ways; to Jesse Pitts, who pulled and refiled hundreds of folders from the military government files in Kansas City, and who readily shared his knowledge about the retired military government records; to Hermann Bauer, Eugen Siebecke, and Ludwig Mütze, who in addition to giving me many hours of their time for interviews also shared their personal papers with me; to the numerous other Americans and Germans who gave me as much as eighty hours of their time for interviews, and who answered long questionnaires and detailed letters; to Earl Pomeroy, Eric Kollman, Eugene Davidson, and my colleagues at Luther College and Humboldt State College, who read all or portions of the work in its various stages; and to my wife, Gisela, who typed, translated, read, and encouraged whenever the occasion demanded her services. The two chapters on denazification, Chapters 9 and 10, have appeared in much the same form in the *American Political Science Review* for March 1960.

Among those who contributed materially to this project are

the University of Oregon, with a Carnegie Fellowship in Social Science; the U.S. Government, with a Fulbright Research Grant in Germany; the State University of Iowa, with a summer research honorarium; and Luther College and the Board of Christian Education of the Evangelical Lutheran Church, with a grant-in-aid and other material assistance.

J.G.

Contents

A GERMAN COMMUNITY
UNDER AMERICAN OCCUPATION

1

Introduction

This book is more than a case report on the occupation of Marburg. Although it does not pretend to be a microscopic study of the American occupation as a whole or a detailed object lesson for those who may find it useful in the future, it does have a number of definite objectives.

It examines, in detail, the activities of an American military government detachment at the lowest administrative level to suggest what an analysis of a larger unit might reveal.

It attempts to elucidate the political thinking of Americans who tried deliberately to direct the course of postwar German development toward peace, democracy, and free enterprise.

It describes the impact of the occupation on a German community and shows how that community responded to produce, if not a complete eclipse, certainly the effective disillusionment of those forces that might have aided in the reconstruction of a peaceful, democratic (probably not free-enterprise) Germany of the type Americans seem to have sought. Further, it shows how the disillusionment of certain groups permitted the assumption of leadership, at the local level, by others whose political, social, and economic views bear a striking similarity to those of the leaders of the same community who proved so ineffective in the face of the Nazi challenge.

Finally, it shows that in failing to attract a German leadership sympathetic toward the American program in Germany, in fact succeeding in disillusioning what leadership potential of this sort there was, the American occupation gave rise to a strain of anti-

American sentiment among even the most democratically inclined Germans and provided them with a convincing rationale for that sentiment.

The detailed study which follows attempts, first, to show how such unexpected developments occurred and, second, to suggest why they took place. The analysis seems to require a summary, at the outset, of both the aims and the method of military government. The method employed is reasonably clear, and included four basic elements:

1. Identification and removal of the ruling Nazi elite.
2. Identification and destruction (or modification) of the institutions by which the Nazi elite maintained itself in power.
3. Substitution of new or transformed institutions within which a new leadership could grow and function.
4. Encouragement and support of a new leadership to take the place of the removed Nazi elite.

The objectives that this method were supposed to achieve and the assumptions upon which it rested are much more difficult to discern. There was the long-range objective of a peaceful, democratic Germany, expressed in the two major policy statements governing the occupation and apparently impressed on the hearts of those who crusaded for democracy in Europe. But the ultimate ideal was obscured by intrusions of the more eclectic immediate objectives and by the vacillations of military government policy. Denazification, which began as an American purge, became a German-administered program in 1946, lost its emphasis upon vengeance and became narrower in scope during 1946 and 1947, and was eventually abandoned abruptly as an American program in 1948. Decentralization, which Americans pressed upon Germans and flouted in practice, gave local German administrators a close-up of the dichotomy of American theory and practice. Demilitarization, which was accomplished with dispatch in 1945, was forgotten after the final collapse of four-power control in 1948 and gradually changed to rearmament about 1950. Industrial dismantlement proceeded apace until differences in interpretation of the Potsdam reparations agreements brought a partial halt in 1946 and final abandonment as first the Bi-Zone, then the West Zone, and finally the Federal Republic resumed production. Americans hoped to achieve civil service reform, educational reform, and democratization first by influencing their appointed and elected German counterparts and the agencies created by Germans freely elected at the local and state level. But, about 1948, the American emphasis changed to political rehabilitation and reorientation, which would occur at the grass-roots level and go over the heads of local officials and agencies.

The changes in American policy and its application between 1945 and 1949 are crucial to the interpretation of American objectives. One obvious and important reason for the change was the all-pervasive problem of the increasing East-West conflict not only in Germany, but also in France, Italy, Greece, Turkey, Czechoslovakia, and Asia. Had this been the only reason, Americans could rightly be accused of deliberately and systematically adjusting their occupation policies to promote their more important long-range national and international interests; they could be charged with having changed their emphasis from vengeance and security to one of reconstruction and friendship to win a new and powerful Germany as an ally in the cold war.

But, if the intentions found in the case study are typical, Americans in Germany seem to have been truly motivated by a passion for democracy. Accordingly, the policy changes may be interpreted as being based in part upon internal considerations. Denazification was placed under German control because it was felt that the local institutions were sufficiently revived by 1946 to permit German participation at this level. Moreover, it offered Germans the opportunity and the privilege to purge their own communities of Nazis, to assume responsibility under their new leadership, and to have a stake in the changes that would ensue. Reorientation was a logical, positive democratization effort following upon the more punitive, negative programs of denazification, demilitarization, and decentralization. Industrial dismantlement could not continue in a divided Germany, one sector of which needed to import large quantities of food to exist. Thus, it may be argued, the program of the early years of the occupation was altered by new directives emphasizing reconstruction in accordance with changed conditions. The later policies were only possible, of course, after the passions aroused by violent ideological warfare had been somewhat subdued.

Despite the fact that the changes in American policy were conditioned by a combination of the cold war's influence and changed conditions in Germany, Americans in charge of the local community were unable to convince a significant number of Germans that the changes in policy would achieve, or were even designed to achieve, the long-range ideal of peace and democracy. The basic reason for this failure in communication escaped both Americans and Germans at the local level. To be sure, a host of studies on various phases of military government have explained the failure in terms of faulty method: Americans conceived their policies too cavalierly, applied them too haphazardly, and publicized them inadequately. Nevertheless, a more fundamental reason impresses itself upon the researcher. In applying their policies at the local level (perhaps also in formulating the policies) Americans proceeded as though the origin and evolution of democracy is a natural process that needs only to be guarded against evil agents who would block that process. They seemed to hope, in vain, that a new democratic leadership would arise in Germany and freely and readily (instinctively?) accept the American image of democracy and thus also accept the American administrative necessities and policy changes as prerequisites to the attainment of democracy. Philosophically stated, Americans hoped that the new democratic leadership in Germany, once freed from the *Gleichschaltung* of totalitarian Nazism, would translate—or permit and aid Americans to translate—the "general will" into concrete social, political, and economic action.

Americans at the local level apparently neither tried to identify the organized, powerful, traditional German interest groups who had an important stake in the results of the occupation, nor offered concessions and rewards to such groups to gain their support and acceptance. Instead, they chose to remain relatively neutral toward

German political, social, and economic groups, except when the latter presented a threat to the occupation. In effect, military government stood above these groups, in part because of the passions of the recent war and its resultant theory of collective guilt, but also because of military government's apparent operating assumption that such groups were in essence "general" interest groups, good government groups, "family affairs," dedicated to the promotion of the general welfare and needing only to be purged of Nazi influences to restore them to their natural purposes. The effect, at the local level, was to cause a tremendous struggle within and among local interest groups for power and status, causing Germans who participated to believe that military government deliberately and systematically perpetuated the chaos of 1945 for the purpose of achieving either its long-range national interests or a social, economic, and political revolution—an "artificial" revolution, in the words of one American analyst. For example, denazification and personnel policies in Marburg seemed to play into the hands first of Communists and other radicals, later of conservatives, nationalists, and ex-Nazis, all groups with which military government obviously did not identify itself. None of these groups sympathized with the ideals of the American occupation, and the liberals and moderates who did sympathize found themselves unable to move into positions of power and leadership. Thus, the effect of American efforts was to disillusion the occupation's most loyal supporters and to bring forth people who disagreed with Americans about the extent and intent of denazification itself; people who disagreed with Americans about municipal and county government codes, the nature of the civil service, the structure and purpose of education, the proper political party organization and proper electoral procedures, the extent of industrial disarmament, the value of grass-roots political activities, and many other things.

A backward look at the occupation of Marburg might prompt the conclusion that Americans in Germany after 1945 might well have proceeded differently; that they should have treated German organizations that they found as "special" interest groups, veto groups, check-and-balance groups, who struggle for power and position regardless of Nazis although not oblivious of Nazis. Accordingly, Americans at the local level might have decided which German interest groups could be used to further the general principles of the occupation and pledge them military government support. In Marburg such a course would have meant supporting a coalition of Social Democrats, Liberal Democrats, and Christian Democrats. Since these were also the parties that dominated the political committee early in the occupation, this course would have been realistic.

Obviously, the concessions that military government would have had to make to achieve an operational compromise with these forces are important. It appears reasonable to assume, for example, that a good many people whom denazification laws defined as Nazis would have been left untouched provided they collaborated with the new regime; industrial dismantlement would have been curbed to give the new regime a sound economic base and provide employment for refugees; a certain amount of nationalization of industry might have been necessary to hold the Social Democrats in a powerful political coalition; the civil service would probably have been modified, but not to permit—in contradiction to deeply held German convictions—certain equalities in the higher and lower ranks or advancement from the lower to the higher positions as demanded by Americans early in the occupation; educational reform would have been much less pronounced than Americans desired—it probably would not have abolished the differentiated schools from grade five on—but it would have included some curricular and structural changes; and last, political activity at the grass roots would undoubtedly have followed the traditional German pattern, rather than the grass-roots town-hall and public-forum type of activities promoted by Americans.

The historian who presumes to pass upon the errors of the past and suggest alternatives that might have produced other results cannot ignore his more important role of analysis. The analysis of military government operations at the local level leads to an understanding of the events, conditions, problems, and contingencies that perhaps led Americans to choose the course and produce the effect they did, rather than to choose an alternative that might have produced other results. The early emphasis upon collective guilt, nonfraternization, and denazification—in fact, the impact of the violent ideological war just completed—precluded any serious cooperation between military government and German political, social, and economic interest groups, no matter where the latter stood. The same factors also precluded the possibility of a military occupation accompanied by responsible local government. By the time the impact of the ideological war had become less and the Americans had begun to work through German groups by granting local self-government, the cold war was a fact and it appeared, to Germans, as if Americans had merely changed their enemies.

In addition to the assumptions noted above, the contingencies of the occupation are important to the analysis of its course and its effectiveness. The immensity and complexity of the task of military government were themselves staggering. Denazification consumed tremendous amounts of time and energy and seemingly would have required supernatural powers of judgment and organization to function smoothly and justly for such large numbers in such a short time. The problem of mustering both American and German public opinion to support the entire American program was immense. The recruitment, training, and retention of personnel adequate for and dedicated to the task of military government were extremely difficult. The personnel who served in the field detachments were chosen because they possessed some special skill, but not necessarily because they had been trained to administer, control, or supervise a unit of German government. Many had experience as civil affairs officers in France, in Belgium, or in the other liberated countries; but the complete collapse of organized government in Germany was a novel situation. *Kreis* (district) detachments were relatively isolated and almost always far removed from command headquarters. They operated in a strange land where people spoke a language foreign to their comprehension and use. They had to draw upon Germans as interpreters and investigators. The specific information available to them about the area to which they were assigned was limited and out of date, and what they gathered on the spot contained biases which escaped their attention. Detachment officers were deluged by Germans who denounced their compatriots, and by denouncers who denounced the denouncers. They were busy accommodating troops and refugees in the crucial first months of the occupation when they needed manpower, time, and energy to study the local political situation. They were hampered by the rapid turnover in personnel occasioned by officer and enlisted personnel who sought quick demobilization and by others who wanted transfers into military government. They were perplexed by Germans who expressed sympathy with the occupation's general aims, but who disagreed with the details of military government administration. Many of them asserted that they had been unable to do anything about the rise of Hitler; and they avowed they knew nothing about the atrocities in the concentration camps; yet some of them admitted that they had made application to join the Nazi party.

Although the assumptions and the particulars are important to the analysis, the dilemma faced by both military government personnel and the German potential leadership is probably basic. It is the age-old dilemma of liberals and moderates not new in Germany or in the postwar period. Scattered on the political continuum between extremists on both ends, liberals and moderates have always been forced to define and redefine their criteria for action in the light of conditions over which they have no immediate control. In Germany they were dedicated to the task of installing democracy under grossly unfavorable conditions: the ideals of democracy did not enjoy widespread acceptance, the threat of Communist revolution was strong, and the agents of power held office by military force. As a result they took action which did not conform precisely to the very ideals they were trying to promote. As in the past Robespierre (and Babeuf) called forth different action from liberals and moderates than did Louis XVI, Daniel Shays than George III, Louis Blanc than Louis Philippe,

Winstanley than Charles I, so in Germany the threat of Nazism
and the threat of international Communism called forth actions
from Americans and Germans that changed as the occupation
evolved. The point, and central to the thesis developed, is that
liberals and moderates in each of the instances were forced by the
actions of their primary enemies to adjust, redefine, reappraise,
even compromise, their own criteria of action and seek coalitions
to gain power or maintain themselves in power.

The complication arose, in Germany, because Americans
seemed to change their point of reference (their primary enemies)
and thus their policies on the basis of their evaluation of over-all
world politics, whereas the German liberal and moderate, whose
status as an occupied enemy gave him no voice in foreign affairs
and who had to live in the community long after the occupation
would end, necessarily had a stronger domestic and provincial
interest than Americans. The Americans, bearing the responsibilities of power and faced with the immediate administrative
problem of removing Nazis and Nazi institutions, concentrated
their efforts first upon totalitarian Nazism as the *chief* enemy of a
future democratic Germany. The liberal Germans at the local
level agreed, but at the same time they saw a distinct danger in
the fact that Communists and left-wing Social Democrats were
using the denazification program to achieve power locally. Eventually, as American emphasis on vengeance and safety turned to
reform and recovery, as four-power control in Berlin failed, and
as the cold war developed, the Americans saw and admitted officially that Communist totalitarianism was the *chief* threat to a
future democratic Germany. The same Germans agreed again,
but now they saw a distinct danger from the right; conservatives
and ex-Nazis regained political stature (having suffered little economically and socially, they had little to regain) as denazification
passed into limbo and the rearmament of Germany assumed
paramount importance.

It goes without saying that Americans were not oblivious to
the local problems their policies raised; nor were Marburgers
oblivious to the international problems faced by the Americans.

Nevertheless each had to choose between alternative actions on the basis of their judgment about the past, the present, and the future. Neither can be expected to have chosen a course that would bring them defeat or annihilation. Accordingly, the American decision to denazify thoroughly was basically no better or worse than the German liberals' opposition to the purge; the Americans' decision to permit and promote a strong West Germany was basically no better or worse than the German liberals' opposition based on fear of a revived conservative-Nazi coalition, and so on. The evidence from the case study suggests that each group—military government's representatives and Marburg's liberals and moderates—was prone to identify its own hopes and interests with the general welfare. However, since effective power resided with the occupation forces, they, rather than the German liberals, were in a position to make concessions which they could withdraw because they had power. Thus, military government bears the responsibility for failing to adopt a position permitting an operational compromise with the socialists, liberals, and moderates who might have come a long way (not all the way) toward the idea of peace and democracy sought by military government.

One other purpose seems to be served by a detailed examination of a German community under American occupation. It provides a basis for clarifying certain portions of two recent significant studies of the occupation. Lewis J. Edinger's statistical studies* of the present ruling elite in the Federal Republic seem to leave one important question unanswered. If the elite was neither strongly Nazi nor strongly anti-Nazi, if it was neither a strong supporter nor a strong opponent of the Nazi regime, what is its essential characteristic? The case study of Marburg suggests the possibility that Edinger's "coalition of elites" is rather strongly anti-American and that it has available to it—even though unused at present—a convincing rationale for its anti-Americanism. Second, John D.

* Lewis J. Edinger, "Post-Totalitarian Leadership: Elites in the German Federal Republic," *The American Political Science Review*, LIV (March 1960), 58–82.

Montgomery* has presented the thesis that American policy in Germany—albeit haphazardly applied—was in effect a design for an artificial revolution. American policy was punitive in the sense that it removed the Nazi elite and permissive in the sense that it created reformed institutions within which a new elite could function, even if that elite had to be created or encouraged by the occupation. By this subtle method, Mr. Montgomery tells us, Americans hoped to force Germans to be free. The details of the case study do not support Montgomery's thesis, which seems to minimize the intended scope of denazification (by telescoping its chronology and by looking to actual practice) and which ascribes to American policy an order and rationality that is not discernible in the haphazard attempts at American reform and reorientation in Germany.

* John D. Montgomery, *Forced to Be Free, The Artificial Revolution in Germany and Japan* (Chicago: University of Chicago Press, 1957).

PART ONE

The Setting

2

Marburg, March 1945

A short two hours before Marburg capitulated on March 29, 1945, a handful of people waited anxiously at the station for the early-morning train from the south. They were eager to learn whether it was true that advancing enemy tank columns had arrived in Giessen, or whether the passengers had seen enemy patrols. Some of them hoped and most of them were convinced that the war was lost and that an early end of the fighting would forestall needless death and destruction. They had not long to wait. The last broadcast of the Giessen air observer station that morning had warned that American forces were in a small village between Marburg and Giessen and that the main road was cut off.

Marburg revealed great diversity of opinion, behavior, and expectations on the day it surrendered. There was at once an atmosphere of normalcy and of confusion. Although they knew that invasion was imminent, the mayor and most of his staff went to the city hall. The courthouse staff went to work as usual. The police reported for duty. A university professor, unconcerned with reality, spent the morning writing in his study, from which he could see the broad, peaceful Lahn River Valley extending toward Giessen. Later he wrote that he saw the American troops come up the valley. A Social Democrat who had been politically active in the Weimar Republic walked out to meet the American tank column that the Allied radio reported to be near Marburg. A free-lance writer and former Nazi party member who had been asked to leave the party in 1932 sat in the garret of his house watching for a sign of approaching tanks. Marburg's first postwar *Oberbürgermeister* (Lord Mayor) sat frightened among his beehives in a small nearby village. He feared not the Americans but the Nazis who, he believed, would make one last, determined effort to wipe out their opposition before the enemy arrived. Families living near the railroad station had, wherever possible, moved in with relatives or friends up on the hill and farther away from this target of American planes. The foreign laborers in the camps in and around Allendorf—the location of one of the largest explosives manufacturing plants in Germany—were restive but still worked. But there were rumors that they planned to release both criminals and political prisoners from the Marburg prisons. In a village near Marburg a citizen who during better times had erected a high flagpole from which he proudly flew the swastika stole out on the eve of capitulation and sawed the pole off near the ground. In Marburg a couple committed suicide. The first military government officer in Marburg thought they had been Nazis and that they feared punishment by their neighbors. Some members of the *Volkssturm* (home guard) deserted and returned to their homes. Leading Nazi party officials and members of the Marburg military post had fled—some in hope of continuing the war, probably most of them simply out of despair. Not all of them fled. The *Kreisleiter* (district Nazi party leader), who was also the *Landrat* (county executive), remained. To keep alive hopes of resistance he publicly wore the uniform of a Volkssturm noncommissioned officer. But he did this, it was reported, only after his wife had safely fled eastward by automobile. Most Marburgers, however, seemed to have resigned themselves to remain, to surrender, and to place themselves at the mercy of the invading armies. Among the latter were a few who had proposed to the Oberbürgermeister and the Landrat that Marburg surrender peaceably. The remainder prepared for surrender by keeping bedsheets, or anything large and white, ready to hang out their windows as soon as enemy troops reached Marburg.

Marburg capitulated without resistance. The troops that might have defended the area had failed to return after leaving toward the south during the night of March 24–25. The Oberbürgermeister had secret orders to defend the city, but the remaining troops, and the Volkssturm—spiritless, old men who were convinced of the futility of further struggle, and impetuous youths who might have spoiled the efforts to surrender without battle— were ineffective because the weapons they hastily gathered had no ammunition. Sporadic fighting took place on the outskirts of the city. From a hillside forest overlooking the Lahn Valley a machine gun opened fire on the advancing American spearhead. The gun was soon silenced, and the Americans entered the city. The police journal for the day contains the notation that shots were heard within the city at nine o'clock. The mayor sent three policemen to investigate. An American patrol captured them in the square immediately below the old university and on the main thorough- fare of the city. Keeping two policemen as captives—and perhaps hostages—the major in command instructed the other to go up the hill to the city hall and tell the mayor that unless Marburg surrendered peacefully the city would be bombarded. The police journal records that by noon the city was in American hands. A few villages and the city of Kirchhain were captured only after minor skirmishes.[1]

Marburgers accepted the occupation of their city with mixed feelings. They were impressed by the apparently endless columns of tanks, trucks, half-tracks, jeeps, and other vehicles of the Ameri- can Army that passed through Marburg's narrow streets. Those who later reflected upon Allied military might declare that the decision to surrender without resistance was a wise one indeed. The German radio propaganda, declaring that Marburg fell only after courageous defensive action, that the mayor chose suicide rather than captivity, and that there was still a chance to regain the offensive, served chiefly to convince the people that they had been given less than the truth in the past.

Many children and some women welcomed the incoming troops. Soldiers distributed chewing gum, candy, cigarettes, and other goodies to the welcomers and the curious indiscriminately. As noted above, some Marburgers actually came out of the city to meet the troops. The Hessian Military Governor's recorded recollection that Hessian towns were "deathly quiet," that they

---

[1] Numbered notes (primarily source citations) will be found at the back of the book, on pages 215-42.

smelled "of death and destruction," and that "faces could be felt, not seen, behind barricaded windows" does not apply to Marburg.[2] It is true though that most people did not appear in the streets and squares when the invading troops entered. Some feared violence. Others believed the propaganda they had heard regarding the ruthlessness of American soldiers. Probably most of them remained momentarily inconspicuous because they did not know what to expect. Some recalled later that they were busy hiding cameras, silverware, clocks, and other portable valuables.

Conditions in Marburg in March 1945 illustrate the confusion of a community under enemy attack. There was a strange mixture of normalcy on the one hand and bewilderment on the other; of loyalty to National Socialism on the one hand and of hope for a new order on the other; of fear and uncertainty on the one hand and of confidence in the future on the other. Since there were no active political and social groups, it is helpful to construct a continuum of political and social types from the sources available to the researcher.[3] Five types emerge clearly.

Marburg's Political and Social Types

The first was the National Socialist functionary who had actively promoted the program and policies of the Nazi regime. He was justly apprehensive of the American occupation of Marburg. Few of his type remained in Marburg when it was occupied. The ones who did were soon arrested and confined by American troops.

The second type that can be constructed was one who accepted, with varying degrees of enthusiasm, the Nazi state and its entire program because it had offered him something in return. It had offered him employment, security in his position, in-group participation, an outlet for nationalistic feelings, personal social prestige if he joined the Nazi party, and a feeling of grandeur. He and his type had apparently associated themselves with the Nazi regime for a variety of reasons, not the least of which was the feeling that "everybody else was doing it."[4] Milton Mayer, who spent a year studying ten "representative little Nazis" in Marburg, concluded that they did not know about the horror of the concentration camps, that they did not do anything Americans would consider morally wrong, and that they actually believed in the state of emergency that had been declared in 1933. In March 1945 this type of person was disillusioned. His hopes had come to naught, and he learned the awful truth of the concentration camps. He might have been won over to another regime, or to an occupying power, that could offer him something tangible, as the previous regime had done. Unless he was an opportunist, he did not welcome the occupation.

Third was the politically indifferent Marburger. Germans and others mark him by his *"ohne mich"* attitude toward public affairs. The basis for his attitude is a matter of contention. German political leaders attributed it to ignorance, thereby assuring themselves that they were correct in governing without regard for public opinion. The younger party members disagreed. They said the parties discouraged young people, because the party leaders demanded long periods of training and years of service before they placed new members on the ballot. The politically indifferent Marburger expected little change from the occupation. He expected little personal attention from military government and he was unprepared to offer it his own support. He appeared to want to be left to live his own little life.

The fourth was the non-Nazi who wanted little help from abroad in reconstructing Germany. In Marburg he was usually a nationalist, sometimes an internationalist. He had in the past affiliated with either the Social Democratic, the Democratic, the Center, or the Communist party. Regardless of Germany's past mistakes he wanted to rebuild as he thought German history, tradition, and culture demanded. For example, he usually wanted indirect rather than direct political representation, a stratified civil service, with strict entrance requirements for the higher positions, and an educational system with separate schools for the various curricula.

The fifth type was the pro-Allied democrat. He was most willing to cooperate with the incoming occupation troops. He was prepared to give the Americans information about the Nazis in

Marburg and he expected Americans to use his services in rebuilding Germany into a peaceful, democratic state. He was pleased
when the city fell. Some of his type actually went out of the city
to meet the incoming American forces.

One day after Marburg capitulated, an American military government detachment entered the city, to remain some seven years
as the visible hand of the American occupation. The detachment's
impact is the subject of later chapters. We need first to describe the
area over which it had jurisdiction.

The city and county of Marburg have a distinct rural, Protestant, politically conservative character which is typical of north-
central Hessian communities. The city is approximately ninety
miles east of Cologne and lies on the trunk railway some sixty miles
north of Frankfurt am Main and about sixty miles south and west
of Kassel. The Landkreis is surrounded by the rural Landkreise
Frankenberg, Biedenkopf, Wetzlar, Giessen, Ziegenhain, and Als-
feld. Its landscape is generally rolling, divided by two important
river valleys. The Lahn Valley, which enters the Landkreis from
the northwest, passes through Marburg and extends southward in
the direction of Giessen. It is comparatively narrow north of Marburg but broadens to form a rich agricultural plain between Marburg and Giessen. The Ohm River enters the Landkreis from the
east, flows in a northwesterly direction, and empties into the Lahn
a few kilometers north of Marburg at Cölbe. Its valley is very
broad in the Amöneburger Basin east of Kirchhain. The landscape
is further broken by three forest-covered ridges rising to about
twelve hundred feet: the Burgwald in the north, the Marburger
Rücken along the right bank of the Lahn, and the Lahn hills on
the left bank. Wooded areas of lesser elevation, including the
Oberwald, the Seift, and the Herrenwald, in the south and east,
further break the continuity of the landscape.

Transportation and Communication

Marburg's relatively limited demands for transportation are
adequately met by railways and highways. As noted above, Marburg lies on the main railway line that links northern and southern

Germany. A secondary railway, leading from Marburg to Siegen, connects it with cities in the Ruhr industrial area and the Rhineland. Secondary lines also link Marburg with the smaller communities to the north, south, and west. Although the area does not benefit directly from the *Autobahnen* built during the Nazi regime, the Autobahn leading from Frankfurt am Main to the north and east is accessible at Giessen. Marburg is served directly by the Frankfurt-Kassel federal highway, and by highways entering from the west, the northwest, and the north. The railway lines provide the best means of communication and transportation for the area.

Civil Administration

The *Stadtkreis* and the *Landkreis* are separate administrative units of Land Hessen. The Stadtkreis is the municipality of Marburg. During the Weimar Republic municipal government was by an Oberbürgermeister, a Bürgermeister, a *Magistrat* (collegial executive), and a *Stadtverordnetenversammlung* (city council). The Landkreis is a rural administrative unit, comparable to the American county. During the Weimar Republic government was by a Landrat, a *Kreisausschuss* (executive committee), and a *Kreistag* (county legislature). Under the Weimar constitution the Stadtkreis and the Landkreis had achieved a marked degree of self-government. The foundations of local government were universal, equal, direct, and secret suffrage and representative councils—chosen by proportional representation—in the Landkreis, the Stadtkreis, and the Gemeinden. But the positions of the Landrat and the Oberbürgermeister were anomalous. The incumbents were at the same time local officials and state functionaries. The Landrat was appointed by the state, whereas the municipal officers were selected by the Magistrat. The Nazi regime made revolutionary changes in local administration. The local government act of 1935 made the Oberbürgermeister of the Stadtkreis and the Bürgermeisters of the Gemeinden nonelective officials. In practice they were chosen by the Nazi party. The Kreisleiter of the Nazi party became the Landrat of Marburg and other local officials were often Nazi party officials.

After 1945 Hessians patterned their municipal and county government codes after those of the Weimar Republic. Municipal councils (*Gemeindevertretungen* in the villages; *Stadtverordnetenversammlungen* in the city) and the Kreistag are elected by proportional representation. These bodies select the municipal and county officials from applicants who are solicited through public advertisement. The village councils normally select the Bürgermeister from within the council whereas the city council and the Kreistag select municipal and county officials from candidates who have been solicited. The Bürgermeisters (Oberbürgermeister in the Stadtkreis) and the Landrat still function in the dual capacities of local officials and state functionaries. Each is accountable to supervisory officials (*Aufsichtsbehörden*): the Bürgermeisters to the Landrat and the Landrat and the Oberbürgermeister to the *Regierungspräsident,* a district administrator comparable to a French Prefect. The Hessian Minister of Interior is the highest supervisory official. The Hessian municipal code of 1952 states that the supervisory officials can review municipal ordinances, observe municipal government in action, call for oral or written reports, files, and other documents, and generally inquire into municipal affairs. They can participate in municipal council meetings, and can call such meetings for specific purposes. The code gives the supervisory officials authority to nullify resolutions of the municipal councils if they violate the law. Such nullification can be made retroactive. Furthermore, supervisory officials may assign third parties to perform the duties of the municipal government if the elected government fails to do so. Should the need arise, the higher officials can administer a municipality through a commissioner (*Staatskommissar*). The county government code of 1952 permits the supervisory officials to dissolve the Kreistag if it fails to pass resolutions. In that event a new election must take place within three months.[5]

Political Parties

Politically Marburg has had a conservative, nationalist complexion, though in the period since 1945 the Social Democrats have increased their strength in the Stadtkreis and in the Landkreis. Prior to the fall of the Weimar Republic Marburg revealed strong currents of nationalism, conservatism, and anti-Semitism, which apparently provided fertile ground for the early political programs professed by the Nazis. Analyzing the reasons for the success of the Liberal Democratic party in the Marburg elections of 1946 a Marburg military government employee noted that Marburg sent a conservative to the first all-German parliament in 1871. The parliament was predominantly National Liberal, with only three of the twenty-one conservative members coming from west of the Elbe River. He concluded his analysis with the statement: "It is no exaggeration to say that at the moment of the foundation of Bismarck's Reich, Marburg was the most reactionary town in Germany, outside Prussia proper." In 1884 Marburg sent the founder of the local anti-Semitic movement to the Reichstag. But in 1903 "it elected the apostate scion of an ultra-conservative Prussian family, who represented the extreme left short of socialism."[6]

During the Weimar period the German National People's party (Deutsche Nationale Volks-Partei) and the German People's party (Deutsche Volks-Partei) dominated the political scene in the Landkreis and the Stadtkreis. The two parties received approximately 50 per cent of the votes in the Reichstag elections between 1920 and 1928. In the election of 1930 each lost approximately half its support to the Nazi party. In the two elections of 1932 the German National People's party received less than one per cent of the total votes cast. Throughout the period from 1920 to the last election, held on March 5, 1933, the Social Democratic party, the Communist party, and the Center party continued to control approximately 15 per cent, 6 per cent, and 7 per cent of the votes in the Stadtkreis. In the Landkreis the Center party consistently received approximately 20 per cent of the votes, and the Social Democrats and the Communists controlled approximately 17 per cent and 4 per cent, respectively. The growing popularity of the Nazi party after 1928 did not affect the total votes cast for the Socialist, the Communist, and the Center parties.

In the elections held since 1946 the Socialists have made significant political gains in Marburg. The Liberal Democratic party (Free Democratic party after 1948) carried the Stadtkreis in every election, except in 1952. In the latter year the Social Democratic party emerged victorious, partly because of the personal appeal of its candidate for Oberbürgermeister. He was a war veteran, a native Marburger, and a successful Bürgermeister since 1946. In every Stadtkreis election that it did not win, the Social Democratic party ran second. In the Landkreis the Social Democratic party led all other parties in the postwar elections, with the exception of 1949, when the Free Democratic party won. The popularity of the candidate proved to be the determining factor in that election also. The victor was a farmer, a leader in the local *Bauernverein* (farmers' union) and a champion of the agricultural interests of the Landkreis. The Christian Democratic Union ran second in the Landkreis elections prior to 1949, but the Free Democratic party ran second after 1949.[7]

The Nazi Party

The Nazi party had been active in Marburg after the organization of a local eleven-man group in May 1925. Party membership increased very slowly until 1930 in spite of an active recruitment program which included personal appearances of Robert Ley and Otto Strasser in 1928. Between 1925 and 1929 new memberships were partially offset each year by resignations and transfers. The typical year is 1927, in which twenty-six members joined and twenty-two left. In 1929 party membership stood at fifty-six in the Stadtkreis and ninety-seven in the Landkreis.

A successful election in 1930, a personal visit from Göbbels in 1931, and a birthday speech in Marburg by Hitler in 1932 helped to increase the size of the party in Marburg. When the rolls were closed to new members in May 1933 there were over 1,300 members in the city and about 2,000 in the county.

Marburg's enthusiastic support of the Nazi party may be demonstrated more readily with comparative election results than with membership statistics. The Stadtkreis and the Landkreis gave a much larger percentage of votes to the Nazi party than did the rest of the nation in the two elections in 1932 and in the election of 1933. In July 1932, 37 per cent of the German voters declared for the Nazis; in November 1932, 33 per cent; and in 1933, 44 per cent. In Marburg the percentages of votes cast for the Nazi party in the same elections are as follows: Stadtkreis: 53 per cent, 39 per cent, and 57 per cent. Landkreis: 48 per cent, 46 per cent, and 56 per cent.[8] The election results also show how easily the German National People's party and the German People's party shifted their votes to the Nazis. On the other hand, the Social Democratic party, the Communist party, and the Center party held their ranks secure, even in the election of 1933, when the voters had little choice except to approve or disapprove Hitler's assumption of power earlier in the year. The 34 per cent and the 27 per cent of the voters in the Stadtkreis and Landkreis who declared for the Socialists, the Communists, and the Center in 1933 cannot all be classified as anti-Nazis, however. Probably only the Social Democrats and the Communists would fit this classification. The former cast 13 per cent and 11 per cent of the votes in the Stadtkreis and Landkreis, respectively; while the latter cast 5 per cent and 3 per cent, respectively.

An Economic Profile

Marburg is a relatively backward small-farm area. Agriculture is diversified, but concentrates heaviest in small grains, beet crops, animal husbandry, and fruits. Farms are family-size and employ hired hands only under exceptional circumstances. Farmers do most of their own service, maintenance, and repair work, and often make their own shoes and clothing.[9]

The small plots of land that surround the villages of Landkreis Marburg are mute evidence that the owners and operators, most of whom are freeholders, engage in handicrafts, industry, or other activities to supplement their meager agricultural returns. The average farm size in Marburg in 1949 was 5.33 hectares. This compares with the average size of 4.78 hectares for all of Hessen and 6.84 for the Federal Republic of Germany. According to the agricultural census made in 1949, there were 17,099 agricultural and forestry units in Landkreis Marburg. Forty-nine per cent, or 8,418, of these were smaller than one-half hectare in size (less than one and a quarter acres). Thus, 49 per cent of the agricultural units, cultivating a total of 850 hectares, farmed less than 2 per cent of the total cultivated acreage of the Landkreis. The remaining 8,674 units, cultivating a total of 45,831 hectares, included 3,125 units under two hectares, 2,654 units between two and five hectares, 2,463 units between five and twenty hectares, and 338 units over twenty hectares. A comparison of the foregoing figures with similar statistics for other *Länder* of Germany and for the Federal Republic of Germany reveals that farms in Landkreis Marburg and in Hessen are generally much smaller in area than those of the rest of Germany.

The social and economic consequences of such small-farm agriculture upon the community is probably illustrated best by additional figures from the agricultural census of 1949 and the industrial census of 1950. In 1950 Landkreis Marburg had a total employable population of 47,170. Of this total, 28,408 were engaged in agriculture and forestry, but 30,529 were engaged in industry and handicraft, 10,000 in trade and commerce, insurance and transportation activities, and 10,807 in public services.[10] This obviously represents a considerable duplication of economic activity.

The rural, unindustrialized character of Marburg is evident from sources other than agricultural statistics. The population of Marburg had increased at a slow rate in the period of rapid industrial expansion in Germany. The Marburg population of 9,835 in 1871 had increased to 24,676 in 1925 and 27,883 in 1939. In the Landkreis the increase had been from 50,666 in 1871 to 60,503 and 65,629 in 1925 and 1939, respectively. The population of the Stadtkreis and the Landkreis increased substantially after 1945, but this increase was not due to industrialization. The first postwar census, taken on October 29, 1946, reveals that Marburg had 11,268 persons and the Landkreis had 25,168 persons who had emigrated to the territory after the census of 1939. Most of the newcomers were refugees and expellees who came to western Germany from Russian and Polish occupied territories. As a result of the influx of population between 1939 and 1946 the density of population increased from 1,269.1 to 1,699.2 per square kilometer in Marburg, and from 74.9 to 106.2 per square kilometer in the Landkreis.[11]

Many Marburgers are determined to preserve the rural, agricultural character of their community. Attempts to establish industries in the area after 1945 have been opposed by Marburg University and by the inhabitants of some of the villages. A case in point is the attempt of a refugee from Thuringia to establish a tool factory in a small village near Marburg in 1946. Despite the village's thirty-five registered, unemployed workers the community opposed the plans to establish the tool factory. The community revealed a more general resistance to change by its objection to the refugee's tool factory because he was Protestant and the village predominantly Roman Catholic.[12]

Social Democratic politicians who have tried to promote industry in Marburg report that one of the reasons the city has failed to attract industries is the political influence of the University upon other political parties. It is true that one of the most hotly contested political issues in the city since 1945 has been whether the city should invite new industries or remain an academic center and a commercial center for the surrounding farms. Those interested in preserving the city as an academic center argue that smoke stacks and factories do not fit into such a community. Spokesmen for the working classes believe, however, that the opposition to industrialization is in part motivated by social considerations: the "bourgeois interests" who support the University fear that their social status and their political power will diminish if Marburg becomes industrialized and attracts large numbers of workers.

The Landkreis and the Stadtkreis lack major industries. During the Second World War the explosives industry located near Allendorf was the largest enterprise. It employed a maximum of five thousand persons. The chemical and biological industry located in the small village of Marbach, immediately to the west of Marburg, was the second largest in the area. The firm employed 545 persons in 1938. Within Marburg, a tobacco factory, a rug and drapery factory, several construction companies, a firm producing laboratory and hospital supplies, a hardware factory, and several print shops each employed more than twenty persons in 1945. Several construction firms, a clothing, quilt, and mattress factory, a small furniture factory, a toy factory, a nut and bolt factory, and an electrical supply factory are some of the larger new industries that have settled in Marburg since 1945. In the Landkreis the larger industries include the Marburger *Kreisbahn* (county-owned railway), a construction firm in Cölbe, a sheet-metal factory in Cölbe, an electrical equipment factory in Gisselberg, and a small ironworks in Gossfelden. In the buildings and plant formerly occupied by the explosives industry in Allendorf a few small industries have grown. These include a glass and pottery works, a furniture factory, a textile-weaving plant, and a soap factory.[13]

War Damage

Compared with many other cities of Germany Marburg suffered very little war damage. Shortly after the military government detachment arrived, the Public Health and Welfare Officer estimated that about 10 per cent of the city had been destroyed or seriously damaged. An early estimate by civilian officials was 25 per cent. Approximately three and a half years after the end of the war the municipal housing office reported that forty (about .6 per cent) of the 7,198 dwellings in Marburg had been completely destroyed by air raids, while 2,139 (about 30 per cent) had been partially damaged. In the Landkreis the damage was most serious in the city of Kirchhain (1939 population: 3,049). That city reported as follows: fifty-two buildings completely destroyed; two, 80 per cent destroyed; one, 50 per cent destroyed; three, 25 per cent destroyed; and one, 10 per cent destroyed. Thirty-four other villages and cities in the Landkreis reported bomb or combat damage.

In the Landkreis most of the damage had been caused by ground action. Marburg's decision to surrender without resistance had saved the city from siege, but it had suffered earlier from aerial bombardment. It had been bombarded once in 1944 and three times in February and March 1945. In the first of these raids the northern sector of Marburg had been damaged seriously. Of the estimated one hundred bombs dropped, two had hit the railroad station, and the remainder fell among the University's medical clinics, killing approximately one hundred persons. The railroad station was the target in the later raids, which were more effective because of the complete absence of antiaircraft fire.[14]

Slightly Damaged Marburg, a Refuge after 1945

Marburg became a haven for refugees and expellees during the war and immediately afterward. Refugees and expellees were attracted there by the hope of finding housing and by the knowledge that the rural economy provided a source of black-market food. Trading directly with farmers for food was a normal, though illegal, method used by most Germans after 1945 to supplement their food rations. The census figures for 1946 show that the population of the Stadtkreis increased by 43 per cent between September 1, 1939, and October 20, 1946. During the same time the Landkreis population increased 37 per cent. The rate of population growth is extremely high compared with the 33 per cent for Regierungsbezirk Kassel and the 26 per cent for Hessen.[15]

Assimilating the refugees and evacuees, a difficult problem under ideal conditions, was unusually difficult. Housing was extremely scarce because of the war damage, the influx of Germans, and the large numbers of Americans and displaced persons in Marburg. Food and clothing were inadequate. Prospects of supplying more to the area were slight immediately after the war because of the poor transportation and communication between the occupation zones of Germany and between different areas within the occupation zones. Marburg had few industries in which new citizens could be employed and her farms needed few workers except during the harvest and planting seasons. Even where work was available few of the refugees could be employed. A study made by the Office of Military Government for Germany showed that of the expellees destined for Hessen early in 1946, 51 per cent were women, 26 per cent were under fourteen years of age, and only 23 per cent were men.[16] According to the Landrat's reports most of

the men were old and sick. Because they numbered so many un-
employables among them, the refugees were a heavy burden upon
the public welfare institutions. In February 1947, 70 per cent of
the persons in Marburg who received public welfare were newcomers to the community. They received 74 per cent of the public
welfare money spent in the city.[17]

The new citizens of Marburg (*Neubürger*) seemed to intensify
the social stratification that is apparent to Americans. Even without the presence of newcomers the social distinctions in Marburg
were well defined. In part this was due to the presence of an academic community within an agricultural community. An American sociologist who served in Marburg as Military Government
University Officer has written that "Germans high and low, by
contrast [to Americans], with faithful consistency, are prepared
. . . to defend the station in life to which vocation, tradition, or
'destiny' has assigned them."[18] Besides the usual distinctions made
in Germany between university professors and the common people
(*Die kleinen Leute*), Germans distinguished between new citizens
(*Neubürger*) and old citizens (*Altbürger*). The religious affiliation
of most of the refugees also set them apart from Marburgers. The
Office of Military Government for Germany reported that more
than 80 per cent of the expellees who were settled in Hessen by
1947 were Roman Catholics. The indigenous population of Marburg was about 80 per cent Protestant.[19]

The task of governing Marburg after 1945 would have tested
the most carefully planned policy and the abilities, ingenuity,
imagination, and diligence of its administrators. We turn now
to an examination of what that policy was and who its administrators were.

3

The Americans
and Their Mission

The military government detachment that occupied Marburg on March 30, 1945, was a unit of a combat organization. Its primary mission was to help the tactical forces achieve military success. The detachment (F1C2), six officers and nine enlisted men strong, was activated on September 17, 1944, as one of the detachments designed to take over the government of a Stadtkreis. After a brief training period F1C2 was attached to the Thirteenth United States Army Corps to continue its training program, perform various civil affairs functions for the Corps, and await the capture of its objective in Germany. As they were needed, the detachment added specialists from the European Civil Affairs Division specialists pool and from tactical units. By the time it reached Marburg the detachment numbered fourteen officers and eighteen enlisted men; on July 1, 1945, it numbered twenty-seven and twenty-two, respectively; in November, sixteen and ten; and by mid-1946, when it became a Liaison and Security Office, the detachment strength was reduced to two officers and two enlisted men.

Organizationally, Detachment F1C2 was part of Company C of the Second Military Government Regiment. But during the combat phase of military government it was attached to the Thirteenth Corps, then to the First United States Army, and finally to Headquarters, Western Military District. In each of these assignments the detachment received directives from the military government staff officer (G-5) of the headquarters to which it was attached. Thus, between March and October 1945 the detachment governed

Marburg according to directives it received from the three units mentioned and from its parent organization, the Second Military Government Regiment. Later in 1945, when military government was reorganized and when Land Hessen was placed under the command of one military governor, the detachment received orders from, and made reports to, the Office of Military Government for Land Hessen.

The Mission

When it arrived in Marburg the detachment had few policy directives on how to govern a community whose civil agencies had ceased to function. It had a *Handbook of Military Government in Germany* that had been distributed to all military government detachments, but conflicts among military government planners at higher echelons had not yet been resolved in March of 1945 and the *Handbook* reportedly had a somewhat indefinite status.[1] It did, however, provide a convenient check list of duties for military government officers when they entered a city. The ill-defined character of the detachment's general orders early in the occupation is perhaps best illustrated by the statement made in the official history of military government in Hessen that detachments had standing orders to go into their assignments with a view toward removing Nazis and "getting things going."[2]

Directives that the detachment got while in the field did little to clarify the policy. Harold Zink has concluded that detachments were needlessly confused because they received directives through various army command channels rather than directly from military government headquarters.[3] The Marburg detachment was no exception. In a historical summary report for July the Military Governor wrote that administration in his city was more orderly in July than it had been in June, when the detachment passed from one command to another. He stated that in June "jurisdiction was a subject about which its [the detachment's] officers could only guess."[4]

Burdened with the details of local affairs and isolated from his headquarters with only vague and contradictory directives to follow, the local military government officer easily concluded that he was the stepchild of the occupation. Typical of the attitude is the answer Drew Middleton got when he asked a detachment officer what military government policy in Germany was: "Brother, I don't know. Maybe the big wheels in Frankfort can tell you. They snow me under with all sorts of papers. How'm I going to read them when I'm doing forty-eleven different things to get this burg running again?"[5]

In the absence of a clearly defined mission the Marburg detachment made its own policy at the local level. In keeping with its primary mission of contributing to the total war effort it kept German civilians and displaced persons from hampering army units. It repaired waterworks and sewage systems for the benefit of the troops quartered in Marburg, as well as to prevent diseases that might have affected the American Army. It had bodies buried and it confiscated food supplies, gasoline supplies, and motor vehicles. To facilitate troop movements and prevent disease, the detachment organized civilian work crews to clear the streets of rubble. It denazified by removing Nazis from public office, arresting those who were considered to be a threat to security. It gave some attention to the future reconstruction of civil government, but that was definitely secondary in importance.

Late in 1945, after military government commands had been reorganized, policy directives flowed through military government channels and affected the original policy stated in the *Handbook,* that Landkreis and Stadtkreis military government should be supervisory rather than executive in nature. In October the Hessian Military Governor directed that, effective January 1, 1946, "no orders or instructions concerning Military Government with the exception of . . . [property control, military government courts, political activities, and some aspects of denazification] will be issued by Regierungsbezirk or Kreis Detachments to officials at any level of civil government unless an emergency arises requiring immediate action." He ordered detachments to restrict their other activities to inspections and reports required by higher headquarters. Six months later, in accordance with general policy, he redesignated the field detachments as Liaison and Security Offices. They retained functional responsibility only in public safety, denazification, military government courts, and general security.[6]

Accustomed to government by decree while they were isolated from higher headquarters, pressed into action by higher-ranking military commanders in the area, and driven by a crusading zeal to reconstruct Germany, Marburg's detachment officers found it difficult to limit themselves as directed. Two illustrations are somewhat typical. Late in 1946, after Marburg's freely elected civil administration had functioned for several months, the commanding officer (a colonel) of the Marburg replacement depot demanded and got an interview with the Oberbürgermeister. In the presence of a military government officer (a captain) the colonel threatened to dismiss the city administration if the German attitude toward the occupation forces and their employees did not improve.[7] Although military government directives prohibited such action the captain left no record of his protest.

The second illustration types the strong pressure exercised by the detachment upon local officials who were supposedly responsible only to their civilian counterparts at higher levels. As late as 1949 the official county information bulletin (*Kreisblatt*) carried the notification that the director of the American military government office demanded that town hall meetings be held in midmonth. Five months later the Landrat informed his mayors that they were not required to hold town hall meetings in May because farmers were busy haying and seeding. He said he would notify them again "when it is necessary to hold them." Speaking before a training conference in 1950, the chief of the Hessian Field Operations Division told an audience of Kreis Resident Officers that "in dealing with Bürgermeisters and Landräte that oppose us or give only 'lip service' [to the democratization program], remember that there is a possibility of certain ECA aid being withheld from communities that have such officials."[8]

In their failure to limit themselves to liaison and security activities the Marburg detachment was no exception either. In May 1946 a military government team studied local detachment operations in two Bavarian provinces and reported that the detachments were confused regarding their proper duties and functions. Some detachment officers, the report said, interviewed long lines of people daily, and some had adopted a closed-door policy after civilian agencies resumed authority in January 1946. Officers settled problems on the spot and acted in cases that were not emergencies. Detached as they were from headquarters, the report concluded, Americans who varied in their personal attitudes from unrelenting "Kraut-haters" to sympathetic Samaritans who bemoaned the fate of the "good German" considered a directive to be a guide rather than an order "nine times out of ten." The research team recommended that the Liaison and Security Officer should "be fully acquainted with his new task as observer, as liaison, as representative of Military Government, but not for Military Government. . . . It will require some time to orient this personnel to enable it to understand the true function which it performs, to make it realize that Military Government exists only at Land level and, below that level the primary task of Military Government personnel is to report, again and again all factors."[9]

The published standing operating procedure for Liaison and Security Offices stated clearly the mission of local detachments after they had lost executive authority. Detachments were responsible for ensuring compliance by Germans, allied nationals, and Americans with military government laws, quadripartite agreements, and American occupation policy. Liaison officers were to help the occupying forces carry out basic military government policy, to observe, assist, and advise (but not direct) German governmental agencies in the administration and enforcement of German laws, to help promote the development of a democratic system in Germany, and to aid effectuation of the four cardinal principles of military government policy: demilitarization, denazification, decentralization, and democratization.[10]

The standing operating procedure listed fifteen duties of the Liaison and Security Officer. Ten of these called for observation and reports, four demanded vigilance, cooperation, advice, or liaison, and one required action as a summary court officer. The

duties detailed to the Public Safety Officer were similarly investi-
gatorial, supervisory, and reportorial. He too could be directed
to serve as a summary court officer, and he was required to issue
hunting and fishing licenses to Allied personnel. His other duties
were to investigate black-market activities, supervise the German
police and civil law-enforcement agencies, and establish liaison
between agencies concerned with refugees, displaced persons, and
civilian internees.

Detachment responsibilities changed little after control shifted
from the Army to the Department of State in 1949. There were,
however, certain changes in emphasis toward democratization that
had begun in 1948 under the Liaison and Security Offices. The
Kreis Resident Officer functioned chiefly as the High Commissioner's representative in the field. He had a democratization mission, an economic mission, a political mission, and an administrative and liaison mission. They included such duties as fostering
and encouraging the democratic potential of the German people,
publicizing American efforts to restore and rebuild the German
economy, and describing political parties and analyzing their political activities, and preparing reports. The Resident Officer was
specifically charged with observing the "machinations of Communists, who are anti-American, anti-democratic, anti-Marshall Plan
—in fact, anti-everything which constitutes the fundamental mission of the U.S. Government." His administrative and liaison
duties were to establish liaison between Germans and the occupation forces, prepare intelligence and reorientation reports, issue
hunting permits to Allied personnel, control issuance of temporary
and semipermanent interzonal passes to German applicants, and
attend all official functions required by his position.[11]

The Marburg Resident Officer described his position in 1951.
He listed 157 activities that a new Resident Officer might expect
to perform. Approximately 90 per cent of the activities he listed
involved reorientation and re-education of the German people.
The other 10 per cent were activities he performed as the High
Commissioner's representative in the field, as the liaison representative between Germans and the occupation forces, as ob-

server and reporter, and as administrator of routine detachment affairs.[12]

American and German Personnel

How successfully the American occupation effected its mission in Marburg depended partly on the type of personnel assigned to the task. Harold Zink has written that "the record . . . is reasonably good in matters of personnel on an over-all basis. However, some bad mistakes were made and far too much indifference was exhibited by some very high ranking officers, especially as regards enlisted personnel."[13]

When the detachment came to Marburg in March, its commanding officer considered it well staffed with experts in public health, public safety, food and agriculture, public utilities, and monuments and fine arts. In other specialties, notably in civil administration, education, and displaced persons, he thought the detachment lacked adequately trained officers. As the detachment grew in size after Germany's surrender, the proportion of specialists decreased because more and more officers without civil affairs experience or without military government training came to Marburg.[14] But even in the early phase the detachment could not always use its specialists effectively. Local civil government had ceased to function. Displaced persons who had been freed from work camps formed bands that threatened not only the civilian population, but also the security of the American troops in the vicinity. Army units had to be billeted and hundreds of small tasks had to be performed. Thus many of the specialist officers had to assist in civil administration, in the control of displaced persons, and in the maintenance of general security.[15]

If they are viewed collectively, the Marburg detachment's officers and enlisted men from 1945 to 1952 appear to have been representative of what America had to offer to deal with the difficult problem of military government. A good cross section of upper middle-class America, they were zealous crusaders for a future democratic Germany. Educated, trained, and experienced specialists were always numerous, but specialists who also spoke German were scarce. Except for one man, the detachment never had people who might be classified as generalists because of their broad experience and training or their adaptability to unusual situations. During its seven years in Marburg the detachment had only two men who were adequately trained in German history, politics, and culture.

Biographical information about seventy-three former Marburg detachment members shows that of the fifty-six whose prewar civilian occupations are known at least thirty were well-trained specialists in various military government fields. At least seven officers had attended an Army civil affairs training school, at least six enlisted men had attended an Army specialist training school, and at least twenty-two had had previous experience in civil affairs and military government in Europe. Nine others had had civilian or military experience and training that qualified them for positions peculiar to military government. Of the sixty-three about whom definite data are available, seventeen spoke and understood German, five probably spoke and understood enough to converse casually but not enough to conduct affairs without an interpreter, and forty-one understood and spoke no German. Only five of forty-seven reported that they still have friends among Germans, and six maintain business or professional contacts with Germans. Four others married German women. At least four of the *Standesamt's* 151 recorded marriages of occupation personnel and Germans from August 1946 to December 1953 involved members of the detachment.*

Even if we make the improbable assumption that those for whom data are not available had similar training and back-

---

* The breakdown of civilian occupations that I have been able to determine is: six lawyers, two agricultural economists, one chemist, four engineers, seven teachers, two police officers, two journalists, two accountants, one sculptor, two administrators, one analyst, ten merchants, businessmen, or salesmen, two regular army soldiers, six university students, two clerks, one farmer, three high school students, one professional baseball player, and one truck driver. I have been unable to assemble reliable information on at least fifty-two other former Marburg detachment personnel. Many of those in question stayed in Marburg only relatively short periods of time late in 1945 when the turnover was great.

grounds,* and that all members of the detachment possessed such desirable qualities as courage, honesty, endurance, maturity of judgment, and a sense of devotion to duty under difficult circumstances, there are several highly significant personnel factors to consider. The detachment never solved the problem of finding adequate replacements for those who were redeployed to the United States or those who were withdrawn to headquarters because they possessed special ability for policy-making positions. Zink has written that one of the most serious weaknesses of the officer personnel program of military government was its failure to provide for replacements. He wrote that military government officers and men were just as anxious to get home after the war as were their counterparts in tactical units. Even though the Army placed military government officers in critical classifications—therefore they did not come within the point system of release—many of them were able to get out of the Army shortly after V-E Day. Marburg's personnel presented no exception to the general preoccupation of Americans with plans and desires to get home.[16]

Military government lost trained personnel rapidly after the war, and the field detachments suffered more than headquarters from the loss. The Military Governor of Hessen reported, late in 1946, that "the ever current personnel problem" was made even worse by promulgation of a rotation policy establishing a normal overseas tour of duty of thirty months and a maximum tour of thirty-six months. The military government specialists who had been brought to Europe early in 1944 thus had all completed their normal tours of duty in 1946. The report stated, in addition, that "none of the ASTP trained enlisted men remained except those who had converted to civilian status."[17]

The military government officers and enlisted men who remained in Germany found it difficult to become thoroughly acquainted with their jobs and their communities. The standing

---

* It appears improbable that they had, because those who answered my questionnaires and my letters were chiefly those who took some pride in their work with military government, or those who held responsible positions. Former enlisted men responded much less readily than former officers.

operating procedure specified that military government officers and men be rotated at least once a year if they did not elect to be demobilized. An article in the *Marburger Presse* showed the adverse effect of the American demobilization and rotation policy. It listed the succession of military governors in the city from April 1945 to October 1949. The list included twelve persons, some of whom had remained for such short periods that the editor could hardly remember them.[18] The twelve had remained in Marburg an average of three and one-half months each. Thirty-seven other Americans for whom tenure data are available stayed an average of six months each between 1945 and 1952. It is reasonably certain that more complete data would correct this average downward. The average length of time that an American stayed in Marburg permitted little more than a cursory study of the conditions there before he was demobilized or rotated to another assignment. With American personnel thus constantly in a state of flux, the Marburg detachment relied heavily upon its civilian employees and upon German officials. Newly arrived military government officers were especially dependent upon the more permanent German civilian employees of the detachment for background information upon the tasks they performed. In addition, officers who did not speak German relied upon civilian employees perpetually. Indeed, if the obvious Germanic word order and sentence structure of numerous detachment reports—including classified reports—are sufficient evidence, some officers preferred to let their German employees write their reports for them.

A description of the civilian employees upon whom the Marburg detachment depended for much of its intelligence information provides an additional insight into the detachment's ability as a reporting and observing agency. A study of twenty-six German employees—fifteen office employees and eleven investigators—of the Marburg detachment between 1945 and 1950 indicates that they were not drawn from the stable, long-term residents of the community and that they were all classified as minor employees.[19]

The fifteen office employees included ten females and five males. Six of the fifteen were permanent prewar residents of Marburg, three came to Marburg during the war, and six arrived after 1945. One of them, an Austrian, came with the detachment. Nine of the fifteen were still residents of Marburg or the Landkreis in 1954. But of these nine, only four had resided there prior to the war. The occupations listed on their city registration forms were: interpreter (2), secretary (1), book dealer (1), clerks (*Angestellte*) (10), and orchestra leader (1). Only one had a university education.

The eleven investigators were more permanent residents of Marburg. Only four had not lived in Marburg prior to the war, and six still lived there in 1954. Occupationally they represented a motley group. They included a lawyer, a butcher's helper, a gardener, two students, a merchant, a teacher, an author and historian, a janitor, a clerk, and the young son of a Marburg merchant. Six of them were Communists and two were Socialists. One of the latter described himself as a leftist-Socialist. Another joined the National Democratic party in 1947 and actively criticized the occupation. He was later arrested for car theft and also sentenced as an informer by the Marburg denazification tribunal. The other two appear to have had no political connections, but one of them, military government later discovered, had a criminal record with twenty-two entries.

Civil officials were the second major source of intelligence information for the Marburg detachment. A thorough analysis of a representative group of these civil officials will be found in Chapter 5 of this study and frequent references to their attitudes and opinions are found throughout the study. The Landrat, the Oberbürgermeister, the police, the political parties, and others had to submit periodic reports to the Marburg military government detachment and resident office. The information gathered in the reports provided the basis for detachment reports to higher headquarters. Some officials said they made reports only as directed. They did not strive for thoroughness and volunteered no information that was not specifically requested by the detachment. Marburg officials believe that, with the exception of denazification, the Marburg detachment knew very little about local affairs over and

above that which Marburgers told them in their reports. Political
leaders believe that military government collected a tremendous
amount of paper (*"Es muss sich viel gesammelt haben"*), but they
said it was common gossip among friends that the reports were
false, biased, or incomplete. One of them said they thought the political party reports were nonsensical (*Blödsinn*).*

The Marburg detachment relied heavily upon the parties' reports in making its own political activity reports to higher headquarters. For example, in 1947 and 1948 it submitted several such
reports late, explaining that it could not dispatch them earlier
because local political parties had failed to report to the Marburg
office on time, and once the detachment submitted an incomplete
report because one of the parties had failed to report for the period.
One other illustration shows how much the detachment depended
upon civilians for political information. The Public Safety Officer
noted in the Daily Journal in September 1945 that a soldier from
the regional detachment in Kassel had visited Marburg to inquire
about the political parties that were forming in the area. He said
that he instructed the soldier to go to Robert Treut, the chairman
of the political committee, for detailed information.[20]

Marburg's civil officials deliberately withheld information from
military government officers. Occasionally they apologized to each
other for passing information to American agencies. An example
is a memorandum from the head of the police department's special
investigation office to the chairman of the political committee ex-

* Hermann Bauer, interview, June 22, 1954; Jakob Römer, interview, June
15, 1954; Erich Kroll, interview, June 29, 1954. Römer said he and his friends
considered the reports a chore, and that the Kreis committee of the LDP used
to prepare the report by asking each other: "What can interest military government anyway?" I have read the political activity reports on file in the SPD,
LDP/FDP, and CDU offices in Marburg, and I agree that they do not reveal a
great deal about the parties. Another example of the practice of German agencies was described in a report made by the Office of Military Government for
Hessen. The report stated that the Hessian Minister for Political Liberation had
reported a backlog of some 7,000 cases on May 1, 1948. A footnote to the report,
written in May 1949, stated that the figure was misleading and that military government had discovered later that the Ministry had reported the figure "because they felt that it was approximately the figure that MG wanted to hear."
OMGH, Historical Report, 1948, I, Narrative, 9 (mimeographed), OMGUS
Papers.

plaining how a denazification report on a teacher inadvertently fell into the hands of the Counter Intelligence Corps.[21] Landrat Eckel, who was later commended by military government for his fine spirit of cooperation, withheld information from military government and directed his staff to do likewise. In at least two instances, both in 1947, he sent military government employees away when they requested access to files in his office. A subsequent investigation by an American field officer disclosed that Landrat Eckel had called a meeting of his department heads and ordered that "no information from their files will be given to any outside agency including military government."[22] The Landrat wanted only authorized information sent to American agencies.

Not only did local officials withhold information, but they submitted biased or highly subjective reports to the Marburg detachment. The Landrat's reports reflect a distinctly Social Democratic political point of view, Oberbürgermeister Bleek's a Free Democratic bias, and Bürgermeister Gassmann's a Social Democratic bias. Although military government could hardly expect anything else, it is especially significant that some detachment officers were unaware of the political preferences of these people and designated the Liberal Democratic editor Hermann Bauer a Communist and the Social Democratic Bürgermeister Georg Gassmann a Free Democrat. The reports themselves are interesting especially for the technique they reveal. The Landrat's report on refugees shows it clearly. He reminded military government that it had made him responsible for providing housing, employment, and relief for refugees and evacuees and that he had been criticized for not providing adequate services. Then he outlined plans that his administration had made to settle about eight or nine small industries in the Allendorf buildings to provide employment for refugees. But, he continued, military government prevented his administration from going ahead because it would not tell him what parts—or how much—of the plant would be spared. He emphasized that the Allendorf area provided the only place in Marburg where refugees might be gainfully employed. But in a less conspicuous section of the report the Landrat described how shocked Marburgers were with the methods of the Allies from the East because they had permitted only women, children, and the old and the sick to enter Western Germany. He stated that the farmers in Marburg were especially disappointed because few refugees were employable, and that the local administration considered each new refugee a potential welfare case.[23] The Landrat appealed to military government to retain the Allendorf facilities, but he apparently had few refugees who were employable.

Whether or not the Americans—trained, educated, and experienced as they were—succeeded in accomplishing their mission in Marburg only an analysis of the detachment's operations can tell. They were immediately faced with complete collapse of civil authority and had to begin at the beginning. They were hampered by their own personnel policies and by the fact that they had to rely upon German employees with little training, little experience, little stake in the community, and with strong leftist political leanings. As time went on they were further frustrated by the lack of cooperation from their civilian counterparts whom they had first appointed and who were later freely elected.

PART TWO

Military Government
and the Community's Response

4

The New Order Emerges

The military government detachment's primary mission during the combat phase was to contribute to the war effort. What it did to achieve this cannot be separated completely from the early denazification program, the reconstruction of civil government, the restoration of transportation and communication facilities; in short, the long-range objectives of military government. For the sake of convenience, however, these long-range objectives are discussed separately in later chapters.

Security and Order

A member of the Marburg military government detachment's advance party stated later that the detachment enforced maximum security because it was a "well known fact" that Marburg was "a hotbed of Nazism." The policy is understandable. The war was not yet over and even though the *Handbook for Military Government* predicted that German civilians would not resist occupation, cautious military government officers could not discount the possibility of violence. Americans maintained security by methods that appear to have varied with the local situation and with the opinions of local security officers. In the city of Neustadt former Nazi party members were assembled in camps at night and released under guard during the daytime to do clean-up work. In the smaller villages, where no troops were stationed, there appear to have been no restrictions whatsoever. Even the published restrictions, such as the curfew, were constantly violated by civilians and soldiers alike.[1]

The failure to enforce curfew regulations may suggest the false conclusion that enforcement of law and order was lax in Marburg.

Systematic arrests of Nazi party members and those believed to be threats to the security of the American forces kept the situation well in hand. The prisons were filled. The notations after the names on the police rosters submitted daily to the military government prison officer indicate that many of the arrests were made merely for purposes of investigation, but others were based on violations of military government regulations, and many were made for activities during the Nazi regime.

Germans who had been appointed to fill administrative and police force vacancies aided military government in the arrest program. The Military Governor appointed a police chief on April 3, 1945, and instructed him to organize a force. His recruiting was limited by military government to candidates who had not been Nazi party members or who had not served in public office during the Nazi regime. The police chief later complained that the restrictions left only "uninstructed, sick, weak, and old people" to fill the ranks of the newly organized police force. But the Military Governor was fully aware of the consequences of the limitation and, in fact, considered the chief of police himself a provisional appointee, not fully qualified to do the job permanently. But speed was essential, and in the absence of a more suitable candidate he had appointed Erich Kroll, a naturopath and a Communist and later recommended to his successor that a more suitable man be sought.[2] Kroll called himself *Stadtkommissar*.

Whatever the new policemen lacked in training and experience they made up in authority and enthusiasm. Without informing military government or the Counter Intelligence Corps, they ordered all former members of the Nazi party and its affiliated organizations to assemble on Sunday, May 6, 1945, in one of Marburg's public squares. They required those who came to register their names and addresses as well as the names and addresses of any other persons they knew to fall within the registration requirements.[3] The large gathering attracted the attention of local military personnel. When informed of the intent of the meeting, military government and Counter Intelligence Corps representatives approved it.

The Marburg arrest program was part of a larger program that Americans carried out in their zone of Germany. Official reports state that seventy thousand persons were being held under arrest on July 16, 1945, and that "the arrest program has proceeded apace." Local activities were supplemented by zone-wide security check-ups such as the operation "Tally-ho" of July 21–22, 1945, in which eighty thousand Germans were arrested in two days.[4]

The job of maintaining order and security was bigger than that of arresting those considered to be dangerous to the occupation or the war effort. During the early days of the occupation, groups of more than five were forbidden to assemble in public. Later, military government officials required prior approval for any civilian meeting that would have more than five in attendance. The wisdom of the prohibition, from the American point of view, cannot be denied. It did reduce the possibility of organizing underground activities and it restricted political activities which were prohibited. It appears, however, that the literal enforcement of the regulation—longer than it was needed—aroused Germans unnecessarily.[5] Clandestine political groups met regularly in the homes of former political leaders. No military government officer has admitted as much to the author, but it should have been obvious that such meetings took place, because the candidates whom civil officials recommended to military government to fill vacancies invariably were people who were of their own political convictions.

Partly to provide security, military government declared a policy of nonfraternization between Americans and Germans. Nonfraternization in Marburg, as everywhere in Germany, became a farce and was soon discontinued. The policy never worked with reference to women and children and often failed to prevent other associations. In August 1945 the Office of Military Government for Germany reported that "partially as a result of the success of the arrest and removal from office programs, it was decided to order the relaxation of the non-fraternization policy in the U.S. Zone, which took place on 15 July."[6]

The report apparently conceals more than it reveals. Denazification had hardly begun in earnest by July 15, 1945. In fact, the first directive outlining a systematic denazification program for the United States Zone of Occupation was dated July 15, 1945. It would appear, from the failure of the nonfraternization policy in Marburg, that other factors were equally important. Certainly, fraternization between military personnel and the local officials, who were the only people affected by early denazification and removal policies, was never the chief problem. In fact, officals appointed by military government constantly complained long after the ban was lifted that they could not work effectively because Americans did not trust them. The police chief of Marburg, reporting to his civilian superiors, stated that the chief effect of the relaxation of the nonfraternization regulations had not been to ease the difficulty of liaison between the civilian administration and the military, but rather to bring about a "catastrophic" increase in the venereal disease rate, which had been rising rather steadily ever since the beginning of the occupation.[7] The man who later became editor of the *Marburger Presse* said that the relaxation of the nonfraternization rules benefited only "little girls," whereas those Germans who considered themselves to be philosophical brothers of the Americans were still shunned by Americans as they had been from the beginning of the occupation.[8] These complaints indicate that occupation personnel associated very little with officials even after the removal of the fraternization ban.

Military government eliminated a potential threat to security by having the Oberbürgermeister collect weapons, ammunition, binoculars, and radio-transmitting sets. But Germans were somewhat confused because they got different orders from tactical commanders than from military government. Military government officers reported that they did not order cameras collected on March 29, but a notice from the Oberbürgermeister a few days later shows that someone had ordered Marburgers to surrender them.[9] The Daily Journal of the Marburg military government detachment reveals that military personnel also ordered village mayors to collect cameras. In every instance recorded in his journal the Military Governor directed the mayor to secure the cameras and return them to their rightful owners. But Marburgers apparently felt compelled to obey anyone in uniform if he claimed to represent military government. Thus, as in the case of the cameras, Germans often blamed military government for unauthorized actions of individual members of the military forces. Germans still make disparaging remarks about "military government" because Americans requisitioned and failed to pay for radios, furniture, supplies, and labor.

Marburgers who had voluntarily cooperated with military government officials during the early days of the occupation often suggested that better discipline might have precluded many of military government's problems.[10] Often such criticism sprang from a general dislike of the occupation and ignorance of military government's own efforts to control requisitions. Even before requisitioning policies were crystallized, military government officers often intervened to protect German property. The Monuments, Fine Arts and Archives Officer prevented an army unit from defacing a building that Germans had protected because of its rare architectural design. But often military government officers, limited by inadequate rank and authority, looked with dismay upon "the inexcusable misbehavior of American troops, particularly during the combat phase." Commanding generals, who were often the superior officers of the military government detachment, were reportedly lax; they "seemed to condone all but the most serious crimes."

As part of the security program all former members and employees of the German military forces were transported to prisoner-of-war camps. In Marburg the detachment directed those who had not been formerly discharged to assemble and be taken into custody. Judging from the large number who reported and the fact that few former soldiers without proper discharge papers were later apprehended, the project succeeded as a security measure. Yet there are people in Marburg today who take pride in having violated the order. Hermann Bauer has admitted that he lived through the early days of the occupation without discharge papers from the Volkssturm by stating that they had been lost. After he

had become editor of the *Marburger Presse,* Bauer told a military
government officer that he had failed to report for proper discharge.
He said the officer laughed.[11]

Both Allied and German observers have criticized military government's early security measures. They argue that a revolution
would have solved many problems which military government
failed to solve properly; that a rapid annihilation of the Nazis
would have eliminated the opponents of a postwar democratic
reconstruction more successfully than the attempt at a legal, artificial revolution through the program of denazification.[12] An
American sociologist, who was the University Officer in Marburg,
has stated that a "night of the long knives" before the establishment of law and order might have resulted in a rapid purge at
German hands, leaving few, if any, Nazis to be martyrs of the occupation. Gustav Stolper, a student of German history and a member of the Hoover Commission to Germany, wrote in 1948 that
"millions had been waiting . . . millions had made up lists of
their enemies, thought out catalogues of measures to eliminate
those at whose hands they had suffered," but they were never given
a chance. Another has written that Americans should have permitted "the Germans themselves to take care of their war criminals
. . . permitting a certain amount of bloodshed and disorder in
the interests of the catharsis to be achieved."[13]

There is some evidence to support the critics' assumptions that
the Germans would have revolted and that they were stopped by
American security measures. Recent studies of the German underground during the Nazi regime described the nuclei of organizations intent upon revolutionary activity.[14] Military government
officers in many sections of Germany reported, in 1945, that anti-
fascist organizations (*Antifas*), intent upon violent denazification,
were forming. Supreme Headquarters, Allied Expeditionary
Forces, directed military government detachments to disband such
groups and organizations.[15] Whether the decision was based upon
fear of Communism, as Warburg has suggested, or upon fear that
any violence might impair the occupation cannot be determined
from available sources. A military government report said that

some such groups "undoubtedly" included democratically minded persons, but that more often their leaders were persons primarily interested in advancing their own welfare, or minority groups who claimed to speak on behalf of the entire community. The groups were, the report stated, "almost wholly of leftist orientation led principally by former Social Democrats and Communists."[16]

Except for a small, insignificant group in Kirchhain there is no evidence in Marburg to support the belief that military government prevented a purge by Germans themselves. Even though Marburgers have repeatedly expressed the belief, it cannot be documented by facts.[17] In Kirchhain a group of men, led by a former Communist party member, organized the Antifaschistische Demokratische Vereinigung Kreis Marburg-Lahn. The organization achieved publicity in the summer of 1945 when it attacked the former mayor of the city and threatened other Nazis. But before military government recognized the Kirchhain *Antifa* as a threat to security and order, the more conservative citizens of Marburg went into action. One of the leaders of the Marburg political committee invited the Kirchhain *Antifa* to work together with it in a united front against the fascists, and as a result the committee in Marburg had the organization under control when the detachment's Civil Administration Officer ordered it to disband.[18]

In the rest of Stadtkreis and Landkreis Marburg there was no plan for revolution. None of the persons interviewed by the author participated in or knew of groups intent on acts of violence. The editor of the *Marburger Presse*, who would have known about them if they existed, said that no such plans existed even though the Nazis would probably have considered it just and correct that they be punished without trial. According to a leading political figure of the Weimar Republic and the postwar era, the only thing that might have happened under less careful scrutiny of the military forces is that Germans might have lived up to their "tradition of going to extremes" and shed some blood among the former Nazi party members. He was careful to point out, however, that it would have occurred on a purely personal basis and not as an organized effort.

The criticism of military government for preventing a revolution in Marburg, or in Germany, arises from an afterthought. As former Nazis returned to their old positions and as it became clear that neither American nor German denazification would alter the center of political power in Germany, it began to occur to some that dead Nazis could not have returned. The afterthought ignores the fact that during the early months of the occupation Germans themselves said it was "impossible for Germans even to think deeply."[19] It ignores the conditions described in Chapter 2: the confusion, indifference, disillusionment, fear, and despair of Marburgers in defeat. Besides, the leader of the Marburg Communist party repeatedly told his more conservative friends after 1945 that a revolution would have been absolutely impossible in Marburg even without the interference of military government.[20] The Social Democratic party reportedly discussed revolution from time to time, but only considerably *after* April 1945 when its members had become disillusioned with the denazification program.

Other Early Military Government Activities
Housekeeping and Accommodations

The Marburg military government detachment, to which the area commander had given the extra duty of providing accommodations for the Army, requisitioned houses, schools, clinics, and hospitals. It assigned German Army and Nazi party property and facilities to military units. It usually tried to restrict requisitions to Nazi property. Accordingly, it instructed the mayor to prepare lists of houses owned by Nazi party members and it had "Off Limits" signs posted on property that was to be exempt from occupation by troops and displaced persons.

The detachment's requisitioning policy was not always successful during the early phase of military government operations. The Daily Journal of the detachment contains many entries describing actions taken to prevent tactical units from expanding their living accommodations without proper authority and contrary to the detachment's policy. Some military units demanded whole sections of the city in order to separate military units from the civilian population. Late in 1945, when Marburg was designated as a dependent housing area for American military and civilian personnel, the Army demanded a whole section of the city for an American enclave. The result was that Nazis and non-Nazis alike were removed from their homes. On December 11, 1945, the *Marburger Presse* published a report on the American Army demands for housing. It stated that the Army needed seven seven-room houses, fifty-five five-room houses, 375 three-room apartments, a school, garages, market buildings, a gymnasium, an athletic field, a theater, and an officers' club. All of these were to be within a separate compound.

Often the detachment's decision whether to requisition or not was based upon the facilities that a particular home or building provided rather than its previous use or the political background of its inhabitants. The detachment itself set up a kitchen and mess in a building that had been protected by Germans for its rare architectural design, and the detachment billeting officer apparently saw no harm in converting the University library into a transient billet. The library was spared only because the major who sought the billet deemed the facilities "inadequate for his needs."[21]

In the early period of the occupation Americans demanded comfort. They took Nazis' homes first, but if a non-Nazi lived next door and the unit needed another home, the non-Nazi family usually had to move. The dispossessed Marburgers had to leave their furnishings and their personal belongings behind. Once, it was reported, a military government officer requisitioned the dog along with the home.[22] When a unit required additional furnishings, military government directed the mayor to provide them. He often had to get them from non-Nazis because the demands were so great. The detachment's own demands were not small. It ordered the mayor to provide office equipment, including desks, tables, typing tables, typewriters, easy chairs, one "especially beautiful desk with lock drawer and chair," and "one bookcase with books." The requisition did not specify the language in which the books were to be written. For its kitchens and dining rooms the detachment ordered 125 soup plates, sixty-five cups, sixteen vases, one hundred settings of silverware, 175 wine glasses, and thirty-six champagne glasses among a total of thirty-eight items.[23]

Marburgers criticize the requisitions of homes and facilities more than any other aspect of the occupation, except denazification. The persons whom the author interviewed were usually careful, however, to distinguish between the fact of requisition and the method of requisition. Most of them agreed that the American Army justly demanded adequate facilities, but they objected—not publicly at first—to American requisition practices for several reasons.

Americans seem to have deliberately made it difficult for the dispossessed families. In the early months of the occupation, even if families were permitted to remove possessions, moving vans were not available immediately because they had either been requisitioned by the German Army or destroyed in the war, or because there was no gasoline. Marburgers thus had to leave the heavier articles behind even though the Americans did not requisition them specifically. Even as late as 1946, when advance planning was possible, German families were hastily moved from their homes months before dependents arrived in large numbers. The Army often left requisitioned homes empty or only partly used. While American quarters were not fully used, German officials were charged with housing refugees who came in increasing numbers after the Potsdam Agreement in August 1945.

Marburgers also objected to requisition practices because American occupants of requisitioned homes could use the gardens themselves or permit Germans of their own choice to use them. They were justly aggravated by American publicity releases describing a project instituted by American women's clubs in Germany to distribute fresh fruits and vegetables from the requisitioned gardens to hospitals, children's homes, and other charitable organizations. Often, however, gardens were left unused—during the severe food shortage between 1945 and 1949—but most frequently Americans permitted their maids and housekeepers to use them. In practice the maids and housekeepers, who generally remained even though the occupants of the houses changed, became virtual tenants of the garden plots.[24]

Last, Marburgers criticized the American housing policy because it segregated Germans and Americans completely. Even though Americans did not use homes fully, Germans were prohibited from living in the unused portions. This condition seemed to affect Germans of higher social status most strongly, as they considered it degrading (*eine Herabsetzung*) to be quarantined from Americans.

Military government officers themselves reported that the methods employed to secure housing were inconsistent with long-range military government policies of reconstruction and re-education of the German people to a more democratic way of life. An intelligence officer stationed in Marburg in December 1946 wrote that long experience in intelligence work had convinced him that "the way in which requisitioning has been permitted to go on in many communities has been one of the most detrimental factors in the success of our mission."[25] Military government officers were the first to criticize American requisitioning practices openly. It was one of the many issues on which military government officers and tactical commanders disagreed. Only later, when a movement developed to promote the return of requisitioned property, did German citizens criticize these practices openly.

Liaison with Military Organizations

The Marburg military government detachment performed important services for the military forces. It ordered English-speaking residents to report to the employment office for assignment to the Army and civilian agencies that had to work with the Army. The detachment had public utilities repaired and put into operation. The electric power plant was in operation by April 7, the water works pumped more water one week after the occupation of the city than it had "during normal times," the ice plant was working in June 1945, and other utilities were brought into operation between April and July, 1945.[26] Military government's job was not made easier by the American soldiers' habit of shooting up the electric transformers and the glass insulators on the poles.

The Marburg detachment directed Nazis to clear the streets of rubble. Many of these draftees apparently shirked their duty by obtaining certificates of ill health from their doctors and others admit that they refused to appear for this so-called honorary service (*Ehrendienst*) when ordered to do so. Because male laborers were in short supply, and because military government ordered rubble cleared quickly, the welfare office called upon women to assist in the work. Few exceptions were made. Women with three children under fourteen years of age, or with two children under five, or with babies under one year were required to work half-days unless otherwise excused. Only fully employed women, and those falling into several other special categories, were completely exempted from clean-up work.[27]

While Americans repaired the public utilities and directed the rubble-clearance program, denazification lagged. The newly arrived commanding officer of the Marburg detachment wrote a scathing letter to the Landrat on October 30, 1945, pointing out that the city looked unsightly. He said there was debris in the streets six months after the end of the war. He ordered the Landrat to force Nazis and some of the able-bodied men whom he had observed walking the streets to do clean-up work. He thought that Nazis should work on Sunday and he demanded action immediately.* But three weeks before, the Marburg detachment had reported that Marburg still employed sixty-six public servants who fell under mandatory removal classifications of the denazification regulations. Besides these the detachment reported sixteen with the same classification in quasi-public enterprises and at least three in private positions of importance. Seventy-seven persons whose employment was left to the discretion of the local military government officers by the denazification regulations, but who had received "adverse recommendations" according to the

* OMG, Marburg, to Landrat, October 30, 1945, Stadtkreis Marburg Papers. The letter is probably most significant because it reveals the apparent lack of training of the Military Governor. He ordered the Landrat, who had no authority in the municipality, to institute a clean-up program there. The Landrat is the county manager, whereas the Oberbürgermeister is the highest official in the city. The letter is found in the Oberbürgermeister's files with the Landrat's letter of transmittal attached.

regulations, were still in public office. Furthermore, at least six persons with "adverse recommendations" were employed in quasi-public enterprises, and eleven persons so classified still practiced their professions. On the very day that the Military Governor issued the order to clean up the city, an official in the Oberbürgermeister's office had an interview with the Public Utilities Officer of the Marburg detachment. In a memorandum for the files he noted that the officer permitted employment of persons with mandatory removal classifications and "adverse recommendation" classifications in subordinate positions if it was necessary to keep public works going.*

The Long-Range Program

During the early phase of occupation many activities of the Marburg detachment prepared for the future long-range German occupation. The Marburg detachment knew that Nazis were to be removed from public office and that a civil administration would be formed. Military government officers assumed, generally, that the ultimate purpose of the occupation was to give the German people an opportunity to reconstruct their life on a democratic and peaceful basis, as it was later stated in the Potsdam Agreement. Thus, fully aware of the provisional nature of their work, Americans prepared to, or actually began to, denazify, demilitarize, confiscate property and to reconstruct the civil administration almost from the first day they entered the city.

Early Denazification and Demilitarization

The detachment rooted out traces of National Socialism in various ways. Late in April the Military Governor ordered the Oberbürgermeister to collect all pictures of leaders and events

---

* OMG, Marburg, to OMGH: Weekly Denazification Report (Corrected Copy) for period from October 7 to October 12, 1945, October 13, 1945, OMGUS Papers. Aktenvermerk für Volkspflege: Besprechung mit Captain Fexi, October 30, 1945, Stadtkreis Marburg Papers. See Robert Engler, "The Individual Soldier and the Occupation," *The Annals of the American Academy of Political and Social Science*, CCLXVII (January 1950), 77–86, for the argument that American officers were more interested in getting their areas cleaned than in denazifying Germans, partly because their success as military governors was measured by Army standards.

of the Third Reich. On May 5, 1945, the mayor reported that only ten posters, five etchings, five albums, and thirty-seven pictures had been turned in.[28] He said he would try again. The failure of Germans to comply is not simply proof of Nazi convictions, although they certainly were a factor. Many Germans had already burned or destroyed Nazi pictures. Others chose to retain them as insurance, because they still believed—or hoped—that German counteroffensives might recapture Marburg. It is difficult, however, to reconcile the latter argument with the conviction that many Germans expressed after the capture of Marburg that the war would be over in a short time.

To remove Nazi propaganda from public places military government ordered lending libraries cleared of National Socialistic and militaristic literature. It directed the mayor to change street names, park names, building names, and other designations that glorified the German military, nationalistic, or National Socialistic past, and it instructed him to have someone remove the placards of the Third Reich that had called for unified efforts in the war.

The Oberbürgermeister assigned these tasks to the Marburg political committee. The committee drew up a list of objectionable street and park names and prepared substitutes, which it sent to military government on September 4, 1945. It appointed a three-man subcommittee, consisting of two book dealers and a policeman, to screen the lending libraries.[29] The subcommittee was never absolutely certain of its mission. It did not know if literature was to be destroyed completely or if it had a right to confiscate literature from private libraries. The detachment could give no advice, because top-level military government planners disagreed on the issue.* Eventually Marburg's private lending libraries were cleared of Nazi literature. The University library

---

* Marshall Knappen, *And Call It Peace* (Chicago: University of Chicago Press, 1947), pp. 164–68, describes the conflict between three schools of thought on Nazi literature: one to leave libraries intact, one to destroy all Nazi literature, and one to forbid bookshops from displaying or selling such literature, but not to destroy it. See OMGUS, Monthly Report, No. 11, June 20, 1946, p. 1, which states that the Allied Control Council in Berlin ordered Nazi literature destroyed along with certain war materials and war maps.

was required to segregate it from other literature, while private libraries were left intact. Before the Allied Control Council ordered literature destroyed, private persons were requested to surrender their Nazi literature for pulping; afterward they were "responsible" for doing so.[30]

The attempt to remove Nazi literature failed in Marburg, in no small measure because of the failure of military government to prescribe specific methods for doing so. In 1954 the University library still withheld Nazi literature from general circulation, but private persons were able to retain it. The former editor of the *Marburger Presse* has been successfully collecting Nazi literature from private sources "for scholarly purposes."

Confiscation of Nazi Property

Military government detachments had standing orders to locate, confiscate, or place under guard the property that had belonged to the German Army, the Nazi party, and any of their affiliated organizations. With the help of its civilian investigators the detachment engaged in a continuous search for such property. Toward the end of April the Civilian Supply Officer hired three civilians whose chief task was to collect stores and locate warehouses. The task was difficult because German civilians and displaced persons had looted the Army and the party warehouses just after the first troops arrived in the city. Displaced persons continued to loot after military government arrived, because German police lacked jurisdiction over them and because some local unit commanders apparently sanctioned it. Military authorities stepped in only after the displaced persons began to threaten the security of the local area by robberies and murders. They stopped looting by putting the displaced persons into camps where they could be observed, controlled, and then processed for repatriation.[31]

Typical of most undertakings of military government during the early phase of occupation, property was confiscated hastily and unsystematically. The displaced persons who had been hired as investigators often sought vengeance rather than justice. The

German civilian investigators could not always be relied upon,
even though military government and the Counter Intelligence
Corps had screened them for employment. For example, one of
the civilian investigators hired to locate and confiscate Nazi property was a Marburg merchant who had sold office equipment to
Nazi organizations. One Marburger recorded a current belief
when he wrote, sarcastically, that this man "brought back everything that he formerly delivered to those organizations." Another
investigator who had been appointed to work in a village adjacent
to Marburg took it upon himself to distribute some of the clothing
and supplies he found in a German Army warehouse in Marbach.
He also exchanged some goods for butter.[32] In spite of the difficulties during the early period of confusion, Nazi properties came
under military government property control and higher military
government headquarters decided upon their disposition, especially after Kreis detachments were relieved of functional responsibility for property control in December 1945.

Preliminary Administrative Reconstruction

To provide bases for reorganizing the civil administration,
military government officers made surveys of and wrote detailed
reports—some apparently in a hurry—on fire defense, civil defense,
the police situation, mining, the tobacco factory, trade and industry, communications, finances, fine arts, monuments and
archives, civilian supply, transportation, and agriculture.

Forming a civil government was related closely to denazification. The finance office, the customs office, and the post office
which the detachment closed were not reopened until military
government had screened the personnel and removed the Nazis.
Since these offices were formerly national, the Marburg detachment only observed them. Their operations were subject to review from the outset by higher civilian officials, who in turn
received their directives from higher military government detachments. In the city and county offices military government specialists acted directly to replace those Nazis who had fled prior to
the occupation and those who were removed or arrested after the

city was captured. Less than a week after Marburg capitulated, the Oberbürgermeister listed twenty-six persons whom he had removed on his own initiative and six whom he had removed on orders of military government. The first Military Governor of Marburg said he removed "fully seventy-five per cent of the Stadt-kreis and Landkreis officials above the rank of clerk or laborer" during the first week.[33] Military government officers tried to fill the vacancies with persons who could present acceptable *Frage-bogen* (denazification questionnaires) and who were otherwise acceptable to military government and the Counter Intelligence Corps.

The Military Governor of Land Hessen has written that form-ing a civil administration was singularly successful in those areas where military government appointed a reliable Bürgermeister or Landrat and told him to choose non-Nazis to fill the other positions in the public administration.[34] But there were several very serious difficulties inherent in such a practice, the most ob-vious being that a Landrat or Bürgermeister, even if he accepted the principle of denazification, had no idea what military govern-ment believed a Nazi to be.[35] The definition of who was to be considered sufficiently implicated in the Nazi movement to merit removal came from military government authorities only in mid-1945, when most of the officials had already selected the personnel that they would use to fill the offices under their jurisdiction.

In Marburg the appointment of a Bürgermeister and a Landrat proved that the plan the Hessian Military Governor considered so successful was not easily implemented. Both the Landrat and the Oberbürgermeister had to be removed during the first year of the occupation because they disagreed with military govern-ment regulations. Military government permitted the former to resign in October 1945, ostensibly because of ill health, probably because he denazified very reluctantly and because his views on militarism and government did not agree with those of American officers.[36] A well-known Marburger has said that his personal friend, the former Landrat, died—as he had lived—convinced that monarchy was the best form of government and that the Prussian three-class franchise was best for Germany. The Oberbürgermeister, who had been appointed provisionally in April 1945, was nevertheless retained in office until early 1946, when he was arrested by military government for falsifying his denazification questionnaire.* He had been kept on even though the first Military Governor of Marburg told his successor that the Oberbürgermeister should be replaced by a more suitable person.†

During the first year of occupation the Marburg military government detachment apparently was unable to find suitable candidates for the two most important civilian posts in the area. In the villages of the Landkreis, where military government exercised less care in the selection of Bürgermeisters and officials, the situation was even worse. Many of the public officials in the villages were not even appointed by military government or the Landrat. The Landrat did not know who some of them were during the first months of the occupation.[37] He and military government later discovered that some had been appointed by the military forces that captured the villages, some had been designated as mayors by the local population, and others had continued to serve in the positions they had held prior to 1945.

The detachment reviewed the records and the qualifications of village officials throughout 1945. Those who could not present acceptable denazification questionnaires were summarily removed or arrested and military government appointed their replacements.[38] But owing to the rapid turnover in military government personnel, the need to rely upon civilian investigators, and the

---

* Siebecke was charged with failing to report his connections with a DAF school during the thirties and with threatening an American officer. Technically he was guilty. There is evidence that military government wanted him removed for other reasons as well. He was reportedly an egotist, an opportunist, and a dictator. Besides, military government officers reported that he was suspected of having been implicated in a number of "misdemeanors, fast deals and crimes, including two murders." None of these charges was proved. Siebecke is convinced that he was "framed" by military government officers because he knew too much about military government corruption.

† Richard J. Eaton to author, January 27, 1955. Eaton, who still has the journal he kept in Marburg, was surprised to hear that both Siebecke and police chief Kroll had been retained in office until February 1946, long after he left Marburg.

noncooperative attitude of the Landrat, the Marburg detachment could not scrutinize village and city officials in the Landkreis as closely as it did the Marburg officials. Indicative of the lack of control by military government is the instruction that the Landrat gave to the mayors of the villages regarding the first election to be held in January 1946. He informed them that they were to be the election committee chairmen in their districts. He continued, however: "Mayors who were members of the Nazi party, and who have been formally removed, but still perform the duties of mayor in an advisory capacity, cannot be chairmen of the election committees."[39] Such mayors, the Landrat suggested, should be replaced on the committee by a "politically clean" and "democratically minded" (*"unbelasted und demokratisch gesinnt"*) male citizen.

In Marburg the military government detachment had to exercise a large measure of direct control over local affairs during the first year of the occupation. Theoretically, as time went on, civil officials were to assume more and more direct powers while military government was to supervise. But civilian officials could not be relied upon completely to denazify or to carry out military government directives. Military government employed a number of civilian investigators to review the actions of civil officials. Acting upon the findings of the investigators, upon information from denouncers, and upon information gathered by military government personnel, the detachment assumed more and more direct responsibility for the government of Marburg. It ordered rubble cleared, ordered removals and appointments, demanded translations of newspaper articles, and it even reinvestigated the civil officials it had formerly approved. Further, it continued to arrest Nazis, denazify, maintain security and order, confiscate property, observe political activities, assist in reopening the schools, and act as liaison representative with the military forces in the area. Marburgers who observed the detachment's actions in the first months of the occupation formed definite and lasting opinions about the occupation and the future of Germany. What these opinions were and what effect they would have upon the detachment's work only time would tell.

5

The German Looks
at His Future

The records left by the military government detachments for Marburg and Land Hessen seem to show that Marburgers were reasonably cooperative during the early phase of the occupation. As might have been expected, many Germans were disappointed with certain military government actions; but there is no indication in the American reports that the detachment's sources of voluntary assistance and information were drying up. The Marburg detachment apparently first noticed German reluctance to cooperate with Americans more than a year after the occupation of the city. In July 1946 the Liaison and Security Officer reported that the "readily obedient and submissive attitude of Germans toward occupation" had recently changed. About two months later he added that certain Marburgers revealed definite anti-American attitudes and conduct. They had reportedly sneered at administrative officials for cooperating with Americans and they exerted pressure upon military government appointees whom they wanted removed. All three of the anti-Americans named in the report had cooperated fully with military government at the outset of the occupation.

The records retained by the city and county of Marburg and the private papers of some of Marburg's leading citizens reveal attitudes and actions quite different from those the Americans reported. This difference is highly significant for at least two reasons: the attitude of Marburgers toward the early phase of the occupation conditioned their judgment of all military government poli-

cies and actions, and the former executive officer of the detachment
for Land Hessen has asserted that about 90 per cent of all policy
decisions made at that headquarters was conditioned by intelligence information received from field detachments.[1]

Expectations and Realizations, 1945

Marburgers had only vague ideas about what military occupation held in store for them. Some of them later stated that they
awaited the Americans as liberators. A few remembered the American occupation after the First World War, considered it to have
been a mild occupation, and expected the Americans to follow
their precedent.[2] Few, if any, welcomed the prospect of military
occupation. But many knew something about the democratic idealism of Americans and thought it would be a mitigative influence
upon the occupation. A few brave ones who had listened to the
Allied radio during the Nazi regime believed that the principles
expressed in such documents as the Atlantic Charter would govern
American military government practices. Most of them drew as-
surance from the proclamations posted in their city when the first
American troops entered: "We come as conquerors, but not as
oppressors." In general, Marburgers believed that the Army of
Occupation would be well behaved, disciplined, and "correct," as
they imagined the German army had been in occupying other
countries.

Many Germans expected to play an active role in the reconstruction of Germany. They had heard from Allied radio broadcasts that military government detachments would occupy each
German town. Men and women who considered themselves to be
anti-Nazis and in agreement with the ideals of the Allied forces
anticipated that these detachments would search them out.[3] A
very small group of political leaders, believing they could strive for
their goals independently or at least with only limited military government direction or interference, formed a political committee
whose function and purpose is the subject of a succeeding chapter.
A few presented themselves to the occupation forces, declaring their
readiness to serve in the cause of rebuilding and to assist actively in

the complete destruction of all traces of National Socialism and militarism. Some of them were encouraged, but others felt rejected because military personnel often sought different counsel.

Military government officers, eager to gather facts, heard the reports of those Germans who volunteered information. But the officers were extremely cautious. Finding it difficult to distinguish between objective reporters and the denouncers and opportunists who apparently were far more numerous, they also exploited other sources of information. They interviewed the people whom the military government white, black, and grey lists designated to be reliable non-Nazis and anti-Nazis, and they relied rather heavily upon displaced persons "who disliked the Germans with varying degrees of hostility."[4] Americans who had attended the University sought out their classmates, sometimes without apparent discretion. Hermann Bauer stated that when one officer learned that a friend he sought had been an active Nazi he replied that she was still "a good girl." In addition, the detachment officers called upon Marburg's clergymen, from whom they expected to receive valuable information.

Relying upon the clergy appears to have been a serious miscalculation based upon American rather than German conditions. Presumably military government officers took it for granted that the clergy would be a neutral, nonpolitical source of information and advice. They failed to realize that the German clergyman is also bound closely to the state, which appoints him and which allocates tax money for church budgets. Marburg's clergymen apparently did not ignore the dual character of their positions. A month after he was first interviewed by the Military Governor, and subsequent to his use of the interview as a basis for asking military government for five special favors for clergymen and for a more just requisitioning procedure, the superintendent of the Protestant clergy still entertained serious doubts as to the message that the clergy should bring to the people. He addressed himself to the theological faculty of Marburg University and requested clarification of the status of the clergy under the occupation. He and his colleagues were troubled by the responsibility they felt to the Nazi state. He asked if the clergy should continue to preach obedience to the National Socialist government, which still existed, in spite of the stories of atrocities that were now generally known. In view of the teachings of the Lutheran church to obey the powers that be, the superintendent declared, the clergy found it extremely difficult to preach to those who were still bound to the National Socialist government by an oath of loyalty. The answer he received, one day later, was that the American Army was to be obeyed as the power in existence, and that Lutheran Christians were no longer bound by conscience to obey the National Socialist government. The faculty referred to the atrocities committed by Nazis and to Luther's own statement that a soldier need not obey in an unjust war.[5]

Troop Behavior

Reports abound of incidents that undermined the faith of those Germans who had had confidence in the American occupation; of those who had looked upon it as a liberating influence; especially of those who expected the soldiers to be disciplined and "correct" in their behavior.

The combat troops who entered the city took watches, cameras, radios, and furniture promiscuously. They opened the doors of the prisons and released criminals as well as political prisoners. They were kind to children and friendly with women, but hostile toward men. They apparently respected the nonfraternization regulations only in their dealings with men.

During the first year of occupation, when Marburg was crowded with troops awaiting redeployment, Germans reported many unprovoked attacks by American soldiers upon civilians. The Rector of the University alleged that Marburgers were afraid to walk on the streets at night even before curfew hours. An American survey disclosed that troops attacked even cripples and the war blind. A girl suffered a fractured vertebra when she jumped from a third-story window to escape from soldiers who had followed her into her apartment. The victims of two attacks were totally blinded. The dean of the theological faculty reported that he escaped serious injury at the hands of irresponsible soldiers only because the soldiers were distracted by a woman. He reported that one day as he walked through the narrow city streets a truck loaded with American soldiers approached. The soldiers on the truck amused themselves, as they were sped along, by trying to hook girls' ankles with a cane. When a man came within reach they used the cane as a club. The dean declared that he might have been struck, except that the soldiers saw a woman whom they tried to hook.[6] One of the leading book dealers of the city described other incidents and concluded that these and similar occurrences were the subjects of daily conversations among the citizens of Marburg. He said it was risky to appear on the streets in the evening. He observed that the last insignificant traces of the "joyous reception" that the occupation forces had received were disappearing, and he believed that the democratic ideals that some Germans had had at the beginning of the occupation were being systematically undermined.[7]

The Plight of Germans Who Wanted to Play an Active Role

Germans who believed they had a right to expect military government to use their services, or hear their counsel, were disillusioned and discouraged early. Military government seemed to treat them the same as it treated Nazis, informers, opportunists, and those seeking personal favors. The Landrat, the Oberbürgermeister, the members of the political committee, the chief of police and his assistants in the special investigation branch, as well as many other German civilians, considered themselves to have been ideologically—if not always practically—out of harmony with the Nazi regime. Many of them had lost their positions and some of them had been arrested during the Hitler regime. Although not all of them opposed the Hitler regime actively, and some even applied for membership in the Nazi party, such Germans believed they had a right to expect military government to distinguish between them and Nazis or "ohne mich" Germans.*

* Oberhessische Presse, November 8, 1951, p. 3, carries a report that one such official signed an application for Nazi party membership in 1940. He had been removed from his position in 1933, had been arrested several times by the Gestapo, and had spent four weeks in a concentration camp. The party rejected his application.

But American officers and men in Germany appear to have considered Germans to be as similar as peas in a pod. During the first few months of the occupation American radio broadcasts emphasized the collective guilt of Germans for Nazi atrocities.[8] The Hessian military government detachment filed its miscellaneous correspondence from civilians in a folder labeled "Crank Letters"; a label that was later changed to "Public Opinion," probably after American attitudes and policies toward Germans had changed.[9] Even as late as 1950 the American Resident Officer in Marburg wrote that the opposition to American reorientation programs stemmed essentially from former Nazis and beneficiaries of the Nazi regime.[10] We shall see that the most serious opposition came from non-Nazi sources.

Evidence piled up to convince Marburgers that the attitude of the occupation forces toward Germans who felt themselves qualified to take part in German reconstruction was anything but cooperative. The radio broadcasts emphasizing the Germans' collective guilt were one thing, but there were other examples closer to home. Three American soldiers searched the house of a University professor whom Germans had sentenced to death in 1943. He survived because the sentence had been commuted to five years imprisonment. When he showed them the document in his possession testifying to the fact of his arrest, the soldiers threw it into his face and remarked that it meant nothing to them. When an American general visited Marburg early in July 1945, the Oberbürgermeister informed him that a political committee, consisting of members of all former political groups, had been organized for the purpose of rooting out Nazis. "The American said he could not believe it was possible in Germany and promised to report it as a novelty to General Eisenhower." At another time the Finance Officer of the Marburg detachment refused to interview the man appointed by the Oberbürgermeister to take charge of the municipal finance office, telling him that military government wanted to deal with the Oberbürgermeister only, and ordered him to leave and not reappear in the military government offices. Incidents of this type were apparently so well known among Germans that in 1947 a popular account of German life under the occupation stated that Americans lumped all Germans together as second-class human beings and that from General Clay to the lowliest private in the United States Army there was evident the same spirit of absolute sovereignty of Americans over Germans.[11]

In spite of the fact that Americans regarded them as collectively guilty for Nazism and regardless of how American troops behaved and of how little actual power they themselves could wield, German civilians who professed a sense of responsibility for the future of Germany had a few clear alternatives during the first few months of the occupation of Marburg. They had to work with military government in some way, since a German state no longer existed. They might seek employment with military government or accept a military government appointment in the civil administration. They might form a citizens' group—such as the *Staatspolitischer Ausschuss*—to work with military government. They might, if motivated by selfish, personal interests, turn to denunciation and become agents or informers for military government teams or officers.

In Marburg the possibilities for employment with the local detachment were exceedingly limited for persons desiring responsible positions. The detachment came prepared to furnish its own functional specialists and make its own policy. With few exceptions Germans trained in administrative and executive work found no employment with military government at the Stadtkreis and Landkreis level. Even if a man with such training would have agreed to work for military government in a minor position, he usually was not asked unless he could speak English. Thus, active collaboration was generally restricted to clerical and minor administrative employees who spoke the English language.

German civilians who accepted military government appointments in the civil administration often felt unduly restricted. If they assumed the role of minor officials, took orders, and governed as military government personnel wished, their positions were tenable. During the detachment's first year of operations a civil administration officer kept a desk in the Landrat's office so he could more easily supervise the activities of appointed officials. The

Military Governor required the Oberbürgermeister to appear at the military government offices each day at noon to receive specific instructions. The former Oberbürgermeister has asserted that in addition to the daily visit he was subjected to call by the Military Governor or any of his functional officers whenever they deemed it necessary.[12]

Detachment officers interfered directly in municipal and county affairs without knowledge of or against the wishes of the Oberbürgermeister and the Landrat. They ordered civil officials dismissed for being inefficient or unqualified or because they were hard to get along with. A case in point is the removal of August Eckel, who later became Landrat, from an administrative position on the public utilities commission. The Public Utilities Officer ordered Eckel removed because he was "unable to do the job in a satisfactory manner and usually has an argument about anything that he is told to do."[13] The Oberbürgermeister and the members of the political committee believed Eckel to be qualified and considered the dismissal unjust.

Detachment officers frowned upon independent action or evidence of initiative on the part of their appointees. For example, the Oberbürgermeister's request for permission to publish a handbook of military government laws with English and German commentaries was never answered.[14] Although scavengers at the garbage dump were pushing each other under the wheels of garbage trucks in 1945, the police hesitated, they said, to post rules that might conflict with regulations that military authorities might already have made.[15] Even after the municipal officials were elected in accordance with military government policy, American Army officers threatened to change the administration if American-German relations did not improve.* The Landrat was apparently so well conditioned that in 1948 he still felt obliged to ask the Liaison

* Protocol about the conference with Colonel Kilgore which took place September 19, 1946, with Oberbürgermeister Müller, n.d. (trans. by Bürgermeister's staff); Niederschrift über eine Besprechung am 29. Oktober 1946, n.d., Stadtkreis Marburg Papers. The colonel reported that Americans were bringing a great deal of food to Marburg and prophesied that the Germans would be sorry to see the troops leave. He said the Americans were doing their duty

and Security Officer for permission to establish a riding and driving school.[16]

Germans who did not collaborate directly with military government—either because they felt they were not needed in their specialties, or because they did not want to do so directly—formed citizens' committees dedicated to denazification as well as to physical, political, educational, economic, and spiritual reconstruction of the city and the Landkreis. The most important of the committees in Marburg was the political committee (Staatspolitischer Ausschuss). The activities and the difficulties of that committee are discussed in the chapter that follows. From what has already been said it is clear, however, that any person wishing to play an active role in the reconstruction of Germany found little opportunity to realize his desires at the local level. If he became an employee of military government he could only play a very minor role. If he accepted appointment as mayor, Landrat, or administrative official, he was constantly told what he could or could not do.

The impact of such conditions may help to explain the presence of unusually large numbers of informers among the Germans. Some of those Germans who said they had hoped to punish individual Nazis had already been frustrated because of the early establishment of law and order.[17] Attempts at peaceful collaboration were also being curbed indirectly. There was hardly anything left for Germans to do but become informers or agents for military government. But a significant number of Marburgers who were purportedly willing at the outset to support denazification, demilitarization, and democratization of Germany considered this type of activity morally inexcusable. In fact, the *Marburger Presse* often carried articles and editorials on the evil of denunciation, even if practiced after 1945. It gave a great deal of space to

---

and that the Germans should "watch their language." He told the Oberbürgermeister to order the labor office to send better workers to American units and not only those who wanted to pick up cigarette butts. He observed that the housing situation in Marburg was relatively good and complained that the housing office often sent Army secretaries to apartments that were already occupied. The colonel ended the interview by expressing the hope that relations with the city would improve, but threatened the municipal government with removal if they did not.

the first two cases tried by the Marburg denazification tribunal, involving persons accused of having denounced their fellow citizens during the Nazi regime. The priority and publicity given these two cases creates the impression of deliberation to provide a moral lesson in the evils of denunciation.

Eventually Marburgers who refused to work with military government under the conditions described withdrew from active public life. They followed their personal inclinations and awaited the time when they might successfully assume the role that they believed should have been theirs in the reconstruction of Germany. We shall see that the political committee voted to dissolve itself. Some of its members had resigned earlier, to concentrate on their special interests and professions. The head of the special investigation section of the police department (Sonderabteilung U) reported that he was "fed up" (*"Ich hatte die Nase voll!"*).

Some German Thoughts about the Occupation in 1945

Some of the leading citizens of Marburg left records of their reactions to the American occupation in its first few months. Although the reports which follow cannot be considered typical—their authors were not—they do provide an excellent review of the thoughts Marburgers had in 1945 as they looked forward to an indefinite period of American occupation. The authors had been among the first to volunteer their services to military government or to organize independently for the purposes of denazification and reconstruction. As such, they were probably the only people in Marburg familiar enough with the occupation to write reports about it.

The Mütze Report

Toward the end of June 1945 a man in American uniform came to the home of Ludwig Mütze and asked him to prepare a report of his reactions to the occupation of Marburg. Mütze had been an outstanding school administrator prior to the Nazi regime. Before the Democratic party was dissolved by the Nazis, Mütze had been one of its leading members. He was a member of the voluntary political committee that organized in April, and after September 1945 he helped found the Liberal Democratic party in Marburg. With the approval of military government the Oberbürgermeister had appointed him *Schulrat* in 1945. In that position he worked together with the military government educational specialist on the program of opening German schools.

Mütze's report is a series of personal observations that illustrate why he thought that many Germans who had expected freedom and law to accompany the occupation were frustrated. He asserted that there were millions of Germans who now, after three months of military government rule, were disappointed, embittered, and, in some cases, hostile toward the occupation.[18] Even though his report described his personal experiences, Mütze declared that it still had general political significance, because many Marburgers had had similar experiences and because "the ordinary man makes his political decisions on the basis of his direct experiences and his immediate environment."

His report must be read with some caution, however. Mütze spoke not so much for the ordinary man as for the group in Marburg that would reconstruct Germany as they thought German history, tradition, and culture demanded. Later in the occupation he revealed a strong dislike for the American programs of direct political representation, civil service reform, educational reform, grass-roots reorientation, and denazification other than that directed against very serious offenders who could be convicted of actual crimes. As a conservative, he feared the innovations which complete military government control or radical denazification seemed to foreshadow.

Attitudes of Marburgers toward military government had changed, Mütze thought, because of the widespread knowledge of occupation injustices, which he illustrated with a series of facts and conditions.

A military unit had occupied Mütze's apartment. The officer-in-charge asked him to leave all possessions behind, assuring him that they would be returned. A month later, when he was permitted to reoccupy his apartment, Mütze found it messy and littered with garbage. Three people spent three days cleaning it up. Besides, furniture and other articles had disappeared and all the light bulbs—which were almost impossible to replace through purchase in normal trade channels—were gone.

Mütze thought the American practice of giving short evacuation notices was beyond comprehension and said that every German, whether he was a Nazi or an anti-Nazi, faced the prospect of having his dwelling requisitioned. He, and he believed other Germans also, would not have objected if the Army required them to give up a few rooms, not because Germans deferred to military authority, but because such a practice would have given the owners an opportunity to watch over their gardens and to report to the proper military authorities when they observed troops removing articles from their houses.

A nephew, who had visited Mütze in 1938, and who was a member of the occupation forces in Marburg for a short time, was not permitted to visit his uncle because of the fraternization ban. He was allowed to talk with Mütze in the military government offices. Mütze meant this as an illustration of the foolishness of the fraternization ban, but his real complaint was that the nonfraternization policy worked a hardship upon men who wanted to cooperate with military government with a view toward curbing innovation and widespread social, economic, and political change.

American Army units destroyed the food they wasted rather than give it to hungry Germans. Prisoners of war, Mütze continued, who had been released from American camps spoke of cruel treatment, shortage of food, and regulations prohibiting civilians from bringing food to the prisoners even after the end of the war. There were rumors in Marburg that about fifty prisoners died daily in a nearby camp. Letters from German prisoners in the United States had ceased to arrive in Marburg, although they had come regularly during hostilities. Mütze believed these conditions to be illustrative of the lack of good will on the part of military government toward Germans and of the Americans' unwillingness to treat Germans in accord with the propaganda releases which had encouraged them to surrender. Whether he knew that the American Army consumed its own imported food and not indigenous food supplies, or whether he knew about Nazi policies in occupied territories is difficult to discern. Even if he had known, however, Mütze would expect Americans to act differently from Nazis.

Continuing his illustrations of occupation injustices, Mütze wrote that in Marburg there was a girl who had had both legs severed by a streetcar when she was seven years old. She was thirty-one in 1945, and had worked in a minor position in the city bank for fifteen years, the city having employed her out of a feeling of responsibility. Military government dismissed her along with all other municipal employees and appointed to her position a "man who was a member of a leading Nazi family in Marburg." Mütze thought the man had performed some service for military government, and remarked that such action was difficult to understand when perpetrated by a nation that fought the war against those who opposed Christian ethics and destroyed the laws of humanity. He felt qualified to criticize, he later told me, because he had no part in the Nazi crimes against humanity.

Last, Mütze wrote that the American nonfraternization policy caused Germans to think Americans considered them inferior to Americans as individuals, that Americans apparently classified all Germans with the war criminals, and that denazification proceeded without apparent rules or regulations and without assistance of the anti-Nazis who knew local conditions and people. Although he wrote that no German expected immediate unrestricted intercourse with the occupation forces, Mütze believed that honorable and honest citizens would not long permit themselves to be treated as helots, to be lumped with war criminals, and to be ignored in favor of leftists and opportunists in the denazification program. Regarding denazification Mütze was at least partly correct in June 1945. The first Military Governor of Marburg wrote that the occupation of Marburg during the early days was a "hectic affair."[19] Specific denazification policies were forwarded to military government detachments in July 1945.

Mütze closed his report with the assertion that if conditions such as those he listed and described did not change there was little hope for a peaceful, democratic Germany. He pleaded for some sign of hope for the future.

The Bauer Report

Two months after Mütze made his report, a member of the information control team in Marburg asked Hermann Bauer to report on what the Germans in Marburg thought of the occupation. Bauer had been a newspaper editor and publisher until his paper was suppressed by Nazis in 1934. In September 1945 he became editor of the military government–licensed *Marburger Presse*, the third licensed German newspaper in the American Zone of Germany. He had been a member of the Democratic party of the Weimar Republic and was one of the founders of the Liberal Democratic party in Marburg. As a political committee member and as editor of the *Marburger Presse* he was able to observe the activities of military government rather closely.

Bauer reported that the relaxation of the nonfraternization regulations benefited only little girls. He thought that those Germans who, like himself, subscribed to the democratic principles of the United States still found that military government officers distrusted them as they had from the first day of the occupation. He believed that the implicit assumption of military government that all Germans were Nazis had disappointed a large number of Germans. Bauer, and apparently most other Marburgers, believed that the fraternization ban grew out of the theory of collective guilt of Germans to which the American-controlled radio and press gave considerable publicity during the first months of the occupation.[20] The criticism of military government for not accepting all Germans who wanted to help is somewhat unfair, however, because detachment officers often discouraged Marburgers for no other reason than that they could not distinguish clearly between opportunists and honest volunteers. Furthermore, higher military government headquarters had warned detachments to be cautious regarding self-appointed committees, because many of them only claimed to be spokesmen for the entire community, and because others were dominated by Communists and Social Democrats.

Last, the rapid turnover of military government personnel often placed Marburgers who had been accepted by the former detachment officers in the awkward position of being suspected by the newly arrived officers, chiefly because the new officers lacked adequate information about them. Thus, even though many military government officers were convinced of the collective guilt of Germans, others only seemed to give that impression because they were doing their duty.

Continuing with his report, Bauer asserted that Germans had never envisaged the American campaign against National Socialism to be a campaign against the German nation. Some Germans had hoped that the opponents of Nazism would be permitted to participate in the denazification of Germany. But, Bauer added, the Americans denazified independently, apparently confidently, leaving the anti-Nazis with the somewhat thankless task of reporting mistakes that Americans made.[21] It was thankless because it caused friction between the anti-Nazis and military government. Bauer cited the controversy regarding the removal of Eckel from his position on the public utilities commission. He concluded that those Germans who had been indifferent to the Hilter regime, while they reaped the benefits of that regime, and who were indifferent to the occupation were actually in a better position than those who were anxious to assume the responsibility of rebuilding Germany upon a democratic foundation. At least they were not rebuffed constantly. He, and some of his colleagues, had often been bitterly disappointed.

The Report of the Political Committee

In November the political committee prepared a top-secret report for the Oberbürgermeister on the reasons for the growing German dislike of American military government in Marburg.[22] The membership of the political committee will be discussed in the chapter that follows. It was made up of one Communist, one Socialist, one Christian Democrat, two right-wing Liberal Democrats, and one left-wing Liberal Democrat. Before the committee was formed, military government reviewed the members' denazi-

fication questionnaires and approved the members for the committee. They were all political leaders of the Marburg community. In
their professional activities and as members of the political committee they were able to observe military government in action
better than the average German in Marburg.

In its report the committee conveniently divided the population of Marburg into two major groups: the anti-Nazis, antifascists, and the democrats who looked upon the Allied victory as a
liberation; and those Germans who had believed in ultimate German victory, who viewed the Americans as enemies and, therefore,
used every opportunity to turn public opinion against the occupation and its democratic supporters. According to the political committee, the second group included not only the former Nazis but
also the nationalists and the militarists. The division ignored the
Germans who had accepted National Socialism for various irra-
tional reasons and who in 1945 realized the error they had made
after they learned of the concentration camps and Nazi atrocities.
It further ignored the politically indifferent who were apparently
willing to go along with the "powers that be." The division into
two groups is obviously methodological. It provides a basis for
listing the reasons why the first group—the anti-Nazis, antifascists,
and democrats—were disturbed by military government practices
and policies. The report conveniently lumped all other Germans
into a second group to be ignored.

The committee's report was also in two parts: the attitudes of
anti-Nazis, antifascists, and democrats after seven months of occupation, and the reasons why the attitudes had become unfavorable toward military government. The committee believed that
Germans who had entertained strong hopes for a democracy were
discouraged because military government, "the first democratic
influence in Germany after the war," provided a poor example of
democracy in action. Military government had left unanswered
their longing for law and legal procedures. The committee thought
American policy vacillated, and that it was inconsistent with democratic principles. They believed that the spirit of law, justice,
humanity, love, and forgiveness that the American President

stressed was not evident in military government laws, measures, and orders after the complete victory over the Nazi rulers. Last, the committee reported that the civil administrators, who had been appointed by military government, felt extremely insecure in their positions because military government constantly re-examined their political records on the basis of denunciations by "uncontrollable elements of society." As a result, officials who had cooperated with military government to the best of their ability were beginning to feel that military government no longer trusted them in spite of their "diligent and courageous support of military government in its program of building a new, clean, and democratic life." There is some truth to the last assertion, but not for the reason given, except in isolated cases. Military government reinvestigated the officials because denazification directives changed, because newly discovered Nazi files were made available to the denazification branches of military government, and because personnel changed so often. It was only natural that a new military governor would review the records of his civil administrators, if for no other reason than to know them better. It might be justly asked why German officials objected to such review if they had nothing to hide, but there is a principle involved. German democrats who had been under attack, and who are still a minority, are probably much more aroused by an encroachment upon democratic principle than democrats in countries in which democrats are in a majority.

The committee's explanation for the changed attitude of anti-Nazis, antifascists, and democrats, and for their loss of confidence in military government for Stadtkreis and Landkreis Marburg is perhaps expressed most clearly by translating and paraphrasing the appropriate portions of the report itself:

1. The military requisitioning policy, although just in its demand that Nazi homes be requisitioned, was unjust in practice. Some Nazis sat comfortably in their homes "and laughed" while the occupation forces and military government requisitioned the houses and apartments of anti-Nazis. Troops senselessly destroyed property in the requisitioned houses. They left houses unlocked and unguarded when they departed, making it

possible for unscrupulous Germans or displaced persons to steal property before the owner could take possession again. The result was that furniture was scattered. Troops took along radios when they moved. They confiscated cameras. They tossed porcelain, pictures, furniture, and other valuables into the street, occasionally to be soaked with gasoline and burned. In some homes the troops destroyed or took stamp collections, paintings, and other works of art. Two cafes that had been requisitioned for troop messes were left stripped of equipment and fixtures. "Dumbfounded and bitter, the population of Marburg stood by and watched their last meager possessions being senselessly destroyed, long after the Allied weapons had achieved total victory."[23]

2. The prisoners whom the American Army released came home half-starved. They reported that the camp commanders had ordered garbage from American messes hauled to the dump rather than permit German prisoners to eat it. Released prisoners from the camp at the Marburg south station reported that they had been beaten.[24]

3. American troops permitted mobs of Germans and displaced persons to loot captured *Wehrmacht* stocks while the normal ration coupons for shoes, clothing, and food could not be honored by the merchants.

4. The American Army did not maintain law and order as it had during the early days of the occupation. American soldiers and displaced persons reportedly attacked civilians and even policemen who were unable to arrest them. American soldiers, or displaced persons dressed in American uniforms and armed with American weapons, attacked and robbed Germans in their homes or on the streets.[25]

5. Marburgers were forced to cut down their consumption of electric power to a minimum, which was "almost unbearable," while houses requisitioned by the occupation forces could be seen to have lights burning from top to bottom both in the night and during the day.

6. Germans reported an unusually large number of accidents involving American vehicles. Pedestrians were run down almost daily. Civilian vehicles had been rammed or forced into the ditches. Many American drivers did not obey civilian traffic policemen.

7. American denazification was based upon a basic misunderstanding of the Nazi regime. The methods used were wrong. Many Marburgers agreed with military government in

spirit, but they thought military government investigators used Gestapo methods. Denazification according to a questionnaire and a prescribed scheme did not take into account the party members who were not Nazis as such. There were at least three denazification cases in which military government had dismissed non-Nazis.*

8. The rural population complained about American hunting rights and practices. The troops hunted at night with spotlights and fished with hand grenades. They drove their vehicles over planted fields.

The political committee hoped that the report would serve as a partial explanation of the causes for the disappointment of many Germans with the occupation. The authors of the report said that they did not want to explain away the guilt of the German nation, nor did they want it understood that they expected friendly relations between Americans and Germans to develop in a little more than a half-year. They believed that Germans had to repent and reform, but they thought that those Germans who would lead this reformation needed "a strong arm to lean upon." Military government did not provide the moral encouragement that German democrats needed. They said their opponents had often chastened those who cooperated with military government with: "There are your democratic friends from America. What have they brought you?"

During the early phase of military government Marburgers seemingly viewed their future with a feeling of utter helplessness. The detachment often reported to higher headquarters that Germans came to military government with problems that they should have solved by themselves. The editor of the *Marburger Presse* wrote that he was ashamed of the attitude of Germans toward the occupation. They expected the Americans to help them, and if help was not forthcoming they complained.[26]

The reports just described illustrate one of the inevitable paradoxes of the American occupation in Germany. To the Ger-

---

* Because the SPA believed that unjust denazification was often linked with denunciations, it recommended that military government make denouncers deposit a 500-mark caution fee that they would forfeit in the event the denunciation proved to be false.

man Americans exemplified an ideal to be realized in the indefinite future. The ideal may have been unclear and indefinable, but Marburgers seem to have expected their lots to improve rather than become worse. But short of a miracle, there was much to be done immediately. In the face of normal social inertia and resistance to change, Americans found themselves using methods that could hardly be reconciled with their ideals. Marburgers who sympathized with American ideals, but who were also the objects of American methods, often found it difficult to keep the ideals in focus. Thus, Marburgers seem to have been overly concerned with criticism while they took for granted the encouraging features of American policy and practice.

Even in the early phase of military government the freedoms that Germans enjoyed are noteworthy. No one feared denunciation, arrest, or reprisals for listening to any radio broadcast.[27] The fact that Americans asked for and accepted the Mütze and Bauer reports is itself noteworthy. The fears that some had had of American troops engaging in widespread violence proved unfounded. Marburgers agree that after a very short period of time they felt freer than they had under the Nazis, and that there seemed to be prospects of better and more regular food rations than during the war. The American Army provided emergency food supplies for Germans from Army stock piles. Military government permitted labor organizations to hold shop-steward elections. It manifested an earnest desire to revive political parties. Officially it cracked down on the black market by apprehending, arresting, and trying black-marketeers. It took an active interest in German youth activities, and it imported American films for German audiences. Last, it maintained law and order remarkably well in a disorganized society.

The American Army, and individuals within the Army, also contributed directly to the improvement of German conditions. Soldiers distributed food, cigarettes, and candies to friends and children despite the nonfraternization regulations. Germans who obtained employment with American units got a ration-free noonday meal.[28] Some soldiers spent their spare time helping German youth. They organized or sponsored recreational groups, provided sports equipment, and served as instructors and advisers for youth activities. Later these activities were made part of official Army policy to support German youth activities (GYA). The interest of military units in physical recovery resulted in rapid repair of electric works, waterworks, sewage disposal plants, streetcar lines, highways, telephone and telegraph lines, and other public services.

Furthermore, during the first phase of military government the lack of a clear policy, the rapid turnover in personnel, and the need to do first things first often resulted in salutary neglect of Germans. For example, the University in Marburg enjoyed a large measure of freedom, more freedom than it deserved because it had many Nazis on the faculty. The University medical clinics continued to operate until August under personnel who later fell under the mandatory removal classifications of the American denazification regulations. Faculty members engaged in research without apparent restrictions and the Oberbürgermeister paid them from city revenues.[29]

Military government personnel changed so often that it was possible for German officials to manipulate it to their own advantage. A letter from one conservative politician to another, in June 1945, indicates how this was done. The writer observed that a new military government officer with "an understanding for many things" ("der Verständnis haben soll für viele Dinge") had arrived in Marburg. He suggested that someone should approach this officer and ask him to authorize the formation of a political committee for the Landkreis. It was further suggested, in the letter, that this new officer might be persuaded to use a "responsible" German to advise him regarding personnel matters, because the "Americans appear to have a rather heavy hand when it pertains to personnel policies."[30]

Marburgers took the positive aspects of the occupation for granted and criticized the negative aspects. A public opinion survey conducted in June 1946 among leading citizens of Marburg revealed ominous reactions. Most of the persons interviewed could think of positive aspects of the occupation only under prodding.

When left to voice their own opinions they discussed the negative aspects.[31] A high Landkreis official stated in 1954 that the American occupation forces deliberately used the confusion and chaos resulting from the war to further their own ends rather than to rebuild Germany. He believed that the Germans needed reforms to show them the way for the future, but he thought that the Americans persistently tried to perpetuate chaos for their own advantage by encouraging informers and opportunists, by denazifying schematically, and by demolishing some of the most productive features of the German economy with the exception of agriculture.[32] Most of the persons whom the author interviewed in Marburg in 1953–54 agreed with the opinion expressed by this civil servant.

Of the many reasons for Marburgers' critical judgment of the American occupation one stands out strongly and clearly: Military government developed its own policies based on its own views about the future of Germany and its administrators carried out those policies in their own time and in their own way. Marburgers had to defer to the greater authority of their conquerors. They did this, however, only after a serious attempt to gain authority for themselves.

The Quest for
Civil Authority

During the late spring and summer of 1945 a sign reading *"Die Staatsgewalt geht vom Volke aus"* (The people are sovereign) hung over the doorway of the small conference room in the Marburg Rathaus. The sign was evidence of a struggle for power within the Marburg civil administration between military government's appointees and a self-appointed political committee that purportedly represented the Marburg community. The political committee thought that the Oberbürgermeister was much too dictatorial and that he used his position to form a ruling clique in the city. They placed the sign above the door to admonish the Oberbürgermeister to consult with the political committee, because it represented the interests of the community.

In view of the frequent military government detachment reports that German officials preferred to apply to military government for help rather than to assume responsibility for unpleasant tasks or to use their initiative to begin reconstruction, it is paradoxical that in Marburg at least two organizations, the political committee (Staatspolitischer Ausschuss) and the special investigation branch of the police department (Sonderabteilung U), tried unsuccessfully to initiate and be responsible for Marburg's reconstruction.

The Political Committee

One day after American troops occupied Marburg some German civilians discussed how they might assist the military forces to govern the city. One of them said they should do something to return life to a more normal basis. By early April they had formed a group to call on the newly appointed Oberbürgermeister. Referring to themselves as the antifascists of Marburg, they said they wanted to form a committee to assist the Oberbürgermeister. In the Oberbürgermeister's presence the group designated itself an *Ordnungs-Ausschuss* (coordinating committee) and elected a chairman. It proposed to advise and assist civilian and military officials, and to act as a liaison between the population and the civil agencies. It prepared a placard to publicize its existence and functions.[1]

During this first meeting two of the committee members who had previously met with American military government officers in Marburg expressed their belief that the committee was politically much too conservative. They argued that more working-class representatives should have been admitted. A few days after the formation of the Ordnungs-Ausschuss a second group, representing the "working classes," came to the Rathaus with a request to form a second working and advisory committee. After conferring with an administrative assistant they invited the chairman of the Ordnungs-Ausschuss to meet with them and eventually elected him to act as their chairman also.[2] Acting upon the suggestion of the chairman, this second committee united with the Ordnungs-Ausschuss.

The Ordnungs-Ausschuss, thus enlarged, adopted the name Stadtrat mit angeschlossener Untersuchungskommission (City Council with attached Investigating Committee). It met initially on April 17, 1945, and elected a former German National People's party member as chairman. In this and subsequent meetings the original Ordnungs-Ausschuss members and the "working class" group fought for control of the committee. The latter was made up of former Communists and Social Democrats, but it included some Democrats (Deutsche Demokratische Partei) and others with dubious political connections. Arguing that their conversations with military government officers convinced them of the necessity for a truly representative committee, the spokesmen for the radical group prevailed upon the committee to replace the conservative chairman. To take his place the committee elected a Weimar Republic Democrat who later helped found the postwar Liberal Democratic party of Marburg. The atmosphere at the meetings was so tense that the new chairman (Ludwig Mütze) and his closest colleague (Hermann Bauer) believed that the original Ordnungs-Ausschuss members would ask military government to have the Stadtrat dissolved. They decided to go to military government, describe the purposes and functions of the revised committee, and secure recognition. In the meantime Mütze warned the Oberbürgermeister to support the group that controlled the committee. At military government Mütze and Bauer avowed that an "old Deutsch-Nationale" clique was trying to establish itself in the Rathaus at the expense of the anti-Nazis represented by former Social Democrats, Communists, and Democrats. The military government officer, who later wrote that military government officers and men were convinced that Marburg was a "hotbed of Nazism," readily supported the new committee.[3]

The Staatspolitischer Volksausschuss

Oberbürgermeister Siebecke dissolved the Stadtrat mit angeschlossener Untersuchungskommission on April 21, 1945. He later said that he did it to solve the internal difficulties before the individual members went to military government with complaints, but Mütze and Bauer's visit to military government probably forced the decision. Siebecke correctly believed that military government officers would grow increasingly suspicious of German civilians who carried their political differences to them. Five days after the dissolution Mütze informed Bauer, who had assisted so ably in having the conservative committee destroyed, that the Oberbürgermeister had appointed him (Mütze) Staatspolitischer Referent. Mütze said he would receive an office in the Rathaus and be given authority to discharge Nazis from office, to denazify business enterprises, and to investigate any underground Nazi activities that might be found in Marburg. Furthermore, he said he would help to organize the civil administration. Mütze suggested that Bauer help him form a Staatspolitischer Volksausschuss (People's Political Committee), which would help carry out these duties.

Under no circumstances did Mütze want the committee to appear to be a continuation of the former Democratic party. Representatives of all former parties, except the Nationalist and the National Socialist parties, were to be invited as members.[4]

The twenty persons recruited by Mütze and Bauer to form the Staatspolitischer Volksausschuss represented a variety of political groups. Eight were formerly, or were to become, Communist party members; six were formerly, or were to become, Social Democrats; four were to become Liberal Democrats; and two were not politically active enough to reveal their political inclinations. Four skilled laborers and four unskilled laborers represented the interests of labor. Three members were master craftsmen with employees of their own. The professions had five representatives. Business interests and white-collar workers had three and one, respectively.

It appears paradoxical that a city with a conservative political history should organize a political committee with such a decidedly leftist membership. It appears even more unusual because the two men who formed the committee later became leading members of the Marburg Liberal Democratic party, which eventually affiliated with other parties to form the conservative Free Democratic party of postwar West Germany. It is noteworthy, however, that the Marburg Liberal Democratic party was not as conservative as the national body it later joined. In fact, Bauer resigned from the executive committee when he recognized its conservative nature on the national level.

Probably most important in explaining Mütze and Bauer's recruitment of leftists is the fact that they had established liaison with the military government team. They told their colleagues that the only possible way to secure recognition from the Marburg detachment was to appear radical and oppose anyone remotely linked with the conservative political and economic forces that military government officers believed to have been the mainstays of support for the Nazi regime in Germany. They recalled later that it was common knowledge in Marburg that persons with leftist political inclinations got most support from military government or obtained employment there. It is true that the Oberbürgermeister was a Social Democrat and the chief of police a known Communist who, with apparent military government approval, filled police ranks—particularly the Sonderabteilung U and the department's "political division"—with his political friends. Many of the investigators and other employees of military government were Communists and Social Democrats.

In this context it is noteworthy also that even after the Staatspolitischer Ausschuss membership became decidedly conservative its correspondence, reports, and recommendations still appeared to be based upon radical leftist premises. For example, in October 1945 the committee took issue with the American practice of punishing Nazis by making them work as common laborers. In a report the committee stated that it valued labor according to "European standards" rather than *amerikanisch-demokratisch* standards. The report continued: to use common labor as a punishment is an insult to the working classes. Moreover, the "proletarization" of the Nazi workers would never be possible because in their family and social relationships they would always belong to the bourgeois classes. Under such circumstances the influence of the bourgeois classes could not be kept out of the working classes.*
Another example of the apparent desire to lean over backward to appear leftist is the expression of a former Center party member when he was accepted into the political committee in May. He deemed it necessary to proclaim that he was not a true conservative even though he was a well-known Center party member. Ideologically, he said, he had been a Socialist all the time.[5]

After the twenty persons agreed to serve on the committee that he was to direct, Mütze prepared an application to military government requesting recognition of the Staatspolitischer Volksausschuss and sanction for its work. The application stated optimistically that National Socialism had been destroyed through de-

---

* SPA: Bericht über die politische Lage in Marburg, October 11, 1945, Stadtkreis Marburg Papers. Ludwig Mütze, Hermann Bauer, and Otto Dula later told me that they did not agree with the report, but permitted its dispatch partly to please the Communist secretary on the committee and partly because they thought it might impress some military government officers.

feat; that military government had arrested most of the remaining Nazis and that little remained for the political committee to do regarding these two matters. However, Mütze thought that the political committee would prove invaluable as an interpreter of American actions and regulations to Marburgers. By authorizing the work of the committee Mütze believed military government could forestall criticisms from Germans who misunderstood democratic ideals as expressed by the American President and "leading members of the occupation forces." On behalf of his committee Mütze suggested further that the American officers could not possibly know all of the people who desired to assist them and that the committee could judge the reliability of persons whom military government wanted to place in key positions. On the other hand it could screen out those proposed employees who did not warrant trust by military government because of their past activities and "their characters." In short, Mütze declared, the political committee could help Americans "to understand local affairs and German psychology." To give added force to the application Mütze pointed out three "mistakes" that Americans had already made in denazification.*

The military government detachment and the Oberbürgermeister objected to the twenty-man committee partly because military directives prohibited groups of more than five persons from assembling at any one time. Thus the committee had to be reduced to five members and one interpreter who would also be a liaison representative. The Oberbürgermeister told the military governor that he objected to the absence of "true conservatives" on the committee.[6] Accordingly, the twenty-man committee asked a local Roman Catholic clergyman to recommend a conservative candidate. This candidate, the Staatspolitischer Referent, and three members from within the ranks of the larger committee were elected to membership in a committee of five.

---

* Staatspolitischer Referent to Oberbürgermeister, May 15, 1945; Ludwig Mütze to Oberbürgermeister, May 15, 1945, Stadtkreis Marburg Papers. The "mistakes" were the removal of three persons whom the SPA considered to have been only "nominal" Nazis.

The Character of the Committee of Five

The committee of five was decidedly more conservative than the committee of twenty had been. Not a single laborer remained and Communists and Socialists were in the minority. One of the members eventually joined the Christian Democratic Union; one member and the secretary-interpreter, who also had considerable authority within the committee itself, later became right-wing Liberal Democrats; another remained in the Liberal Democratic party until its national successor, the Free Democratic party, showed its true right-wing characteristics; one was a Socialist and the other a Communist. The economic interests of its members further illustrate the relatively conservative composition of the committee. One member and the secretary-interpreter were civil servants; one a school administrator and the other a teacher. A book dealer and a publisher represented the business interests on the committee. A master electrician and a gardener, both of whom were employers and merchants, were the other two members. The alternate members, some of whom played active roles as well, were even more conservative than the regular members. They did not differ in their political party preferences, but occupationally two were civil servants of the higher ranks, two were owners of large business establishments, and one was a master electrician with a business of his own.*

None of the committee members understood the words they had placed above the door of their conference room to mean what they apparently did to the military government personnel who were natives of the United States and who probably believed literally that "Die Staatsgewalt geht vom Volke aus." A member's own words are noteworthy. Writing to a friend on the first day of

---

* Ludwig Mütze to Oberbürgermeister, May 24, 1945, Stadtkreis Marburg Papers. Note that the total membership is six, rather than five. The secretary and interpreter assumed an important position because he was the only English-speaking person on the committee. He must actually be considered one of the more influential committee members, because he was its liaison representative with military government officers and was often forced to make decisions on the spot. These decisions were usually adopted by the committee in subsequent meetings.

the occupation, Hermann Bauer said he would like to begin publication of a newspaper because the people were so terribly ignorant and stupid that they would even blame the enemy for the difficulties they had to suffer. The attitude and behavior of Mütze further illustrate this difference. As chairman of the city council after 1946 Mütze constantly criticized the editor of the *Marburger Presse* for publicizing city council proceedings and for asking for public pressure upon councilmen regarding specific issues. He thought that the publicity only encouraged "unfounded" criticisms from the public and tended to hamper the work of the city council.[7]

The different interpretation of the sovereignty of the people by the members of the political committee and by American personnel in Germany is further evident in the cool reception given by the former to the reorientation program which was sponsored actively by military government and Department of State representatives in Germany. Even though Hermann Bauer supported the reorientation program, his position regarding the ignorance of the population has been noted. Ludwig Mütze openly criticized the effects of the reorientation program. Besides his criticism of Bauer's publication of city council proceedings, he related an incident to the author regarding a public meeting on the question of consolidation of schools. He and the Landrat wanted to consolidate the schools of two villages, but in public meeting the citizens of the villages voted the proposal down. His comment: "The officials of the county and even the locally elected city councils cannot do anything anymore unless it is popular." We shall see in a later chapter that the other members of the political committee were unsympathetic toward the reorientation program and its town-hall meetings and public forums. One of the members stated that he was so disappointed with all the other things the occupation forces did that he wanted no part of anything they were promoting.

Another significant illustration of the conservative orientation of the political committee involves a discussion of the other organization in Marburg that was willing to asume responsibility in the job of denazification and demilitarization.

The Special Investigation Branch of the Police Department

On April 21, 1945, the chief of police appointed Hans Frese to head a special investigation commission (Sonderabteilung U). He instructed the commission to combat National Socialistic influences and to discover any plans that might arise or meetings that might be held for the purpose of organizing a Nazi underground (*Werwolf*) movement. The police chief directed Frese to watch certain suspicious persons who might promote Nazi activity.

Frese and his staff worked with a vengeance. Although they were recompensed later, they began without promise of compensation and Frese converted his own home into an office. He interpreted the order to battle Nazi activities (*"Bekämpfung national-sozialistischer Umtriebe"*) to include the following: campaigns against Werwolf activities, location of centers of Nazi activity that might attract youth, suppression of rumors and gossip that might motivate youth to undertake underground activities against the occupation or the newly formed city administration, and negation of the commonly held assumption that the "new people's state" (*"Neuer Volksstaat"*) consisted of weak and incompetent officials. Frese reported that during the first week of activity he made connections, set up a card file of National Socialists, investigated the emergency policemen upon request of the American Public Safety Officer, secured an assistant who "stood near to the Communist party" (*"Steht der KPD nahe"*), and made a series of case studies of individuals by interviewing them and studying their past activities. During the second week he investigated former denunciants, examined businessmen and intellectuals to set up "white" and "black" lists, and devised a card file of information on former members of the Nazi party and its more important affiliated organizations. He reported no Werwolf activity.[8]

Frese apparently never made a third activity report. The political committee, after settling its internal difficulties and cutting down its membership, decided to eliminate other organizations that might threaten the city and the county with precipitous political change. A committee member later stated that the conservatives deliberately became members of the political committee to act as a counterweight to the active leftists in Marburg. He said they were especially afraid that the Communists might gain power by working in conjunction with the investigators of the military government detachment.[9] The members of the Staatspolitischer Ausschuss agreed that the Sonderabteilung U was completely infiltrated with Communists intent upon capturing the city administration with the aid of their Communist confederates employed as special investigators and clerks in the office of military government. It is true that Frese employed an assistant with Communist tendencies and a confidential secretary who "stemmed from a proletarian, communistic milieu."[10]

On June 5, 1945, the political committee devoted a part of its regular meeting to a discussion of the Sonderabteilung U. The committee agreed that every effort should be made to have the organization dissolved. It instructed its chairman to petition the Oberbürgermeister to dismiss the Sonderabteilung U and to order it to turn over to the Staatspolitischer Ausschuss any files, correspondence, and other material that it had collected. The Oberbürgermeister and the chairman of the political committee agreed that it might be difficult to dismiss Frese. Fearing that Frese might even try to assassinate the Oberbürgermeister, they asked the public safety division of the military government detachment to dispatch an American soldier to the interview during which the Oberbürgermeister would relieve Frese of his duties. Arguing that it would be too dangerous, Mütze convinced the Oberbürgermeister to change his plans to have the soldier remain hidden in the background. Consequently, the four men sat around a table. The soldier reportedly leveled his loaded, cocked, sub-machine gun at Frese, while the Oberbürgermeister dismissed him, ostensibly for exceeding his authority by preparing a card file of National Socialists and for attempting to do the work that had been delegated to the political committee.[11]

By June 10, 1945, the Staatspolitischer Ausschuss had eliminated the Sonderabteilung U and had established itself securely. Five days earlier the Oberbürgermeister had recognized it positively. The Military Governor recognized it tacitly by conferring with it, the Public Safety Officer, and the Deputy Military Governor regarding housing, employment policies, financial questions, weapons for the police, and resumption of postal services.[12]

The Staatspolitischer Ausschuss in Action

The Staatspolitischer Ausschuss assumed many and varied duties, often without proper authority from military government or the Oberbürgermeister. Late in May it set up standards and procedures by which the city and the outlying communities could be denazified. The Military government detachment rejected them because detailed directives for denazification were to be prepared by higher headquarters. The political committee nevertheless continued to denazify. It reviewed the applications for employment in the civil administration and asked the Oberbürgermeister to agree not to hire anyone in the city administration without the committee's approval. There is a thick file of letters in the Marburg Rathaus testifying to the fact that the political committee recommended dismissals and reviewed the records of employees dismissed by the Oberbürgermeister or by military government. The committee systematically assembled a list of names of former members of the Nazi party and its affiliated organizations to enlarge the list it had inherited from the Sonderabteilung U. A committee of three directed lending libraries in the city to remove National Socialistic, nationalistic, and militaristic literature. The liaison representative of the committee asked military government officers for permission to employ Nazi party members in the public works as minor employees or to retain some party members for whom adequate replacements reportedly could not be found. The Military Governor informed the committee that the denazification directives received by the detachment precluded such employment. The committee prepared a list of Nazi families as a guide for those who might be called upon to secure furniture and other facilities for the military forces. Completely exceeding its authority, the committee advised the municipal personnel office to make all dismissals under denazification temporary until each case could be reviewed. It was hoped, in June, that Marburg citizens with clean political records would be designated as a final denazification review board.[13] Such optimistic hopes were disappointed by the denazification regulations of higher military government authorities. The political committee also proposed an active denazification of business life in June 1945. In this proposal the committee was apparently ahead of the American planners in Germany. The publication of the military government denazification policies for business and industry came in September 1945. As early as June a council (*Wirtschaftsrat*) had been appointed from within the political committee to prepare proposals for denazifying business enterprises. The committee's files contain a large number of applications from individuals and business firms requesting permission to open new business establishments or reopen old ones. The committee reviewed the applications and gave first priority for resuming operations to those firms whose owners and managers could demonstrate politically reliable backgrounds. Construction firms that had not profited through cooperation with the Nazi regime received priority in the contracts to do reconstruction work for the city. The committee overruled the recommendation of its more radical members that the property of war dead and missing be made public.[14]

Denazification constituted only one interest of the political committee. The chairman reported in August 1945 that the members of his committee held long meetings and spent sleepless nights in the interest of providing food, housing, and transportation; regulating traffic; alleviating the shortages of coal, wood, workers, and specialists; supplementing the limited incomes of widows and pensioners; discussing the problems of youth and the lack of school facilities; reactivating the press; and supplying the needs of ex-soldiers and the wounded.[15] Actually it assumed the duties and functions of the old city council, which the Nazis had abolished. In a sense the Staatspolitischer Ausschuss was a representative body similar to a city council (*Bürgerrat*) as it existed prior to 1933. The members of the Ausschuss were recognized leaders of political groups, which eventually became political parties. Thus, persons who later became members of the Christian Democratic Union, the

Free Democratic party, the Social Democratic party, and the Communist party were all represented. The committee members were not chosen by an electorate, but neither were nor are the members of the city council elected directly under the system of proportional representation and balloting for party lists in use in Germany. Even with the electoral machinery functioning, political party leaders have almost absolute power to determine who will represent the party. Because they are elected proportionately, city councils are usually coalition governments. Accordingly, the political committee might be said to have been a form of coalition government of the city in the absence of a city council. From this point of view the statement, *Die Staatsgewalt geht vom Volke aus,* makes sense to Germans as a symbol of responsible opposition to the Oberbürgermeister and the other officials who served directly under the local military government detachment.

An indication of the range of interests of the committee other than denazification, which we have noted, might be provided by a partial list of the committee's activities during the seven months of its existence. It debated the important question of incorporating four outlying villages into the municipality of Marburg. It designated committees to study labor requirements, finances, public welfare, housing, and cultural and educational matters. The entire committee discussed and made recommendations regarding the curfew regulations for young people. It also proposed that strangers to the city not be allowed to establish businesses or to serve in high administrative posts until the local citizens had been found inadequate to fill the needs.[16] Inadvertently, the political committee helped to prevent the employment of National Socialists in the early days by enforcing this policy. Because of difficulties of communication between the four zones of occupation and between the military districts within the American Zone, it was possible for a Nazi who was known in one locality to move to another, change his name, and then surge into the foreground as an anti-Nazi.[17]

The minutes of the committee's meetings reveal many other problems that were presented to it or taken up by it for solution.

The committee discussed the reactivation of trade unions. It investigated poor-quality work by shoemakers and it ordered the police to close the business of a fortune-teller. It proposed a ban on migration to the city because of the crowded living conditions and the presence of large numbers of American troops. It sought new sources of tax revenue and it reviewed the budget. In addition, the committee repeatedly petitioned military forces to release the tobacco factory from requisition so that it could be placed in operation and thereby provide employment and increased tax revenue. It summoned the Rector of the University to present the arguments upon which the faculty senate based its opposition to the proposed plans to introduce new industries into the city. It expressed readiness to serve as an appeal board under the military government regulations for the denazification of business and industry. Last, it made recommendations for preventing possible Prussian influence upon Hessian farmers' organizations. The committee observed that farmers from Eastern Germany and Prussia emigrated to the Western zones after Poland and Russia confiscated their lands. To prevent these "nationalists" and "militarists" from becoming members of Hessian farmers' organizations, the committee suggested that they be prohibited from purchasing land in Hessen.[18]

The Committee, the Oberbürgermeister, and Military Government

Despite military government's approval of its organization and membership, the Staatspolitischer Ausschuss did not enjoy the detachment's confidence. Individually, or as a committee, the members sought persistently to gain military government recognition and support for its work. On May 11, 1945, the committee petitioned military government for recognition and on May 26 the Deputy Military Governor welcomed its cooperation in personnel policy. The Daily Journal of the detachment recorded another meeting between the Deputy and the committee on June 9, 1945. Two months later the new Military Governor, who had arrived a few days previously, reported a conference he and his deputy had

had with the Oberbürgermeister and the Landrat to discuss the dismissal of the official in charge of Marburg's public works "because he had received a lot of mail regarding it from 'the political committee.' "[19]

The committee was gratified by the recognition that military government seemed to give in these meetings. There were, however, certain ominous features of these early meetings that appeared to be insignificant at the time. Ignoring the committee's desire to govern rather than advise, the Deputy Military Governor suggested that the Landrat serve as a member of the Ausschuss. The Oberbürgermeister objected, saying that the Landkreis and the Stadtkreis are two separate administrative districts.[20] Although the incident was passed over as inconsequential at the time, it is indicative of the fact that military government regarded the Ausschuss as little more than a source of information and service, whereas the committee wanted to serve in an administrative capacity.

To guard against the political committee's ambitions, and acting under specific direction from higher headquarters, the Marburg detachment gave it only tenuous support. New officers sometimes suspected it. In August the new Military Governor met with the committee only after it provided him with a history of its organization, a list of its original members, the changes that had taken place in membership, the political preferences of its members, and the relationship it bore to the Oberbürgermeister.[21] Undoubtedly, the suspicions of the detachment officers were prompted by directives from higher headquarters. Supreme Headquarters, Allied Expeditionery Forces, ordered groups and organizations that had formed to fight Nazis to disband.[22] The first monthly report of the Military Governor for Germany stated that "throughout the U.S. Zone some progress in the restoration of democratic forms of political and public life has been made by the appointment of local citizens' councils to advise the Bürgermeister." But in another section of the same report the voluntary groups that had been formed to assist in denazification and to advise local officials were said to be "dominated by individuals interested primarily in advancing their own welfare or by distinctly minority groups claiming to speak on behalf of the entire community."[23]

Because military government suspected and even distrusted the committee, because the committee assumed authority that had not been delegated to it, and because of personality conflicts, serious differences drove the two organizations further apart during the second half-year of the occupation. Officials appointed to civil posts by military government thus found themselves precariously situated somewhere between the source of their authority and their constituents as represented by the political committee. When German administrators heeded the criticisms of the political committee or German citizens, military government ordered its appointees to ignore all orders or instructions except those of military government. In September 1945 the detachment's Education and Religious Affairs Officer provided the *Schulrat* with a letter stating that the Staatspolitischer Ausschuss was to follow the orders of the Schulrat in school affairs because the Schulrat received his orders and authority from military government. In December the Civil Administration Officer ordered the political committee to limit its activities to advice and counsel in the future. He wrote that the committee had power only to recommend action in matters brought to its attention and that its decisions were not to be binding upon anyone unless approved by the proper civil or military government official.[24] Military government officers insisted that their civilian appointees carry out military government policies as interpreted by the local unit.

As a countermeasure, the political committee exerted pressure upon military government's appointees either directly or by appealing to military government. In July, two committee members, meeting with the Deputy Military Governor, "emphasized that their denazification policy is not the same [as] the one of the Oberbürgermeister and that they are not dependent on his politics." A statement read by Hermann Bauer to the entire committee said that the Oberbürgermeister was dictatorial, autocratic, and desirous of ruling according to the infamous *Führerprinzip* (Leadership principle) of the National Socialists. Siebecke, the

statement continued, thinks he can brush the political committee aside with a smile and a joke: "The committee can meet up
there [in the Rathaus] as much as it likes, but it is not recognized.
Decisions are made by me alone!" The Oberbürgermeister, caught
between his superiors on *Schulstrasse* (military government) and
his critics in the Rathaus, defended himself before the assembled
Staatspolitischer Ausschuss, stating that he could not tolerate some
nine or ten Oberbürgermeister in the Rathaus.[25] But the political
committee, acting in accordance with its interpretation of *Die
Staatsgewalt geht vom Volke aus,* passed resolution after resolution. The Oberbürgermeister, an experienced politician who was
not above using his position to advantage, accepted them, rejected
them, ignored them, or took them to military government for approval or disapproval in accordance with existing policy. The in-
voluntary resignation of the Landrat in October was to him sufficient evidence of the fate in store for an appointee of military government who refused to conform to the policies of the occupation
authorities.

Annoyed by the failure of the Oberbürgermeister and his staff
to act on its resolutions, the Staatspolitischer Ausschuss took action
to ensure the effectiveness of its work. On November 23, 1945, it
appointed an *Überwachungsausschuss* (watchdog committee) to
see that its decisions were enforced. It asked the Oberbürgermeister to approve the watchdog committee and to give written
notice of the approval to all of his subordinates. The Oberbürgermeister took the request to those to whom he felt responsible—the
military government officers. The upshot was the letter, written
hastily and in longhand, by the Civil Administration Officer or-
dering the committee to limit itself to advice and counsel in the
future.[26]

Although conflicting personalities played an unmistakable role
in the difficulties between the Oberbürgermeister and the Ausschuss, the crucial issue was the difference between the proposed
reconstruction policy of the political committee and the policy of
military government as administered by its civilian officials. Many
of the committee's resolutions were contrary to the policies and

practices of military government. Examples to illustrate this are numerous: The committee demanded reinstatement of persons designated by military government to be mandatory removals, provided the committee decided upon review that the persons were not really Nazis. Accordingly, it advised the Oberbürgermeister to consider all dismissals to be temporary until a civilian review board had screened the dismissed employees' records. In August the Oberbürgermeister agreed that no one would be hired in the city administration without the committee's prior approval. In September 1945, the editor of the *Marburger Presse* published an article on the committee's views regarding denazification and the employment of former Nazis. He said the political committee desired "men with character and good qualifications" ("*fachlich geschult*") for the vacant positions. If the applicants had been only "formal" and "nominal" Nazis the political committee recommended their employment so long as they appeared qualified and ready for "democratic cooperation." The committee said such persons must be proved antifascists and must have completely reliable ("*einwandfreie*") recommendations. In this way the injustice of denazification would be minimized.[27] Obviously, the Oberbürgermeister could not follow through with the concessions that he made to the Staatspolitischer Ausschuss in the face of the demands by the military government detachment that he carry out the policies of denazification as they were laid down by higher military government authorities. According to the latter he was obligated to remove all Nazis.

Another instance in which the Ausschuss demanded the impossible of the Oberbürgermeister was in its resolution regarding refugees. The Oberbürgermeister was obliged to accept and provide for refugees coming to Western Germany in accordance with the terms of the Potsdam Agreement. The political committee, nevertheless, resolved that newcomers to the city and county should be restricted in their employment and economic opportunities; local citizens were to have first priority. It advocated discrimination against the farmers who came to the Landkreis from the areas occupied by Russia and by Poland. It refused to accept applications from refugees for employment in the city administration.[28]

The foregoing examples, plus others that might have been cited, give meaning to the observation of a friend of the Oberbürgermeister regarding the difficulties of the position. He asserted that the Americans proceeded in their politics without regard for the views of provincial politicians. He said that what the Germans believed to be mistakes by the Oberbürgermeister and neglect of seemingly important measures should be recognized for what they were: the result of an impossible task [in the sense that it would not please Germans] given him by military government rather than the result of incompetence and lack of insight.[29]

The Oberbürgermeister and the Staatspolitischer Ausschuss agreed on one major issue. It is rather significant that agreement of the two caused military government to curb the authority it had previously granted to both. In October 1945 the month-old Liberal Democratic party of Marburg announced that it would no longer collaborate with the committee. The party's reasons were that the military government detachment had given all important positions in the civil administration and the military government offices to Socialists and Communists. Furthermore, the Liberal Democrats suspected that the detachment had promised to reward its investigators with important positions after the end of the occupation. They feared that the investigators would use their positions—as they reportedly used their powers as investigators—to make room for other members of their parties, with the result that the administration would be dominated by leftists.[30]

We have seen that the political preferences of the detachment's investigators were decidedly leftist. On October 29 the Liberal Democratic party stated that it had verified the fact that, without exception, the investigators employed by military government were members of the Social Democratic or the Communist parties. It was no secret anyway.

A German employee of military government, who served from 1945 to 1952, said that it was common knowledge that leftists had a better opportunity than conservatives to receive employment or clearance for employment from military government. He listed three military government investigators and one counter intelligence corps investigator who were Communist party members. He said that several were Social Democrats. He described himself as a leftist–Social Democrat. He repeated the generally known fact that military government permitted Communist functionaries to organize the adult educational program in the city. The Marburg Criminal Police Commissioner, who had been imported by military government to fill the office in 1947, reported to the author that the police department was full of Communists when he arrived. In its discussion on October 29 the Liberal Democratic party agreed that the investigators could present acceptable *Fragebogen* (denazification questionnaires) to military government, and none of the Germans I interviewed expressed the opinion that the employment and recommendation of Socialists and Communists was a deliberate policy of the local military government detachment. They usually interpreted it correctly as a natural result of the general American attitude toward Germans, Nazis, and those who had suffered political persecution. It is certainly true in Marburg that faithful Socialists and Communists suffered at the hands of the National Socialists. Some Germans intimate that certain detachment officers personally favored Communists or Socialists, but the officers cited appear to have been so few in number and of such little consequence in the matter of employment and appointment policies that they could not have accounted for the large numbers of such persons who received relatively important positions. Probably one of the better explanations of the dilemma faced by the local detachment is the one made by Julian Bach: "Those Germans who would appear to be most acceptable [to the American policy makers] in their international point of view are Communists in their national view; while those most acceptable in their national point of view are German nationalists in their foreign policy."[31]

Yet the Marburg electorate appears to have agreed with the suspicions of the Liberal Democratic party. One of the most widely publicized campaign promises of the Liberal Democratic party in the election of April 1946 was that the city administration would be "de-Communized." Marburg was the only city in Germany that cast a plurality vote for the Liberal Democratic party in the election of April 1946. Hermann Bauer, a leader in the Liberal Democratic party, and the editor of the *Marburger Presse*, in analyzing the reasons for the success of his party in the first postwar free election in Germany said that the party's open plan to "de-Communize" the city administration ensured the victory.[32]

The military government detachment criteria for employment were a clean political record—as determined by Fragebogen and investigation by the Counter Intelligence Corps—and the ability to speak English. These criteria were sometimes passed over, however. In May 1945 the detachment appointed a Landkreis administrative officer who had been a tax inspector until he retired in 1944, explaining that he was acceptable because he was "a member of the Evangelical Lutheran church and [claimed] no political party." At another time the Office of Military Government for Land Hessen apprised the Marburg Public Safety Officer of the fact that he had in his employ four persons classified by denazification authorities as "discretionary with adverse recommendation."[33]

The Staatspolitischer Ausschuss, the Oberbürgermeister, and the Liberal Democratic party in particular, criticized the investigators not for their past political records but for their lack of experience, for their characters and their morals, and for their assumed designs for the future. One German said, in 1954, that he shudders to this day when he recalls the machinations (*finstere Rollen*) of some of the investigators. Another remarked that relying upon a butcher's helper, adventurers, and "mysterious persons with unknown pasts" is no way to organize a smoothly functioning intelligence system. The political committee was appalled because Americans received irresponsible political *Giftmischer* (literally: poison mixers) and denouncers. They said these "intriguers" (*politische Intriganten*) and "hyenas" (*politische Hyänen*) sowed seeds of mistrust and caused Germans to lose confidence in appointed officials as well as in military government.[34]

In October 1945 the political committee and the Oberbürgermeister decided that the investigators would have to be curbed or dismissed if the committee was to continue to function. On October 16, during a meeting with the Military Governor, the committee's liaison representative said there were rumors abroad that the political committee was under investigation.[35] Without answering, the Military Governor expressed continued confidence in the committee, but approximately one week later the committee's suspicions were verified. A military government investigator came to the home of Ludwig Mütze and said he wanted to talk with Mütze. When Mütze's wife told him that her husband was at a meeting in the Rathaus, the investigator boasted: "A bomb will burst in that place soon. The committee will be scattered. Especially Mr. Treut will be removed."[36]

The incident provided the Staatspolitischer Ausschuss and the Oberbürgermeister with the first concrete evidence that they were being investigated and reinvestigated constantly. What they could not have known about was the pressure that higher headquarters placed upon military government detachments just then to do a more effective job on denazification. A student of American denazification policy has reported that the Patton incident in August tended to bring about an intensification of denazification.[37] The impact of this intensification upon the local detachments is illustrated by the fact that Headquarters United States Forces, Europe, is reported to have sent telegrams to the commanding officers of the two military districts of the American Zone, threatening to court-martial military government officers unless denazification proceedings were accelerated.[38]

The Oberbürgermeister and the Staatspolitischer Ausschuss decided to take their mutual criticisms of the work of the investigators directly to military government. The Oberbürgermeister went as the spokesman. He expressed his belief that the investigators were chosen for political reasons and that very little consideration was given to their characters, their experience, or their training. The Oberbürgermeister knew that the American Army had given them several weeks of training in investigational procedures. But, he said, the investigators were comparatively young men and, therefore, somewhat radical. He added: The people who felt themselves to be the true representatives of the local community had had no opportunity to approve the investigators. Yet their power was so great, under military government, that they could influence major policy decisions relative to the community. The public-spirited citizens of the community, the Oberbürgermeister continued, could produce evidence that the investigators were biased and prejudiced and that they tried to secure positions for themselves and their friends.* Even if the investigators were honest, he argued, they could not be completely objective because they lacked training and experience.† Last, the Oberbürgermeister offered his solution: Military government should inform him of derogatory information about outstanding personalities so that he and the political committee might verify it. He said that many of those under investigation were well known and respected and that Marburg would suffer great loss if these people were unjustly defamed.[39]

Military government officers were immovable in this matter. Unknown to the civil officials at the time, investigations were actually increased. When the Oberbürgermeister learned that even he was not immune to investigation, he and the political committee took matters into their own hands. Mütze visited the home of the young investigator who had threatened the political committee with dissolution. Mütze knew the young man as a member of an established family of merchants and tradesmen in Marburg

---

* In his testimony at the Oberbürgermeister's trial Mütze stated that the SPA was cognizant of several investigations that had been made of persons known to the SPA members for as long as thirty years, and that the reports of investigation had been false. It is also noteworthy that the brother of one of the military government investigators, a Communist, was put in charge of the municipal personnel office after military government removed the civil servant who had been there until early in 1946.

† There is a familiar ring to this argument. It was used over and over by Marburgers in their protests against denazification and the filling of the vacant positions with persons who had not had the traditional training that Germans believe to be essential in public administration or the civil service. It was the argument used against school reform and civil service reform. Americans rejected it as an indication of class consciousness, but it appealed to Germans, probably for that very reason.

and he gave him a verbal lashing. When the same investigator was cited for a traffic violation, the Oberbürgermeister had him arrested, apparently hoping for a reaction from military government. The military government officer in charge of the investigators questioned the arrest and the Oberbürgermeister went to visit him prepared to discuss the case as well as the investigators in general. The words that he and the lieutenant exchanged in the military government offices on that evening at closing time are not completely verifiable. Probably the tension, the heated discussion, and the threats from both sides obliterated a great deal. Nevertheless, it is reasonably certain that the Oberbürgermeister demanded forcefully that the lieutenant restrict the activities of his employees and that both men struck the table top with their fists. During the course of the interview the Oberbürgermeister— he is not one to have refrained from doing this—reportedly mentioned some of his important connections in Germany and in Washington and London. The lieutenant said later that the Oberbürgermeister threatened to have him assassinated.[40]

The investigations continued. Early in December the detachment reported that "the chairman of the political committee, who was closely watched already for some time, proved to be a party-member and was dismissed immediately."[41] On December 12, 1945, the Staatspolitischer Ausschuss sent a resolution to the Oberbürgermeister stating that it judged its chairman to be a public-spirited leader. Although the detachment had dismissed him because of his formal connections with the Nazi party, the committee expressed the conviction that he had been a true anti-Nazi. Moreover, he had already been approved for the position by military government and the local Counter Intelligence Corps detachment. Therefore, the Staatspolitischer Ausschuss would interpret his removal by military government as a concrete gesture of nonconfidence in the committee, despite professions to the contrary on the part of American officers. The committee discerned no other alternative to dissolution.[42]

Partly because of the need for a city council to serve as a review board for appeals under the law for denazification of business and industry, and partly because of the need for an advisory body to the Oberbürgermeister, the detachment persuaded the four political parties of the city to organize a Bürgerrat (city council) until elections could be held. On December 17, 1945, a nine-man Bürgerrat was activated to take the place of the Staatspolitischer Ausschuss. Six of its members had been Ausschuss members. The man who had been arrested on December 12 was employed as secretary to the Bürgerrat on January 8, 1946. He reported that he had been cleared by military government and that his arrest had been a mistake.*

The Bürgerrat assumed a much more moderate role in the government of the city than had its predecessor. There is no evidence that it objected to the investigators. The minutes of its meetings show that it confined itself to discussions of political, social, and economic problems of the city that did not fall under military government regulations and restrictions. When such problems were at issue, the Bürgerrat left them to be negotiated between the Oberbürgermeister and the military government officers concerned. The Bürgerrat's lack of initiative, its studied refusal to become implicated with military government, its obvious desire to do only what was possible are demonstrated most convincingly by its resolution regarding the appointment made by military government to fill the vacancy in the Rathaus after Oberbürgermeister Siebecke's arrest. The Bürgerrat recommended the man who had been Bürgermeister prior to 1933. But military government promoted Bürgermeister Dickman to Oberbürgermeister instead. Many of the complaints that the political committee had made against Siebecke it had also made against Dickman. However, the Bürgerrat took no initiative, merely resolving that "The conditions demanding a show of confidence are unfavorable, and [the committee] declares its willingness to cooperate in the interest of the public welfare."[43]

* Bürgerrat, Minutes, January 2, 1946, Stadtkreis Marburg Papers; *Marburger Presse*, December 21, 1945, p. 6. An additional member had been added to the SPA in October 1945. The CDU, a newly formed political party, had asked for representation on the committee at that time.

The two organizations that might have given constructive assistance to the military government detachment thus had been eliminated from the scene. The Bürgerrat, which took their place, assumed a passive role and accepted the decisions of the military government detachment with only formal resolutions of disappointment.

During the first year of occupation in Marburg a significant change took place in the attitude of Germans who might have been the most ardent supporters of military government had they been permitted to collaborate with it without sacrificing their self-respect and their pride. They shifted from a predilection to support almost anything to an inclination to support only that which was obviously beneficial to the Germans, or absolutely necessary because of the demands of military government. Many of them refused to keep up the relations they had already established with military government. Very few of them volunteered information, advice, or criticisms. They studiously reported only those things specifically required of them by military government directives. The effect of the withdrawal of Germans upon the intelligence function of the local detachment, after it relinquished most of its executive powers to higher headquarters or to the local civil administration and reverted to a liaison and security detachment, has been noted in Chapter 3. It is significant because after executive and functional powers were relinquished, military government justified continuation of Landkreis and Stadtkreis offices for their value as intelligence agencies.

Having described the community and its occupation forces and having discussed how military government established itself in control, we can now turn to the specific long-range policies of the Marburg detachment.

PART THREE

The Punitive Program

7

Industrial Disarmament

As a liaison and security organization one of the chief functions of the Marburg detachment was to observe and report the impact of American policy at the local level. Between 1946 and 1948 most of its time and energies were devoted to observing the effect of American preventive and punitive programs: industrial dismantlement, administrative decentralization, and denazification.

American policy directives instructed the Military Governor to prevent Germany from again becoming a threat to world peace. The objective was to be achieved, in part, by industrial disarmament and demilitarization, by removing war production facilities for reparations payments in kind, and by destroying those facilities not transferred for reparations.[1] But the vague and partly conflicting industrial disarmament and reparations provisions of the Yalta and Potsdam agreements gave the four occupying powers in Germany considerable latitude of interpretation and left numerous issues upon which the four disagreed.

The United States' published policy statements suggest, and the actions of its representatives in Germany reveal, that the United States never seriously promoted a policy leading to a completely de-industrialized Germany.[2] Seven months after Germany's defeat the Department of State released a statement to the press declaring that "it is not the intention of the United States wantonly to destroy German structures and installations which can readily be used for permitted peacetime industrial activities or for temporary shelters." Secretary of State James F. Byrnes' Stuttgart speech of September 6, 1946, and the Revised Level of Industry Plan for the American and British occupation zones, which was approved on August 26, 1947, further outline policies designed to retain German industries for peacetime production.[3]

If detail and emphasis in military government reports are valid criteria, it is obvious that from the beginning of the occupation military government modified any plans it may have had to pastoralize Germany. In his first monthly report the Military Governor stated that "far from restraining resurgent German business, great efforts must be exerted to build up industrial, transport, and communications facilities, which are essential for the production of coal required in Western Europe and for the provision of minimum food and other essential supplies."[4] The careful statistical studies made by the military government economics division presage a growing interest in production indices and the general level of production in the American Zone. After 1945, while other functional divisions of the Office of Military Government for the United States Zone began consolidating their reports into bimonthly reviews, and later into quarterly, semiannual, and annual reviews, the industry division continued to publish long reports and statistical reviews each month. For example, the January 1947 reports of the industry division and the trade and commerce division required forty-nine and twenty-seven pages, respectively, whereas the reports for reparations and restitutions, denazification, and displaced persons required sixteen, six, and seven pages, respectively.

The American military government, and later the military governments of the United States, Great Britain, and France together, progressively reduced the amount of industrial equipment to be dismantled and shipped out of Germany or destroyed. In May 1946 the American Military Governor suspended dismantlement of plants that had not already been allocated for reparations payments. In accordance with the bilateral agreement between the United States and Great Britain on a Revised Level of Industry Plan in 1947, the industrial capacity of the Bizone was adjusted to a figure considerably higher than that set in 1946. Later, in 1948 and 1949, Western Germany began to participate in the European

Recovery Program and additional adjustments in favor of increased industrial capacity for Germany were made.[5]

In Marburg the military government detachment found only two industries that were subject to control or destruction under Allied directives. One of these was the pharmaceutical and biological plant located in Marbach; the other the huge munitions industry hidden in the woods near Allendorf, about fifteen miles east of Marburg.

The Marbach Industry: Behringwerke

Military government property control officers seized the *Behringwerke* on July 5, 1945. Technically it was not a war industry, but according to Allied directives its laboratories and research facilities were subject to control, and as I. G. Farben property it was subject to military government decartelization.[6] The I. G. Farben Control Office of the military government economics division supervised the activities of the Marbach industry directly, requiring only incidental observation or special reports on the part of the Marburg military government detachment.

Military government control of the Marbach plant affected Marburgers negligibly if not salutarily. Although its research and production activities were scrutinized by military government inspectors, the industry reportedly produced biologicals at full capacity by July 1945. One month later all other industrial establishments in the American Zone produced, on the average, at 5 per cent of capacity. Six months later the production index for the American Zone was only 26 per cent of the 1936 base.[7]

The tremendous demand for pharmaceutical goods in postwar Germany and the general reluctance of American officers to destroy a going concern made possible rapid resumption of production of the Behringwerke.[8] To maintain adequate standards of health and to reduce the possibility of epidemics that might have affected the Allied forces, military government urged production of pharmaceuticals and biologicals. Military government also encouraged maximum agricultural production at all times and therefore authorized the Behringwerke to initiate research in and production of vaccine for the treatment of hoof-and-mouth disease. Initially military government authorized the Behringwerke to breed its own research animals, but as the supply of research animals became short, military government officers used their superior communications facilities to locate and secure additional horses, which apparently could not be purchased in the normal trade channels.[9]

Immediately after Germany's surrender in 1945 a firm not directly controlled by military government and not engaged in production of critical materials would have met insurmountable difficulties in trying to resume operations as quickly as did the Behringwerke. Most industries that did produce during the first few months of the occupation used raw materials and supplies that they had stockpiled before the end of the war.[10] After the war, communication and transportation for civilians were impossible between the various occupation zones of Germany and difficult within the zones. By virtue of its control of the Behringwerke military government could allocate scarce supplies to it for production deemed necessary for the achievement of Allied purposes.

To summarize: For Marburgers in general, military government control of the Marbach pharmaceutical and biological plant proved to be somewhat of a blessing. Producing with military government authorization, and at times with the assistance of control officers, the industry provided employment opportunities in a city and county faced with a serious unemployment problem. By 1948 the Behringwerke employed more than four hundred persons, 80 per cent of the 1938 figure.[11]

The Allendorf Munitions Industry

Unlike the Behringwerke, the Allendorf munitions industry was built specifically to further the German war effort. It included two plants; one produced ammunition, mines, and bombs for the German Navy, the other produced gunpowder, dynamite, and shell and bomb charges. Construction was begun in 1941, and the installation was approximately 75 per cent completed at the end of the war. The American Army found the installation undamaged

at the war's end. As they were built specifically for wartime manu-
facture of munitions, the Allendorf plants, along with twelve other
similar plants in the American Zone, were marked for destruction.
Prior to destruction, general purpose equipment was to be dismantled and made available for direct reparations payments.

American troops guarded the Allendorf plants from the beginning of the occupation of the Landkreis, and the military government detachment formally placed them under property control
on July 16 and August 21, 1945. The property came under the
immediate jurisdiction of higher military government headquarters, and the Marburg Property Control Officer served chiefly as a
liaison representative for higher headquarters.[12]

Destruction and Dismantlement at Allendorf

On March 15, 1946, American Army Engineers destroyed four
large munitions storage bunkers. Because of its isolation and its
facilities, the Allendorf industrial area was used after March 1946
as a demolition center. The American Army shipped captured
enemy bombs and munitions to Allendorf and German demolition
crews exploded them or broke them down for salvage.

Beginning in November 1946 a Hessian state firm, the Gesellschaft zur Erfassung von Rüstungsgut, dismantled the plants,
shipped equipment and stores to eleven nations, among whom
Yugoslavia, France, and the Netherlands received the largest
shares, and sold the equipment not marked for reparations. It
placed the receipts for materials it sold into blocked accounts to
be used later for reparations payments. According to military government reports the Allendorf equipment was completely dismantled by September 1948. The *Marburger Presse* reported that
the Gesellschaft zur Erfassung von Rüstungsgut completed its work
on March 15, 1949.[13]

The Effects of Policy Changes upon the
Allendorf Industry

After the equipment had been dismantled, the remaining buildings and facilities were not destroyed, as had been originally con-
templated. In part, the Allied policy changes, described above,

were responsible, but the demands of American military units in the vicinity also prevented complete dismantlement and eventual destruction. The American constabulary troops stationed in Landkreis Marburg demanded retention of the waterworks in Allendorf even after they had been marked for dismantling. The waterworks were kept intact and today supply water to several neighboring villages as well as to Allendorf.[14]

In Marburg the policy changes and the solicitude of local military government officers for the community they governed are reflected in several ways. Early in 1946 the detachment tacitly permitted the Landkreis administration to allocate Allendorf facilities to two firms for the production of soap and waxes. Later other firms began to produce in Allendorf with no apparent objection from military government. The civil administration could not grant leases to firms, however, because military government had made public no final plans for the disposition of the buildings. By November 1948 the Marburg detachment reported that twenty-one German firms occupied fifty-six buildings of the former munitions industry. They produced glass products; sweaters and underwear; soap, shoe polish, and cosmetics; ovens and stoves; cement and concrete parts for construction purposes; malt extracts; roofing for railway cars; solder irons; small furniture and store equipment; hair dryers; small motors; vacuum cleaners; blacksmith blasts; textile machinery; post office equipment; wood products; paints and lacquers; and chemical products.[15]

In 1949, after the equipment and machines had been dismantled, the Hessian government assumed control of the remaining buildings and the land. On March 2, 1949, the *Marburger Presse* reported that the Landkreis administration had been authorized to invite German firms to examine the facilities provided in Allendorf and to settle there.

Industrial Disarmament and the Marburg Community

Industrial disarmament in Marburg resulted directly in the elimination of some industrial potential that might have been used for future war production.

The other significant result was that Marburgers came to identify military government with a policy that they believed would
perpetuate unemployment, reduce the standard of living, make
assimilation of refugees and expellees difficult, and generally limit
the economic opportunities of Germans. A military government–
sponsored opinion poll, conducted throughout the American zone
of occupation in 1947 to determine German expectations regarding reparations demands, showed that a large percentage of Germans believed that Allied policy was designed to break down the
German way of life and to depress the German standard of living
for at least a generation. An analysis of the polled opinions concluded that to express public opposition to industrial disarmament
and reparations policies would be politically expedient for Germans and that military government officers should take this into
account in observing political party activities in their areas.

True to expectations, Marburg's political leaders and civil administrators discovered that opposition to military government
industrial disarmament policies helped one to remain in office or
to be elected to office. Local political leaders demanded additional
jobs and homes for refugees and increased industrial output to
pay for food imports on the international market. They told the
Marburg electorate that military government continued to assume
a negative attitude toward these problems because dismantlement
continued until 1949.

One other minor result of the industrial disarmament policy in
Marburg was that it provided still another basis for the growing
suspicion of some Marburgers that Americans trusted no Germans,
not even those they had appointed to office or those elected democratically.

The Political Parties and Industrial Disarmament

Marburg's political leaders opposed destruction of the Allendorf industrial facilities from the beginning. None of the published platforms of Marburg's political parties includes positive
statements regarding the Allendorf industry. It is safe to assume,
however, that the parties were opposed because of their later ex-

pressions and because public criticism of occupation policies was apt to bring reprisals from military government. All parties called for increased industrial production to compensate for the loss of agricultural production to Poland and Russia in the East. They emphasized the need to export manufactured goods to pay for food imports, and they stressed the unemployment problem which resulted from the influx of refugees and expellees into Western Germany after the war. The first coalition government of Landkreis Marburg, in 1946, described its most crucial task as that of retaining enough plant and equipment in Allendorf to provide full employment for indigenous persons and refugees and to provide temporary housing for the refugees.[16] The first published platform of the Marburg Social Democratic party probably stated most clearly the general attitude of the political parties toward industrial disarmament. It recognized the guilt of German industrialists in Germany's war plans, but emphasized that Germany would never be able to pay its international reparations debts and feed its population at the same time, if it were agrarianized.[17]

When American Army Engineers came to destroy parts of the Allendorf industry in 1946, the Landrat, the executive committee of the Landkreis, and the political party leaders tried to stop them. The Landrat sent delegations to the military government detachments for Marburg and Land Hessen. The delegations presented a strong argument by appealing to a problem of great concern to military government: that of providing facilities for employing and housing the refugees who had been streaming into Marburg.[18] The Landrat stated that his administration had already made plans to locate a soap factory, a repair shop, a furniture factory, a glass factory, a fertilizer plant, and a building materials plant in Allendorf.

In March 1946 American Army Engineers destroyed only the four munitions storage bunkers at Allendorf. Whether or not they had originally planned to destroy anything else cannot be determined from unclassified sources. But Marburg's political leaders believed that they had saved the plant from complete destruction. One of them later said he was sure that Americans

"wanted to see the whole thing blow up" because "American bomb-
ers had not been able to locate the plant during the war." Although
he could not possibly have been sure, there is apparently some
basis for his suspicion. In 1947 the Kassel Reparations Office advised that the standing timber around the Allendorf plant be
cut down because "the camouflage afforded by the forests and the
brush planted on the roofs of the buildings prevented location
of the plant by air observation during the entire war."[19] Shortly
after the four storage bunkers were destroyed, the *Marburger Presse*
reported that local civilian leaders had prevailed upon military
government to appoint one German to salvage some of the usable
parts before the destruction. Trying to point out the difficulties
under which he worked and the desire of the Americans to get on
with the task regardless of the consequences, the article depicted a
rather pathetic scene in which the man hastily unscrewed a few
light bulbs before the storage bunkers went up in smoke.[20]

Marburg's political leaders openly told their constituents that
their intervention had saved the Allendorf industry from complete
destruction and that such opposition constituted good democratic
thought and action. In a press release in 1949 Landrat Eckel stated
that one of the chief aims of the Kreis administration since 1945
had been to reopen the former munitions factory in Allendorf for
peacetime production and, failing completely to note the changes
in American policy that made it possible, he wrote that his administration had succeeded partially in spite of the control of the
plant by military government.[21]

Marburgers Relate Industrial Disarmament to Other Military Government Policies

Marburgers who effectively opposed American industrial disarmament policy cited other military government policies to defend their position, to achieve popularity among their constituents,
and to show Germans that either Americans were inconsistent or
they tried to perpetuate confusion in Germany.

The most popular tactic used by Marburgers to criticize industrial disarmament was based upon the assumption that a de-

mocracy functions well only under favorable economic conditions,
The belief appears to be so widely accepted in Germany that it
might conceivably be called a German characteristic by one who
believes in such things. The assumption is the basis for German
statements that democracy as practiced in America and England
may not be adequate for Germany. It appears also to be the basis
for the answers given by Germans in public opinion surveys conducted for the Office of the United States High Commissioner in
Germany in 1950. In one of these surveys approximately 60 per-
cent of those asked replied that they would choose a government
that offered the people economic security and the possibility of
a good income over a government that guaranteed free elections,
freedom of speech, a free press, and religious freedom. They obviously agreed that they could not have both in Germany.*

The belief that Americans defeated their own democratization
program by continued industrial disarmament was presented in an
editorial of the *Marburger Presse* in 1949. Commenting upon the
sentence of six German workers in Dortmund for resisting the dismantlement of German industries the editor wrote: "It would be
funny, if it were not so serious. The Allies criticize us for our
apparent deference to authority (*Man wirft uns unseren Kadaver-
gehorsam vor*), try to educate us to be democrats, but demand respect for Allied authority. They want to make free men of us but
force us to work at that which will destroy our economy. We have
reached a point where it is honorable to have been tried and sentenced by an Allied court."[22]

Political leaders made the most of the theory that Germans had
to resist military government policies to achieve democracy; that
they had to resist one of military government's policies to promote

---

* Surprisingly, American policy appears to have been made upon similar
assumptions, even though some Germans publicly argued that democracy in
Germany had failed before and would fail again for other than economic
reasons. See OMGH, Historical Report, April 1947 through June 1947, I, 24,
for an American expression of this belief, and Erich Kuby, "Die Krise der
Demokratie," *Der Ruf, Unabhängige Blätter der Jungen Generation* (Munich),
III (January 15, 1948), 2, and *Marburger Presse* (guest editorial by W. Lehn,
Arbeitsgerichtsrat, Marburg), March 5, 1948, p. 3, for German arguments to
the contrary.

its others. The Oberbürgermeister from 1946 to 1951, speaking before the Hessian Landtag in 1947, expressed his conviction that German opposition to industrial disarmament was most encouraging because it represented good democratic thought and action.[23]

Local officials compared the effects of industrial dismantlement with the aims of other policies to point out what they believed were serious inconsistencies in American policy. An Allied Control Council law, passed in January 1947, required German communities to facilitate the integration of expellees into the indigenous population with equal political rights and to provide equal opportunity with the original population in obtaining public welfare assistance, employment, and critical items of consumer goods.[24] The Landrat constantly reminded the military government detachment that expellees coming to Marburg in accordance with Allied agreements could be assimilated only by increasing employment opportunities. As Marburg's economy consisted almost exclusively of small farming plots, he emphasized the need for increasing industry in the Landkreis. He reported again and again that he could not plan the refugee program intelligently because he lacked information on the use of the facilities in the Allendorf area, the only place in Marburg that might attract firms that could provide additional employment opportunities in the amount required. As early as April 1946, when the full quota of refugees and expellees had not yet arrived in Marburg, Landrat Eckel wrote that plans to build about eight or nine small industries for peacetime production in Allendorf could not go ahead because he had been unable to discover what parts—or how much—of the Allendorf plants would be saved for future use.[25] He said that attracting large firms was completely out of the question because they would not invest in an enterprise that might have to be moved when dismantlement was completed.

In addition to restricting employment opportunities, American dismantlement of the Allendorf plants took away buildings that the Landkreis administration wished to use for temporary housing. Throughout 1946 and 1947, when refugees and expellees came into the Landkreis individually and with organized transports from the East—there were over nine thousand refugees and eighteen thousand expellees in Marburg in 1947—the Marburg civil officials tried to settle them into homes averaging about one and three-quarters persons per living and sleeping room in 1946. By the end of 1947 each home in Marburg averaged slightly over seven occupants, and each room averaged two and one-half occupants, a density which exceeded the zonal average by two and one-half persons per dwelling and by six-tenths person per room and which in turn was exceeded only by two other cities in the American Zone.[26] According to civil officials the Allendorf facilities would have provided adequate temporary housing for approximately eight or ten thousand refugees if military government had released the buildings for such purposes and if employment could have been provided in the vicinity. The barrack-type buildings that had housed foreign laborers during the war stood empty, with the exception of those that housed displaced persons during 1946 and 1947. Late in 1947 the Landrat informed the Marburg detachment that approximately twenty-five of these buildings had stood empty and had been neglected so long that they could no longer be used for housing unless major repairs were undertaken. The Landrat stated that even if military government were to release the buildings they would have to be moved because he could not settle large numbers of people in Allendorf unless there was some prospect of their finding employment there.[27]

Changed military government policies took effect slowly in the local communities. The unemployment and housing problems were not solved in 1949. The *Marburger Presse* reported that slightly over 20 per cent of all employables in Marburg were not working at the end of 1949. The Marburg figure was twice that of Land Hessen and more than double that of the Federal Republic. Early in 1950 fifteen firms, using former Allendorf munitions plant buildings, employed only about seven hundred persons. Other buildings provided 110 dwellings.[28] Reporting on the visit of an American congressional delegation to Allendorf in September 1949 the *Marburger Presse* described the surprise of the congressmen at the wretched living and working conditions of the

refugees living at Allendorf and quoted—with apparent pleasure—
one of the congressmen as having remarked that if "things don't
change the Reds will find fertile ground here."*

Marburg's civil officials and political party leaders believed
that the industrial disarmament program had serious negative
effects upon their community, upon military government's policy
of democratization, and upon its policy of proper integration of
refugees and expellees. They believed it was impossible to be completely responsible public servants because they could be responsible neither to military government, if they were so disposed, nor
to their German constituents without objecting to some military
government policies.

Industrial Disarmament and Local
Responsible Leadership

In an earlier chapter it has been noted that some leaders of
the Marburg community had expressed a desire to cooperate with
the military government detachment, but that they were disillusioned by many things, especially by the reception they got when
they formed a political committee to assist in the rehabilitation of
their city. The industrial disarmament program provided these
disillusioned Marburgers with still another example of apparent
American distrust of their sincerity.

Marburgers gradually became aware of the change in American
disarmament policy after 1946, even though the effects of the
change were not great immediately. Some political leaders were
encouraged by this change because they regarded it as an expression of faith on the part of Americans in the new political leadership and organization of Germany. But the majority suspected
that the change in American policy was based upon fear of Communism rather than upon faith in Germans. Military government
provided the suspicious ones with political ammunition that others

---

* *Marburger Presse*, September 13, 1949, p. 3. Seemingly pleased by the
American's discovery of the menace of Communism—something that many Germans claim to have known since 1933—the reporter stated that one of the
refugees answered the congressman's remark with: "But Germany doesn't like
the Reds."

found almost impossible to refute. In January 1947 military government for Land Hessen issued an instruction to the reparations supervisor at Allendorf demanding removal of all standing timber within the Allendorf industrial area. Later clarifications of the order asserted that the standing timber had prevented location of the industry by air observation during the entire war and that any large installation so concealed constituted a war potential. The industry was to be brought into the open so that "no large chemical equipment can be installed at a later date without detection."[29] Hermann Bauer later said that it was useless to explain that this was not necessarily inconsistent with Americans' increasing faith in German leadership, because Marburgers generally regarded it as another example of American attitudes so manifest in their denazification program.

Marburgers considered the action to be a verification of their suspicions that Americans still did not trust German political leadership. Some stated, correctly, that any industrial plant is potentially a war plant; that it becomes a war plant as result of a political rather than an economic decision. By the same logic war plants, such as those in Allendorf, can produce peacetime goods when political decisions determine such production. They believed that Americans assumed, when deciding upon their policy, that German political decisions in the future would be to make war rather than to live in peace.

Few Marburgers appear convinced that American distrust of Germans changed significantly even after Americans extended economic aid to Germany in 1948 and even though Germany received a measure of independence under the Federal Republic after 1949. Most of them apparently attribute the change in American policies to the tense international situation that manifested itself in the Communist success in Czechoslovakia and in the Berlin blockade in 1948. It is surprising to an American how many Germans are convinced that international affairs are conducted exclusively on principles of power politics. An observer of the German scene has written that "every schoolboy knows that we discovered our love for Germany the same day we found out that we could not live with the Russians."[30]

Marburgers acted upon the assumption that American aid to Germany was motivated by selfish interest. During the election campaign in 1948—while Americans debated the possibility of extending economic aid to Germany in large quantities—a rumor circulated in Marburg declaring that the United States would certainly speed economic aid to Germany if Germans voted for the Communist party in surprisingly large numbers. The rumor gained such popularity that all other political parties in the area bought space in the *Marburger Presse* to warn their members of the danger of voting the Communist ticket for such reasons.[31]

American activities at the international, zonal, and local level seem to have convinced Marburgers of the verity of their assumptions. Beginning late in 1947 the American information control division intensified its political information program "in the direction of the dangers of Communism."[32] While Marburgers observed American anti-Communist activities at the international and zonal level, local military government representatives began to sponsor reorientation activities to democratize Germany at the grass-roots level. To be sure, reorientation was not wholly a part of the cold war. Military government had not pressed reorientation prior to 1948 because of its preoccupation with the purely negative aspects of military government policy. But the fact that all these activities did occur somewhat simultaneously provided Marburgers with evidence to support their foregone conclusions about foreign affairs in general and American foreign policy in particular.

While it is true that the effects of American policy changes became more noticeable at the local level as the cold war became more pronounced, it is not true, as Marburgers generally believe, that American policies changed only after it became obvious that the other Allies could not cooperate with the Communists. The speech by Secretary of State Byrnes in 1946, which most Germans knew about, and the Revised Level of Industry Plan in 1947 are ample evidence that military government modified its industrial disarmament policies in favor of German industry before the cold war.

This mistaken German belief discloses a disturbing cynicism about America among German political leaders as well as among their constituents. Whenever they believe they can do so without disturbing their coalitions with other political parties, Marburg's political leaders express the belief that Americans continued to treat Germans like second-class people, continued to dismantle German industries, and behaved as if Germans were all Nazis or potential Nazis until such time as it became obvious that America might need Germans in the future to help fight Communists. Failing to take into account the possibility of a humanitarian motive in American policy changes toward Germany—and such a motive certainly existed—one Marburger remarked that "one doesn't get anything for nothing in this world." He said Americans helped Germany in order to help themselves, and that military government began to emphasize the reorientation program so it could prove to the taxpayers back home that Germans were becoming more democratic; that they could be relied upon as democrats in the American sense of the term. The unreconstructed Nazis, even more cynical than the others, generally follow the thought expressed by a civil servant in the city administration. He said the changes in American policy show that Americans became conscious of the fact that they fought the wrong enemy in 1941–45.[33]

The effects of the industrial disarmament program in Marburg show the truth of the prediction made by the American committee that prepared the report upon which the Level of Industry Plan of 1946 was based: "This large program of capital removals is an experiment unique in the history of the world. Its effects cannot be precisely predicted, but many secondary repercussions will result from the wholesale uprooting of industrial plants."[34]

8

Decentralization

One of the basic objectives of American military government in Germany was to destroy, or prevent the revival of, the centralization of power that had been evident in German history in the twentieth century, especially during the Hitler regime. The first general directive received by the Military Governor in Germany instructed him to administer Germany with a view "towards the decentralization of the political and administrative structure and the development of local responsibility."[1] More than two years later the objective remained essentially the same: "You will continue to promote the development in Germany of institutions of popular self-government" and oppose "an excessively centralized government which through a concentration of power may threaten both the existence of democracy in Germany and the security of Germany's neighbors and the rest of the world."[2]

The conditions of utter defeat in Germany and the disintegration of civil government down to the village level in some areas lent themselves ideally to the reconstruction of German political and administrative institutions from the bottom upward. It has already been noted that military government was practically forced by circumstances to begin political reconstruction at the village and county level in Germany.

It is beyond the scope of this study to outline in detail the methods military government employed to achieve decentralization in Germany, but a few key features of American policy are noteworthy.[3] Military government deliberately permitted the formation of political parties, the resumption of self-government, the organization of police forces and trade unions, and the conduct of democratic elections at the village and county level first. It did this in part to strengthen local institutions, but especially to provide Germans with experience and lessons in democratic local self-government.[4] Later, upon completion of its negative program, military government and later the Department of State concentrated upon a reorientation program which concentrated upon the grass roots. Reorientation is the subject of a subsequent chapter, but we should note here that its chief aim was to encourage town hall meetings and public forums at the village and county level "in order to further local autonomy, spread the doctrine of officials' responsibility to the public [and] convince officials of the advisability of community participation in public administration."[5]

Decentralized Civil Government—Centralized Military Government

One of the curious features of American policy in Germany was military government's attempt to decentralize the civil government at the same time that it tried to centralize military government control. To ensure consistency of action and more effective headquarters control over detachments, military government began early to relieve detachments of their functional duties in the Landkreise and the Regierungsbezirke. Harold Zink has pointed out that military government never intended to operate German government directly, partly because adequate personnel could not have been found in the United States.[6] Field detachments governed in the cities and counties during the period of hostilities and the immediate post-surrender period only because of the complete collapse of civilian government and because their directives were not clear. Relieving detachments of the executive powers they had assumed was in accord with long-range military government planning as well as with traditional military practice.[7]

Removing authority from military government field detachments did not automatically promote responsible local self-government. In fact, military government appears to have been more

interested in improving its own control than in permitting greater
freedom to local civilian governmental units. Especially revealing
in this context is the military government study of detachment
operations in two districts of Bavaria. The study concluded that
the autonomous character of detached military government units
made it difficult for higher echelons to command adherence to
orders and directives. In tactical units an order is an order to be
carried out, the report said, but "in Military Government, a directive becomes a guide, nine times out of ten." The report continued: "The small detached command also has a tendency to drift
into sloppy habits, to fake reports and to regard all higher headquarters representatives as disturbers of the peace."[8] Essentially,
the conclusions of the study group were that field detachments
still did not understand that military government policy was made
at Land level.

The military government control office in Berlin also studied
the functions of military government liaison and security detachments throughout 1947 and the early part of 1948 to determine
their contribution to the over-all military government program.
If records of the discussions are accurate, Berlin was more anxious
to concentrate authority at higher headquarters so that military
government directives would be enforced more effectively than
that Germans have more self-government.[9]

The Effect of Centralized Military Government

Beginning early in January 1946, local civilian officials became
more and more independent of local military government detachments. But ultimate military government control was not removed
completely. It was shifted first to the district detachment and then
to the Land detachment. The effect was that Landkreis and village
civil officials became more responsible to civil officials at higher
civil government levels rather than to military government officials
at their own level. They did not become mere community representatives with considerable freedom of action as desired by military government in its decentralization policies. Harold Zink
wrote that "some [of the critics of military government's policy to

reduce detachments' powers] have paid far too little attention to the control which remains. . . . In reality the freedom given the Germans under the new setup may be no greater than that permitted under the system which provided an American military government detachment at each German political unit."[10]

Implementing military government orders and directives by Land civilian agencies required increasing power and authority for these agencies over regional, county, and village civilian agencies. A superficial study of Land government's role in denazification, public finance, education, property control, and food and agriculture provides sufficient evidence of its increasing authority. But it can also be illustrated in the realm of political affairs, where it would appear that removal of military government control should have permitted the greatest freedom.

After the Marburg military government detachment lost much of its authority and, what is more important, most of its personnel, the regional civil government required political parties to make monthly activity and membership reports to the civil government. Land and Regierungsbezirk officials ordered political parties to report periodically to the Oberbürgermeisters and the Landräte. The latter submitted the reports, through civilian channels, to higher civil governments, which in turn wrote political activity reports that were required of them by Land military government. Previously, when local military government detachments had adequate personnel and authority, political activity reports were gathered from the parties by military government detachments and transmitted to higher headquarters through military government channels.

The stigma that such a requirement placed upon opposition parties, for example the National Democratic party and the Communist party, is so obvious that it needs no elaboration. The Communist party, and later the National Democratic party, eventually refused to make the reports to the Oberbürgermeister and the Landrat. After consulting with military government the Oberbürgermeister and the Landrat told the parties they need no longer report.[11] More important to the present discussion is the fact that the Oberbürgermeister and the Landrat, in reporting local affairs to higher civil governments, functioned once again in the traditional dual role of local administrators and state functionaries. Military government had considered such dual responsibility to be so detrimental to the development of local self-government that it prohibited it in the municipal and county government codes written during the early phase of the occupation.[12]

Military government had tried hard to achieve decentralization, but German resistance to major changes in local government codes had been apparent from the beginning of the occupation.[13] The Hessian municipal code of December 1945 and the county government code of January 1946 made the Oberbürgermeisters and the Landräte at the same time local officials and state functionaries. Military government, believing this to be "detrimental to local self-government," demanded a change and settled for a compromise.[14] Civilian administrators nevertheless believed that the compromise decision to elect indirectly, rather than appoint, the Landräte and Oberbürgermeisters was too great a concession to military government's demands. The Oberbürgermeister of Marburg, in an interview with the press, said he would have liked to see the highest officials in the municipalities and the counties remain state officials (*Beamten*) as they had been prior to 1933. Under the new codes, Bleek said, the supervisory authorities could not review the qualifications of those who would "represent the state at the local level."[15]

Faced with continuing German resistance to change, lack of control over its field detachments, and depletion of trained personnel through rotation and demobilization, military government headquarters eventually allowed the German chain of supervisory authority to be linked again. The village Bürgermeister answered to the Landrat, the Landrat and the Oberbürgermeister to the Regierungspräsident, and all of these to the Minister of Interior. Commenting upon the Hessian municipal and county government codes in 1950, an American political affairs officer stated that they provided for somewhat greater interference in legislation by the executive branches than American officials would like to see, "but it is necessary to keep them from evading existing law."[16]   Military government faced the dilemma of permitting centralization, at least at Land level, and ensuring the enforcement of military government directives at the local level, or of forcing upon reluctant Germans decentralization and broad freedom for local government and taking a chance that some military government directives would be ignored at the local level.   The choice that military government made is indicated by the fact that municipal and county government codes give broad powers to the executive and to the supervisory authorities over local legislatures and councils.[17]

9

Denazification from Above

American military government denazified in Germany to achieve
a negative and a positive result: to remove Nazi influence from
German life and to provide conditions under which a more democratic life could grow and flourish. To achieve the former it
liquidated the Nazi party and its affiliated organizations; arrested
and detained influential Nazis and "other dangerous persons"; removed and excluded Nazi party members "of more than nominal
importance" from office and private enterprise; eliminated Nazi
teachers and teaching materials from the schools; and punished
those Nazis who had taken an active part in organizations declared
to have been criminal by the Nuremberg Tribunal. Further, it
eradicated Nazi ideals from German legislation, decrees, and regulations; erased Nazi emblems, insignia, and symbols from public
parks, institutions, buildings, monuments, streets, statues, and
other places; and it seized and blocked Nazi property. To achieve
the positive aim of denazification military government encouraged
political parties, trade unions, and other democratic institutions
to develop, with the enforced condition that they be purged of
Nazis and that they continue to exclude Nazis. In short, denazification was a program for separating Nazis from non-Nazis and
prohibiting the former from exerting their influence on German
life.

According to its administration, denazification in the American Zone of Germany can be divided roughly into two major programs: one administered by military government exclusively, the
other administered by Germans themselves, but under military

government supervision and control. In Marburg the former began with the occupation of the city and ended on May 31, 1946. The latter began on June 1, 1946, and continued until October 15, 1949, when the Land denazification ministry closed the last denazification tribunal in Marburg. For all practical purposes, however, denazification in Marburg ended a year earlier, when military government closed its special branch office and the Germans dissolved all tribunals except one that was to clean up the remaining cases and hear appeals.

Denazification by military government without direct assistance by Germans may be subdivided roughly into three phases, each more comprehensive than the preceding phase.[1] The first, conditioned by the exigencies of war and the adverse publicity accorded to certain denazification difficulties in Aachen late in 1944, was governed by Supreme Headquarters (SHAEF) directive of November 9, 1944, requiring removal of all persons from public office who had joined the Nazi party before Hitler became Chancellor in January 1933.

The more comprehensive second and third phases may be dated from July 7, 1945, when Headquarters, United States Forces, European Theater (USFET), issued a directive setting forth in detail the denazification program for the initial post-surrender period. It listed 136 mandatory removal and exclusion categories and stipulated that membership in the Nazi party prior to May 1, 1937, or holding office in certain of its affiliated organizations was cause for mandatory removal or exclusion from the positions to which it applied. It applied to persons in positions of "more than minor importance" in public offices and persons in "positions of importance in quasi-public and private enterprises" as well as in commercial, agricultural, and financial institutions. A month later, on August 15, 1945, another USFET directive expanded the program by defining persons in "positions of importance in quasi-public and private enterprises" to include those in private business, the professions, and those "of wealth and importance" who were unemployed. On September 26, 1945, Military Government Law

Number Eight extended denazification over the entire German economy except agriculture, and made Germans themselves criminally liable for failure to remove Nazis from positions other than ordinary labor, except when expressly authorized to do so by military government.

For the German affected by the directives, denazification began when military government or his employer required him to fill out a detailed *Fragebogen* (denazification questionnaire). Military government "vetted" the questionnaire according to an elaborate—and ever-changing—evaluating process. In accordance with the July 7 directive it automatically and summarily removed or excluded from certain positions those people whose questionnaires clearly stated that they had been Nazi party members prior to May 1, 1937, or whose answers indicated that they fitted into one of the many other exclusion categories. If a person's questionnaire exonerated him or did not implicate him sufficiently to warrant mandatory removal or exclusion, military government checked the information therein against its own adequate sources of information for possible falsification. The questionnaire was thus the primary basis for denazification proceedings, except for persons who had been placed in mandatory arrest categories. The latter were taken into custody immediately upon recognition.

The American-administered denazification program, through May 1946, affected chiefly those Germans employed, or seeking employment, with the Army and in public offices, and those who came under mandatory arrest categories. In its later stages it also affected persons employed by private industry and in trades, but it is almost impossible to assess the effects of Military Government Law Number Eight because it was soon replaced by the German-administered Law for Liberation from National Socialism and Militarism. When the latter was made public in Marburg, the number of questionnaires received by the detachment dropped off 85 per cent. Even before the new law took effect in June 1946, local German employers and review boards withheld decisions under Law Number Eight in anticipation of the new law.[2]

Scope

Reliable statistics showing the scope of military government denazification in Marburg are not available. Denazification records are not open to private researchers. It is doubtful, however, that such statistics could be assembled readily, because local military government records have been partly destroyed, and because of the methods of denazification. Many persons in Marburg were denazified by higher headquarters. The Land military government detachment directed denazification of the railway, the post, telephone, and telegraph agencies, the University and the churches. The Information Control Division denazified the press and the publishers. In individual cases, Land headquarters also denazified public officials in the Landkreis and the Stadtkreis. Published statistics for the entire American Zone show that 6 per cent of the total population was directly affected by denazification proceedings, and that military government removed or excluded from employment slightly over 2 per cent of the population. Interpolation of these percentages upon Marburg's population figures for 1946 shows that, if Marburg remained true to the zonal average, approximately 7,800 (6 per cent of the total population of 130,000) were affected by denazification and approximately 2,700 were removed or excluded from employment.

Available figures indicate, however, that the Marburg detachment denazified more intensively than the average detachment in the American Zone. The first Military Governor stated that he removed 75 per cent of Marburg's public officials during the first week. In December 1945 the detachment reported that it had received 11,500 denazification questionnaires for processing. The discrepancy between the Marburg figure (8.8 per cent of the total population of 1946) and the zonal average (6 per cent) may be due to the fact that Marburg had an unusually large number of Army employees to process and also to the fact that many questionnaires were duplicates. The zonal statistics are based on individuals, not questionnaires. After nine months of occupation the detachment had removed seventy-one officials and employees (56 per cent) and 120 Bürgermeisters (94 per cent) from the Landkreis administration and ninety officials (30 per cent) from the Stadtkreis administration, the police department, and the city savings bank. These figures show actual removals and do not show how many applicants for civil positions or for jobs with the American Army were rejected. Neither do they show the number denazified under Law Number Eight.[3]

The relatively small percentages of the total population affected by military government denazification (8.8 per cent in Marburg and 6 per cent in the American Zone) may presage the conclusion that denazification made little impact upon the community as a whole. Furthermore, since it was personal in nature, it appears that denazification's effect was primarily personal, unique, and particular to the individual concerned. However, since it applied almost exclusively to persons in prominent social, political, and economic positions, its effects were felt and observed much more widely than the statistics seem to indicate.

The Social and Economic Impact

Although citizens of Marburg agreed (in 1953 and 1954) almost universally that removal or exclusion from office caused serious economic hardship, a study of the conditions between 1945 and 1948 suggests other conclusions. The social and economic impact of American-administered denazification was, in fact, as unexpected and unusual as the economic and social conditions under which denazification occurred were abnormal and unstable.

The most evident and immediate effect of removal for the individual Marburger was that he no longer held a position for which he had spent a lifetime in preparation and which he expected to hold until retirement. Except for Nazis who got their jobs through party connections, businessmen, and some others, it is generally true that military government denazification most often affected persons holding public office with civil service tenure. The strong impact of the psychological shock of removal or exclusion from a position in which he had traditional and legal rights and privileges on the individual public servant in Marburg is probably indicated by the fact that a public opinion survey in the American Zone in 1948 showed that 84 per cent of the Germans who prefer government work to private industry do so because it provides security and pensions.[4]

For many Marburgers the initial psychological impact of removal or exclusion was soon dispelled by the attitude and action of military government's German appointees. Civil officials and political party leaders seem to have encouraged removed officials to communicate frequently with the city and county offices about their future reinstatement. The Landrat wrote to his civilian superior, in June 1945, that he merely suspended his "denazified" civil servants and gave their replacements only temporary appointments.[5] He dismissed civil servants most reluctantly, if at all. In one instance he followed the direct order of military government to dismiss his *Kassenbeamter* (treasury official), but with the consent and advice of a voluntary political committee for the Landkreis, whose members were approved by military government, he assigned the official to a back-room office from which he continued to direct the affairs of the treasury, while a clerk who was acceptable to military government served as a front.[6]

Evasions of denazification were as common in the city hall as in the Landrat's office. There a specialist in the municipal personnel office still managed his office after military government removed him early in 1946. The city transferred his wife to the office as a clerk. She took the files and correspondence pertaining to personnel administration home at night and brought them back in the morning. At times the newly appointed personnel administrator, who was inexperienced, called at the specialist's home to discuss personnel administration. At one time he brought the specialist back into the office as an employee. The arrangement continued until the approved personnel administrator died in office, whereupon military government ordered the specialist dismissed again. Nevertheless, the city council voted to give him six months' retroactive pay for his continued service.[7]

That the personnel specialist was no exception is borne out by numerous examples which testify to the fact that long friendships and loyalties among Marburg's officialdom were not affected by military government directives which divided Germans into "Nazis" and "non-Nazis." In November 1945 the Oberbürgermeister wrote a memorandum for his files in which he wondered "whether such officials could be paid full wages for the period of their so-called honorary service."[8] At one time the city administration hired a group of removed persons to assist in the tax assessor's office. The Bürgermeister furnished them an office in one of the municipal buildings, where they apparently worked without detection by the public or by military government investigators. Two of them have reported that the Oberbürgermeister assured them that they would be employed as emergency workers until they could be reinstated in their former positions. An ex-Bürgermeister, who had himself been in a Nazi concentration camp, reportedly came to visit them often, bringing tobacco that he had received from his American acquaintances. Some officials jokingly referred to the office as the "Nazi Rathaus."[9]

Socially the removed officials in Marburg suffered no ill effects. Those whom the author interviewed reported that they continued to move in the same social circles they had before. In fact, a few believe that the prestige and respect they enjoyed in the community were somewhat enhanced because the occupying power summarily and "unjustly" removed them and because seemingly they were the greatest losers after the war. It is significant that former Nazis and non-Nazis seem to agree on this point. The reasons they offer differ, however. Communists and left-wing Social Democrats who believed a social revolution was needed in Germany argue that the civil servants and the middle class were all Nazis—if not in fact, then in theory—and thus denazification provided no moral basis for social ostracism. Others, especially conservatives, argued that denazification was an unpopular and unjust purge carried out by rogues (Lumpen) and opportunists.

The economic consequences of removal and exclusion from office were negligible when viewed in the context of the immediate postwar German economy.* "In Germany today [1945] . . . the

* It is interesting that most of the Germans I interviewed in 1953 and 1954 gave as their greatest hardship the fact that they lost their income. When I reminded them, however, that they could buy hardly anything with their money in 1945 and 1946—contrary to 1953 and 1954—and that they could secure more

historical role of price has been obliterated," reported military government. "The wages for which men work are far less important than their food rations . . . and men will seek the job which pays the better ration. . . . Those who have accumulated funds, and who cannot work in the better rationed jobs, need not work at all."[10]

Before the currency reform in 1948, after which price again performed an economic function, German employers were unable to prevent employee absenteeism. Early in 1946 military government observers estimated that between 20 and 25 per cent of all workers stayed away from their jobs each day. Staying away from work to barter for scarce commodities and food had become so widespread a practice by 1947 that "thousands of employers [had to] provide consumer goods incentives for faithful work and regular attendance." They provided noonday meals in factory canteens; they secured housing and provided transportation for their employees; they sold at cost or gave away to steady workers a small portion of their own product (compensation wages); and they operated repair services for shoes, clothing, and household articles as incentives to keep workers on the job. In Marburg, the Landrat reported in 1946, commuters found it impossible to board the morning trains at local stations, because people going into the country to barter for food had already filled the trains to capacity in the larger stations.[11]

The ex-Nazi who had been excluded from office had a most advantageous position in the German barter economy between 1945 and 1948. Although some had neither the means nor the inclination to become full-time black-marketeers, most admit readily that they secured goods over and above their rationed allowance by trading with farmers or with "the enemy." The man who had been forcibly excluded from a position could spend as

---

food by going onto the black market for one day than they could buy with a month's salary, they readily agreed. Also they admitted that they could go to nearby farms and trade clothing, jewelry, or other articles for food that they could not buy in normal trade channels at any price. After they were faced with their own admissions, most of them agreed that they did not suffer from loss of income. Nevertheless, loss of income was the standard answer I received when I first asked my interviewees how denazification affected them personally.

much time as he wished traveling to the farming communities near Marburg, bartering one thing for another until he had the desired food and other commodities. As it often required several transactions to acquire, let us say, a pound of butter or a sausage, the advantage lay with the man who had most time on his hands. In addition, the ex-Nazi could, and sometimes did, serve Americans or negotiate illicitly with them for the most prized medium of exchange in all Germany: the cigarette. Marburgers point out that an unemployed person who spent one day at the railway station carrying bags and equipment for American soldiers could expect to earn the equivalent of several months' pay in cigarettes and candy.[12]

Furthermore, as a second-class citizen—which he was under the denazification laws—with few rights and obligations, the ex-Nazi had little sense of moral responsibility to work for the reconstruction of Germany.[13] Indeed, if the return from foraging was so prized that a fully employed worker easily overcame his moral obligations to his employer and society every fourth or fifth day, how much greater was the return for a man who felt fewer obligations and had all his time to barter and forage?

The American-administered denazification program in Marburg scarcely affected German individuals socially or economically. It did not bring about the desired separation of Nazis from non-Nazis, and in fact inadvertently placed Nazis in a more advantageous economic position than non-Nazis. Prospects of reinstatement and the widespread German belief that "little Nazis" should not be punished severely, mitigated and soon dispelled the immediate psychological shock of dismissal. But politically the American denazification program produced a series of reactions that affected deeply the relationships between Marburgers and military government, and which revealed the paradox of American denazification's negative and positive aspects: the use of undemocratic negative means to achieve democratic positive ends.

Political Impact

In a previous chapter we have seen that leading citizens of Marburg formed a political committee early in the occupation.

This committee, made up of non-Nazis and dominated by conservatives in their political, social, and economic viewpoints, expressed to military government and in its minutes what it considered to be the attitude of Marburgers toward American denazification. In June 1945 the committee chairman reported to an American that "denazification proceeded without apparent rules or regulations," and that the anti-Nazi Germans who knew the affected people were given no opportunity to testify. "Denazification," he continued, "apparently classifies all Germans with the war criminals." Two months later, Hermann Bauer, a committee member, wrote that he and his colleagues could not understand the implicit assumption of military government that all Germans were Nazis unless they could prove otherwise. In November the whole committee submitted to the Oberbürgermeister a secret report which asserted that denazification was based upon a fundamental misunderstanding of the Nazi regime, that denazification methods were wrong because they proceeded on the assumption of guilt rather than innocence, and that fixing a date for dividing Nazis from non-Nazis precluded individual consideration of each case.[14]

The political committee's strongest criticism of denazification came late in 1945 when it endorsed twenty-three theses on denazification prepared by the local Roman Catholic priest, who was also a respected adviser on educational and religious affairs for several Marburg military government officers.[15] The priest's theses included the usual German protests against denazification: the law was written after the crime, it was arbitrary, the people affected could not initiate an appeal, it violated fundamental laws which recognized the rights of the individual, its methods were those of totalitarian states, dividing the innocent from the guilty at a specific date was nonsense, and others. The political importance of the priest's theses was, however, that they pointed up specifically eleven ways in which denazification was an outright violation of his understanding of, and Americans' profession of, democratic theory and practice.

Denazification in 1945 and 1946 produced a strange paradox in Marburg. The anti-Nazis and the non-Nazis who were the most active and vocal supporters of military government early in the occupation were also its severest critics. While the Nazis apparently chose, for obvious reasons, to remain silent, the political committee, the Oberbürgermeister, the Landrat, the editor of the *Marburger Presse,* who was also on the political committee, and the founders of the new political parties—some also committee members—were almost the only vocal opponents of denazification. They denounced its theoretical basis and its practical effects. To the critics' dismay Americans often interpreted their criticism as verification of the collective guilt of Germans for the Nazi regime, a judgment which Marburg's political committee rejected categorically. They said they were not Nazis in disguise, even though none of them had suffered seriously under the Nazi regime, with the exception of one whose newspaper was suppressed. None of them had actively supported the Nazis, and especially the conservatives, who had a stake in the existing social-economic system, never forgave the Nazis their destruction of law and justice. Nor did they approve of the "democratic implications of Nazism," which permitted the untrained, the uneducated, the lower classes (*niedrige Schichten*) to become important officials and social leaders because they were party members.[16] To their further dismay, denazification's critics sometimes aroused in Americans a not altogether unfounded suspicion that some of the critics had themselves failed to include everything of pertinence in their own denazification questionnaires. The Oberbürgermeister's actions aroused such suspicion and he was subsequently arrested for falsification of his questionnaire, even though inclusion of the item itself would not have disqualified him from the office of Oberbürgermeister. Other officials, on the other hand, also failed to include some items on their questionnaires—some allegedly with verbal permission by military government officers—but they were never brought to trial, probably because they appeared docile and seemed to obey military government orders.

On the other hand, radicals—the Communists and the left-wing Socialists—apparently endeared themselves with military government officers by their stand in complete support of early military government denazification in Marburg. They had suffered under the Nazi regime as political parties and as individuals, but, in many instances, no more than had some of the political committee members and other democrats and conservatives in Marburg. But they were apparently troubled little by the violations of individual rights, fundamental laws, and democratic principles that the political committee found so odious. The American-appointed police chief, a naturopath by profession and a Communist in politics, appointed a political radical to head a special investigation section of the police department, instructing him to root out Nazis.[17] He also established a political division in the newly organized department and appointed as its chief a radical who said, in 1954, that if he and his friends had had their way in 1945 there would be no more "Nazis" in Marburg in 1954 to be reinstated in their former positions.[18] We have seen that Communist and Socialist investigators outnumbered all others at military government.

Denazification divided Marburgers into two clearly discernible political camps. The conservatives and the Liberal Democrats on the political committee believed that military government denazification permitted—perhaps not purposely, however—a small number of radicals to promote a social and political, and perhaps economic, revolution during the early phase of the occupation of Marburg. They believed that the leftists deliberately used denazification to infiltrate the city and county administrations so they could eventually seize power completely. In opposing this preparation for revolution the political committee and other relatively conservative politicians found themselves defending the Nazis, the politically indifferent, and the opportunists of the past who had once accepted Nazism—or condoned it—for various reasons, one of which was that it purported to stand for order and security. Few Marburgers were surprised when the Liberal Democratic party won the first election on the strength of the slogan that it would "de-Communize" the city administration if elected.

The American denazification program had wide political ramifications. It placed German anti-Nazi and non-Nazi democrats and conservatives under the necessity of either opposing military government or supporting a program that violated their political principles and their social and economic ideals. The political committee was deadly serious when it wrote, in November 1945, that it needed "a strong arm to lean upon" if it would help to rebuild Germany into a democracy. It referred directly to military government's apparent paradoxical policy of using arbitrary means to achieve democratic ends when it quoted the remarks of its opponents: "There are your democratic friends from America. What have they brought you?"[19]

Denazification also cast an unfavorable reflection upon military government policy and its local agents, the American officers. Marburgers suspected Americans of being leftists at worst, or of being politically too naïve to discern the leftist strategy at best. Some Marburgers who had believed it all along strengthened their conviction that democracy is a fair-weather political system which changes its methods in the face of adversity. Others, who probably would have given democracy a fair trial in Germany, report that they were shocked that military government officers and men apparently did not recognize the basic dichotomy of arbitrary means and democratic ends. Still others believed that Americans did understand the conflict, but used their power to promote American self-interests.

It will be noted how easily Marburgers used their conclusions about the Americans in the community to rationalize their own positions under the Nazi regime: If democracy is forced to make adjustments under political stress, perhaps dictatorship alone can fight Communism or get a nation out of a severe economic depression. If military government officers and men did not understand the essentials of their political system, were they any different from Germans who were led by Nazis, not knowing where they were being led, but enjoying the benefits of Nazism? If they (the Americans) did understand, why did they not object to denazification as they expected Germans to have objected to Hitler?

If Americans acted upon power-politics principles, using arbitrary means to achieve their ends, they took a page out of Hitler's book.

Whether Germans could have and would have denazified more justly, more effectively, and more systematically, as their criticisms of American denazification imply they could and would have, need not remain an unanswered question. Beginning in June 1946 they were given a chance.

10

Denazification from Within

The American-administered denazification program reportedly achieved the preliminary objective of removing Nazis from leading positions in government and business.[1] The German phase of denazification, commencing on June 1, 1946, was the comprehensive, long-range denazification program based upon the Law for Liberation from National Socialism and Militarism written by Americans and Germans together. The law was a criminal code on Nazism and militarism. It outlined procedures for judging every German above the age of eighteen according to his degree of responsibility for the wrongs committed by the Nazi regime. It provided that all Germans over eighteen register and upon the basis of the registered information be classified into one of five categories of guilt: Major Offenders (Class I), Offenders (Class II), Lesser Offenders (Class III), Followers or Nominal Nazis (Class IV), and Persons Exonerated (Class V). The class into which a person was placed depended upon Nazi party membership tenure, offices he had held, his economic gains under the Nazi regime, and other specific factual data he had to supply on a questionnaire (*Meldebogen*). The law prescribed sanctions for major offenders and offenders and provided opportunities for rehabilitation through probation for lesser offenders. It removed disqualifications from followers and exonerated persons.

Denazification thus differed sharply after June 1, 1946, from denazification by military government. Military government still controlled, reviewed, and advised, but German tribunals denazified. For the first time denazification affected all Germans over eighteen years of age. For the first time also, Nazis were to be punished rather than merely removed or excluded to make room for more democratic elements in certain influential positions.

In the Stadtkreise and Landkreise, denazification tribunals (*Spruchkammern*), which were directly responsible to the Land Minister for Political Liberation, implemented the denazification law. The law required that each Kreis have at least one tribunal. In Marburg there were, at one time, two each in the Stadtkreis and the Landkreis. The permanent tribunal staff included a public prosecutor, several investigators, and clerical and statistical assistants. The tribunals consisted of a chairman and at least two assessors (*Beisitzer*), who together with the public prosecutor were appointed by the Minister for Political Liberation. In practice the political parties that had been approved by military government at Land (state) level submitted lists from which the Minister appointed the chairmen, the public prosecutors, and the assessors. The tribunal chairman selected the assessors for individual sessions in a predetermined sequence.

The development of denazification by German tribunals also shows a marked difference from the development of military government denazification prior to June 1946. Beginning in July 1946 military government authorized a series of amendments to the Law for Liberation, each of which narrowed the scope of denazification and simplified the process to some extent, whereas under the previous program amendments had generally broadened the scope and complicated the administrative processes. The youth amnesty of July 8, 1946, exempted youths born after January 1, 1919, from denazification unless they fell into major offender or offender categories. The Christmas amnesty of 1946 was extended to low-income groups (less than RM 20,000 in taxable property in 1945 and less than RM 3,600 taxable income in 1943 or 1945) and to persons who were more than 50 per cent disabled, provided they did not fall into major offender or offender classes. By January 1949 approximately 20 per cent of the registrants in the American Zone had been amnestied.[2] The most complete figures available for Marburg show that by March 1948 approximately 29 per cent had been pardoned.[3]

Additional revisions in denazification procedure under the Law for Liberation became effective on October 3, 1947, and March 28, 1948. The first of these permitted the public prosecutors to classify members of the Nazi party and its affiliated organizations, except those found to have been criminal by the Nuremberg Tribunal, "strictly in accord with the evidence" instead of automatically as had been previously prescribed.* The March 1948 amendment was designed to speed denazification because it was "essential from the standpoint of Military Government objectives in Germany that this program be finished rapidly."⁴ Essentially, it gave the public prosecutors complete discretion in filing charges against those who had not yet been tried.

The most complete figures on Marburg's denazification by German tribunals show that by March 1948 approximately 29 per cent of the total population (1946) and approximately 38 per cent of all Marburgers above eighteen years of age had been affected by denazification under the Law for Liberation from National Socialism and Militarism.⁵ To be sure, many of those affected were subsequently exonerated or placed in the lower classifications, but each person of the 29 per cent was in some way affected (*betroffen*).

Marburgers, and some students of denazification, believe that the Law for Liberation provided the basis for a social and political revolution by legal means even though military government had placed specific limitations upon the fines that could be assessed against the guilty.⁶ But Marburg proved to be no place to promote such a revolution with the help of Marburgers themselves.⁷ The anti-Nazis and non-Nazis whom military government found in Marburg did not agree unanimously upon the social, economic, and political changes that denazification seemed to make possible. Nor did they agree upon denazification's means. A few Liberal Democrats and the right-wing Social Democrats who might have supported a mild denazification program as a means to achieve

* OMGUS, Monthly Report, No. 27, September 1947, Denazification and Public Safety, August–September 1947, pp. 1–2. The organizations found to have been criminal by the Nuremberg Tribunal were the SD, the Gestapo, the SS, and the Leadership Corps of the Nazi party.

military government's democratization program were offset by rightists on the one hand and leftists on the other. On the left the Communists and the left-wing Social Democrats wished to push denazification toward social, political, and, perhaps, economic revolution. On the right a powerful majority of conservatives, found chiefly in the Liberal Democratic (presently Free Democratic) and Christian Democratic parties, and radical nationalists, found mainly in the National Democratic party, wished to preserve the socioeconomic fabric of Marburg and denazify to restore the *status quo ante* Nazi.

The newly formed political parties, which Americans had licensed to provide experience in political democracy at the grass-roots level, proved to be the institutions that conditioned the success or failure of the denazification program. In Marburg four parties, the Liberal Democrats, the Christian Democrats, the Social Democrats, and the Communists, were permitted to participate in denazification by virtue of their state licenses from military government. They nominated the tribunal personnel and even distributed tickets for particular hearings during the early days when denazification was more popular. In addition, the tribunals submitted questionnaires to the parties on which the parties supplied information about persons coming before the tribunals.[8]

But the different views on denazification did not follow party lines strictly. Conservatives and some nationalists were active in all three major parties in Marburg, whereas the democrats and radicals were found most often in the Social Democratic, Liberal Democratic, and the Communist parties. In all but the latter, however, they were a distinct—albeit vocal and active—minority. The strength of the conservative non-Nazis was already obvious in the early phase of the occupation when they dominated the political committee. The Marburg political committee was, in fact, a coalition of political party leaders without benefit of election.

Strongly represented in all three major parties of Marburg, those who objected to the revolutionary nature of denazification easily dominated the whole program. At first, when it appeared that the Law for Liberation would be enforced literally at the insistence of military government, they subverted it. Later, as the law changed to include fewer and fewer people, their attitude toward the law itself changed. As early as October 1945, after Military Government Law Number Eight went into effect, the Oberbürgermeister told the political party leaders to advise their members to secure adequate uncontestable attestations (*einwand-freie Gutachten*) for presentation to the proper German denazification authorities. The use of such attestations and recommendations, which Germans later called *Persilscheine* after a leading brand of laundry soap, became so widespread after 1946 that the Marburg public prosecutor, a radical Communist who wanted to enforce the law to the limit, wrote to the *Marburger Presse* that his office had been flooded with affidavits, letters of recommendation, and other evidence to assist the Nazis affected by the Law for Liberation. He pointed out that his task was made most difficult because those in higher social, economic, and political circles could present recommendations and references from respected persons, whereas the "kleine Mann" could not.[9] In the ceremonies at the opening of the denazification tribunal for Landkreis Marburg, the chairman, formerly a Center party member and presently a Christian Democrat, informed the audience that the purpose of German denazification was to convict the guilty and restore the "mere followers" as citizens with full rights and privileges.[10] He said, in 1954, that he believed it was his duty to exonerate those who had made a false political choice under Hitler, because they should not have been included in any denazification process. The chairman in question had been one of the early military government appointees in the Landkreis administration. He had a clear anti-Nazi record, but he is not a democrat in his social and political views.

In practice the Marburg denazification tribunals reduced the classifications of guilt prescribed by the law for certain Nazi activities and membership tenure. The city tribunal exonerated a leading University official who had been a Nazi party member since 1933. Further, it declared a University administrative officer to have been nonpolitical (*ein unpolitischer Mensch*) and merely in-

structed him to reform, although he too had a long party record.
It recommended that his atonement be to serve the University once
again, but this time to prevent "old Prussianism and militarism"
from gaining the upper hand.[11] In numerous other cases the tribunals placed defendants in Class IV or V when they were automatically chargeable as Class II offenders under the Law for Liberation, even though the law proscribed declassification by more
than one degree.[12]

As military government modified the denazification law by
amnesties and amendments, the conservatives gradually gave more
and more support to the law itself. The changes made it possible
to do within the framework of the law what they had formerly
done by subverting it at the expense of apparently cooperating
with the Nazis. During the early phase they interpreted the law
broadly, allowing countless Nazis to evade punishment. But during the latter phase, when the law itself permitted evasion, they
supported it, thus again permitting Nazis to go unpunished. Their
actions were continuously criticized by the active leftists and democrats of Marburg.

From the beginning the vocal, active leftists and democrats objected to the tribunals' lenient decisions. Toward the end the
leftists opposed the law itself, because they believed it to be impossible to denazify thoroughly under the changed law. Early in
1946 the Communist public prosecutor and the Communist special
branch chief of the military government detachment pushed for
thorough denazification according to the letter of the law. They
were joined by the democrat Hermann Bauer, who thought the
law provided a workable solution to the difficult task, even though
it did seem to be somewhat hard on the "little Nazis."[13]

But the few Liberal Democrats, the leftists, and the Communists soon found themselves outnumbered, overruled, and finally
pushed to the sidelines completely. They were attacked by Nazis
and conservatives alike, but for different reasons. The Communist
public prosecutor of the city tribunal succumbed before the full
force of the conservative attack when he publicly announced that
he would bring charges to convict the Oberbürgermeister when his

case came before the tribunal.[14] Although the Oberbürgermeister was technically not chargeable under the law, the public prosecutor insisted that he had used his position during the Nazi period to improve his financial and economic status. Shortly before the trial began, the public prosecutor in question was suspended for alleged membership in the Schutzstaffel (SS), a crime defined by the Nuremberg Tribunal for which he was never charged. A new public prosecutor was appointed and the tribunal exonerated the Oberbürgermeister after it had heard the testimony of several prominent witnesses, including a high government official who was the Oberbürgermeister's personal friend.[15]

The other Communists fared no better in their services with the denazification tribunals. Their efforts had been so completely frustrated by 1947 that all twenty assessors resigned.[16] In the meantime the Minister for Political Liberation had dismissed the Communist secretary of the Stadtkreis tribunal, ostensibly for listening to telephone conversations of non-Communist public prosecutors and other tribunal personnel.[17] The American detachment's German special branch chief, a Communist, whose duty it was to observe denazification and prepare "delinquency and error reports" for higher military government headquarters, complained that he fought a losing battle to uphold the law. Because American personnel changed so often, this special branch chief assumed complete responsibility for supervision at times. In 1947 the Liaison and Security Officer for Marburg told a field adviser that he had "no knowledge whatsoever of denazification" and consequently "the entire section [special branch] is being run by a German civilian chief." The German chief asserted that the tribunals did not enforce the law, that the investigators were inadequate, and that cases were quashed by public prosecutors without proper evidence. When he objected strongly to the exoneration of a Landkreis official who had been a mandatory removal under the USFET July 7 directive, the Land military government office apparently failed to support him. He reported that Marburgers could evade the law without fear of American interference.[18]

Hermann Bauer, a left-wing Liberal Democrat, was undoubtedly the severest and most persistent critic of Marburg denazification tribunal decisions. He believed that denazification provided a means for eliminating the enemies of an infant German democracy. He thought that proper administration of the law would have resulted in punishment for real Nazis and exoneration for "little Nazis," whom he thought the law affected unjustly. He reported in his newspaper, which was licensed by military government, that in practice the important Nazis—the ones who enjoyed high political, social, and economic status—could bring evidence, affidavits, and witnesses that easily swayed the judgment of the tribunals. The "little Nazis," on the other hand, were at the mercy of the tribunals. He often editorialized on his belief that "if all the big Nazis are set free, there are only little ones left to hang."

Bauer, frustrated much earlier than the Communists, resigned his position as deputy chairman for the Marburg tribunal in October 1946, protesting the exoneration of several University officials and professors, the light sentence pronounced against a Marburg merchant, and the more severe judgments against several people he considered to have been only nominal Nazis. Bauer's resignation prompted the Military Governor to name him as a leading Communist, classifying his information reliable and verified.[19] It is true that Bauer criticized the tribunals for being too lenient, as did the Communists, but it is significant that the Military Governor ignored Bauer's political views expressed editorially in the only newspaper in the area and the fact that Bauer was one of the founders of the Liberal Democratic party in Marburg and as such signed the weekly party reports that were submitted to military government.

Although Bauer's resignation aroused undue suspicion at military government and eliminated him from direct participation in denazification, he used the columns of the *Marburger Presse* to point out in detail case after case in which important Nazis—who apparently would have been extremely insulted had they been considered mere followers between 1933 and 1945—were exonerated, declared to have been mere followers, or placed in lower classifications than the law permitted. But in 1948 Bauer's last means of protest was taken from him. The Marburg tribunal exonerated the former owner of the Marburg newspaper and he once again assumed control of the newspaper plant that military government had taken under property control and turned over to Bauer in trusteeship.[20] Eventually Bauer was ousted from the staff of the paper completely.

Bauer's campaign to push denazification according to the spirit of the law brought him bitter rewards. He lost the *Marburger Presse,* as he had lost his newspaper during the Nazi regime. The American military governor believed him to be a Communist. Bauer resigned from the executive committee of the Free Democratic party and continued to have serious political differences with his close personal friend, Ludwig Mütze. By 1952 he had eliminated himself from all positions from which he might have influenced public opinion in the direction of a more democratic Germany, even though he still continues, as a private citizen, to promote democratic causes.

Denazification and Local Politics

The impact of denazification was felt keenly by the newly formed political parties in Marburg, both in their organizational activities and in their campaigns. As noted above, the four major political parties which had military government licenses to campaign at the state level carried the burden of denazification. But they had to compete in local elections with other parties that military government had licensed to operate at the Landkreis and Stadtkreis level in accordance with its program to build German democracy upon a grass-roots foundation.

Several local political parties were organized in Marburg after 1946 and received military government licenses. The most important of these was the National Democratic party. It began to campaign actively in Marburg early in 1947, but it had already been licensed in several neighboring Landkreise. Its leaders claimed that it was the only right-wing party in postwar Germany. Reviving Admiral Dönitz's last-stand maneuver, the party campaigned for a union of Germany and the Western Powers to fight Communism. It encouraged refugees and expellees to believe that they would eventually be returned to their homelands in the East. It attacked denazification violently. Some of its Marburg leaders said denazification could be dismissed as a ridiculous affair (*eine lächerliche Einrichtung*), except that it tended to be more brutal than Nazi justice. The National Democratic party's views on denazification, its extreme nationalism, its anti-Communism, and its claim to be the only truly German party appealed especially to the ex-Nazis.[21]

Competition between the four established parties, especially the more conservative Liberal Democrats (later Free Democrats) and Christian Democrats, with the local splinter parties for members and votes added the final blow to the denazification law in Marburg. With four or five parties competing in every election, the one-third of the electorate that was affected directly by denazification, plus those who for various reasons sympathized with the one-third, represented the difference between victory and defeat at the polls. All Marburg's political parties, with the exception of the Communist party, toned down their emphasis on denazification and even helped prospective party members gain full political rights once more. The Communists themselves were accused of denazifying with a view toward gaining political support while they still participated in denazification.[22]

Political party membership grew tremendously between 1946 and 1948. The secretary of the Marburg Social Democratic party reported that new enlistments in his party and in other parties grew because "being a party member seemed to be insurance for the little Nazis." Another Marburger stated that it was common knowledge that the quickest way to be cleared by the denazification tribunals was to join one of the political parties. Significantly, in 1948, when denazification was coming to an end and the law itself permitted easy denazification, new enlistments decreased and established membership suffered a reduction of "landslide proportions."[23]

The competition among the parties for members was paralleled by the competition for votes. Marburg's local elections after 1946 are best characterized as campaigns which appealed to nationalist sentiment, denounced occupation policies, and attacked denazification. The major parties could not afford to isolate themselves from at least one-third of the future electorate in the face of the appeal made by the local parties. As early as 1946, echoing the theme of the Liberal Democratic party that denazification in Marburg had led to "Communization" of the city administration, a Christian Democrat predicted that denazification prepared the way for "Bolshevizing" Germany. In 1949 the Free Democratic candidate who won the Bundestag election told his party followers that "the unfortunate effects of denazification . . . had defamed and discriminated against millions of guiltless citizens." Behind these and other overt expressions of hostility the parties continually worked for a denazification policy that would allow re-assimilation of ex-Nazis.[24]

Military government itself recognized the danger of party competition to the denazification program in 1948. The National Democratic party participated in the 1948 election even though its temporary license had expired. After the election another local party protested and petitioned for a new election. The Office of Military Government for Land Hessen decided to issue a permanent, retroactive license to the National Democratic party rather than permit a new election, because it believed that a new election might result in an even higher vote for the National Democrats, or force the other parties to stress nationalism and appeal to the ex-Nazis to keep from losing votes.[25]

The failure of denazification to achieve its negative objective in Marburg is manifest in the paradoxes it produced in its application. Evidence of this failure is the fact that in December 1948, 28 per cent of the municipal employees were among those who had been incriminated under the Law for Liberation. The Landkreis administration employed twenty-three officials (18 per cent of the total) who had been affected by the denazification law, and the villages had elected twenty-five mayors (20 per cent) who were likewise incriminated. Furthermore, the Denazification Division of the Office of Military Government for Land Hessen estimated that in 1948 about half of the Hessian high government employees were persons who had been affected by the Law for Liberation.[26]

The positive objective of denazification, to provide conditions under which a more democratic life could grow and flourish, proved even more impossible to achieve in Marburg than the negative one. Although there were many reasons for the failure of denazification, in Marburg, none seems more important than the mistaken American belief that if given a measure of freedom and local self-government, without Nazi interference, Germans at the grass-roots level would emulate Americans: that they would demand individual rights and assume individual responsibilities, willingly eliminate Nazis and other antidemocratic elements, but not initiate radical economic changes. The mistake lay in the fact that many Marburgers apparently chose to assume the indifferent (*ohne mich*) attitude toward public affairs with which politicians, the press, and Americans had characterized "the German." They cast their ballots—diligently and religiously—referring to themselves in conversations and in letters to the editor as voting cattle (*Stimmvieh*), then left public affairs to the political experts. In Marburg those political experts were the conservative, middle-class, protestant political party leaders who were more interested in preserving a "political, economic, social, and cultural system much older than Nazism" than in promoting a legal revolution of society and politics, which would have been necessary—in Marburg at least—under the denazification law, or an economic revolution, which might have been possible under the law.

PART FOUR

The Constructive Program

11

American
Democratization Efforts

Military government's stated long-range objective was a democratic and peaceful Germany.[1] It pushed denazification, industrial disarmament, and decentralization even though they were preventive and punitive, to prepare the way for eventual democratization. During the first three years of occupation the negative programs eclipsed the positive one, but military government officers always tried to impress their own conceptions of democracy upon Germans.

Efforts at democratization lacked systematic organization and direction before 1948. Americans made personal contacts, visited legislatures and administrative offices, promoted youth activities, distributed films, and called attention to American press and radio information programs. In effect, between 1945 and 1948 Americans tried mainly to reorient the German counterparts of military government officials.[2] In Marburg, as in other local detachments, such efforts suffered from lack of personnel. As the detachment became smaller and smaller, in accord with military government policies, personal efforts beyond routine duties necessarily decreased. As military government became centralized, the little active promotion of democratic ideas that there had been was shifted to higher headquarters, away from the Kreis detachments. Nevertheless, the Standing Operating Procedure for Liaison and Security Detachments defined one of the missions of the detachments as that of promoting a democratic system in Germany. But it failed completely to assign to either the Military Governor, or the Public Safety Officer, or the Special Branch Officer duties that might have promoted democracy.[3]

The Marburg Effort

Marburg's military government officers maintained close liaison with their civilian counterparts during the early phase of the occupation. They held daily conferences with the Oberbürgermeister, and, beginning in May 1945, the Public Safety Officer held periodic conferences with Bürgermeisters in the Landkreis.[4] Because of personnel reductions and the greater emphasis upon denazification, the Marburg detachment officers abandoned scheduled meetings but continued to make occasional unscheduled visits when time permitted or the situation demanded them. Available records indicate that officers conferred regularly with county administrators in the food office, agriculture office, the county savings bank, and the county railway and that between August 1947 and July 1948 the Military Governor held monthly meetings with the city administrative officers.

In addition to the liaison between American officers and civil officials in line of duty, military government officers and enlisted men participated in discussion groups, as they were encouraged to do by a memorandum issued in 1946 by the Office of Military Government for Hessen. Marburg students organized such a discussion group, but it automatically excluded many Germans because the discussions had to be held in English. Furthermore, the Marburg Liaison and Security Officer reported that the discussions often nearly defeated their purpose because few qualified Americans attended, and because German students tended to stray from the prepared topics—in the particular cases reported, the Weimar Republic and the Nazi State—in what he believed were attempts to defend their support of the Hitler government. Although he was proud that Americans usually spoke up about "how we do it in the States," the officer felt that the discussion topics should have been prepared more carefully in order to obtain American participants qualified to answer German questions. Nevertheless, the Office of Military Government for Germany listed the Marburg discussion forum among the three most successful in Land Hessen.[5]

Marburg's military government officers made few inroads into the social life of the community. When they did it was usually to associate with Germans in the higher social and educational circles who understood English and who had professional interests similar to those of military government officers. In effect, this meant that, aside from purely personal friendships, military government officers and enlisted men associated socially with Marburgers who generally opposed basic military government objectives such as civil service reform, school reform, social and political democratization, and thorough denazification.[6]

For the most part military government democratization policies before 1948 were designed to permit democratization rather than promote it. American representatives in Germany apparently assumed that the negative policies were permissive policies: they would clear the way for a resurgence of democrats at the grass-roots level. Almost two years before the war's end C. J. Friedrich wrote: "The destruction of the Nazi sector [of the dual state in Germany] will automatically revive the other, giving the latter opportunity to fill the vacuum created by the disappearance of the party."[7]

Based upon the assumption that democracy would grow from the grass-roots level upward, military government policy concentrated upon removing the obstacles to democracy, encouraging political parties to develop, and ensuring free elections and free exchange of opinions. Local initiative, responsible self-government, and elections at the grass-roots level were to be the avenues by which Germany would develop democratically. "American policy," wrote one who was directly involved, "is not 'imposing' democracy, but is imposing restraints upon those elements of the German population who would prevent democracy from becoming established." Accordingly, military government licensed local parties early and directed local communities to hold free elections in January and April 1946 "to give training in democracy and to strengthen local German administration by giving it a popular base."[8]

It is of some interest that Marburg's political leaders thought the elections in January were too early and that they were disappointed when German requests for a delay were denied, presumably by General Clay himself. The Landrat addressed a communication to the village mayors in December 1945, explaining the election procedures, and warned them that the elections were to be held on express orders of military government (*Es sei darauf hingewiesen, dass dies die ausdrückliche Anordnung der Militärregierung ist*).[9]

Political Activities in Marburg

Political parties that formed in the Kreise needed military government licenses. Military government required that the founders fill out denazification questionnaires, prepare party programs, party rules and by-laws, and submit them to military government for review. After a party received a license it could recruit non-Nazi members within the Landkreis, collect money, and hold meetings approved by military government. Later, after November 1946, licensed parties could hold meetings without prior approval. Parties could invite speakers, but those coming from outside the Landkreis only with military government approval, and those coming from outside the American Zone only with USFET approval. The parties were required to submit periodic activity reports; bimonthly first, monthly later on. The reports were to include the total number of party meetings held, the attendance at the meetings, the number of members, amount of money on hand, the source of party income, and a statement of expenditures. The parties were also ordered to describe important meetings, significant developments in party organization and finance, and to give sketches of important personalities.[10]

But military government discovered after 1946 that permitting German political parties to organize and campaign at the local level did not ensure the results it desired. The local political parties were controlled from above rather than from below. The political apathy of Germans did not disappear even though most Germans voted in the elections. A public opinion poll conducted for HICOG in 1950 revealed that of the Germans interviewed 75 per cent of those between fifteen and nineteen years of age, 65 per cent of those between twenty and twenty-five, and 62 per cent of those over twenty-five expressed absolutely no interest in politics. Seventy-nine per cent of the first age group and 82 per cent of the latter two age groups said they would not take a responsible position in political life even if they were asked. The political leaders, even at the Kreis level, disdained public opinion as a guide to action. They refused to push vigorously the American suggestions for civil service reform and school reform and they procrastinated regarding American demands for changes in local government. The political parties united in their opposition to industrial disarmament. They subverted the denazification law. They became the sounding boards for widespread opposition to the occupation in general. In fact, the parties were not only agencies of democracy, but also agencies through which Marburgers opposed and attacked military government policies looking toward democracy.

The Marburg detachment had neither the personnel nor the authority to do anything about the matter after 1946. It continued to receive reports from the parties themselves, and it was charged with observing political party activity. But members of all Marburg's political parties have stated that they considered the military government reports to have been a chore (*eine Sorge*), and that they reported only what they thought military government would like to hear. Lacking personnel, the detachment apparently relied heavily upon the official party reports and upon other information that it received, but which it did not seek systematically. At least one reason that Americans did not achieve the results they desired was that they expected too much. Americans were unable to admit "that democratization did *not* mean Americanizing Germany," wrote one observer. Another has said: "Had there been the considered Allied attention to democratic minima which the gravity of the large scale occupation required, much . . . provincialism might have been avoided and the general effort made more successful as a result. The essentials of political democracy . . . do [not] demand the existence of an independent civil service commission after an American model styled to meet the patronage needs of a political situation without German parallel."[11]

Marburg's political leaders were active long before military government authorized them to form political parties in August 1945. One day after the occupation of the city Hermann Bauer corresponded with his political friends, and together they formed a political committee out of party cells.[12] The Oberbürgermeister and the Landrat conferred with political leaders before recommending appointments to military government. Landrat Eckel called Social Democrats together in his home even before Germans were authorized to assemble in groups of more than five. Hermann Bauer, Gottlieb Pfeil, and Ludwig Mütze met occasionally with others between April and August 1945 to discuss the formation of a liberal political party.[13] Erich Kroll depended upon the Communist party to fill the ranks of the police department. Other parties developed more slowly, but a leadership corps was represented in the political committee after military government and the Oberbürgermeister rejected a few of the more extreme nationalists and conservatives. The four major political groups had coalesced and maintained personal liaison so that in August 1945, when military government authorized political parties to form, they quickly established formal organizations.

Marburg's Major Political Parties

The Social Democratic Party

The Social Democratic party (SPD) organized most thoroughly, with the possible exception of the Communist party. It divided Marburg into two districts (*Bezirke*): Marburg and Lohra, to the south. Each of the districts sent delegates to the party conventions (*Kreisgeneralversammlungen*). The party divided the Kreis further into fourteen functional party districts (*Arbeits- und Werbebezirke*). Each of the functional districts had an organization composed of a leader and a working committee (*Arbeitsausschuss*). The working committees included specialists in organization and recruiting, finance and administration, education and cultural affairs, village administration (*Kommunalpolitik*), agriculture, women's affairs, youth activities, and social welfare (*Sozialpolitik*), including refugee problems. The party work at the local level was coordinated with general party activities and programs by the Kreis committee (*Vorstand*) and the Marburg party office (*Geschäftsstelle*). The published program of the Marburg SPD corresponded with the SPD program for all Germany. It advocated socialization of basic industries, co-determination for workers in management, farm cooperatives and land reform, parliamentary representative democracy, and a unified socialist Germany. Locally it favored increased industrialization, integration of refugees and expellees, and denazification.[14]

In practice and in election campaigns the Marburg Social Democrats opposed many military government policies and practices. They were represented on the political committee that criticized the early occupation. Oberbürgermeister Siebecke opposed military government employment standards vigorously. Landrat Eckel constantly reminded the detachment of the negative effects of industrial disarmament. The party helped "little Nazis" in their denazification trials. It opposed military government civil service reform, which, among other things, would have required civil servants to be nonpolitical. It called for the unification of Germany. It gave lip-service to educational reform, but it did not want to change the German school system.[15] The Social Democrats especially portrayed military government's objections to a socialistic and planned Hessian economy as an American violation of democratic principle. Military government's opposition manifested itself especially in two ways: the American insistence that trades and crafts operate on a free-enterprise basis with freedom of entry; and General Clay's requirement that Hessians vote separately on their constitution (1946) and on Article 41 of that constitution. The latter established the constitutional basis for socialization of basic industries.[16]

The Liberal Democratic Party/Free Democratic Party

The Liberal Democratic party (LDP), which began as the Democratic People's party (DVP) and is today the Free Democratic party (FDP), never organized so carefully down to the village level as did the SPD. Its district headquarters in Marburg served as an umbrella organization (*Dachorganisation*) for relatively independent local groups throughout the district. In Marburg a Kreis committee gave direction to party activities in the area. The committee included persons who specialized in youth activities, community affairs, women's activities, social welfare, agriculture, and the like. These experts (*Referenten*) represented the district organization at local party meetings and recommended party platforms in their fields of interest. Within the Kreis local party groups formed village committees (*Ortsgruppen*), while in the villages the party designated one or more persons as observers and workers (*Vertrauensmänner*).

The published programs of the party changed between 1946 and 1952. While it was a local group, the DVP platform, although rather vague, called for "true political democracy," the re-education of youth, a "progressive farm program," the recognition of "private property and private initiative as the source of human progress," and the political, social, and economic reassimilation of those who were "misled or forced followers of the Nazis."[17]

After the Marburg DVP joined the Hessian LDP, its local platform specifically advocated a continuation of the professional civil service, improvement of housing, a just welfare and assistance program for refugees, evacuees, and disabled persons, and graduated tax schedules. The platform stated that denazification was a matter of law. But the LDP believed that in the best interests of the community the Marburg administration should also be "de-Communized." With reference to purely local affairs the LDP wanted to keep Marburg a cultural center, allowing only that industry to settle which would not change the zones and the building plans of the city.[18]

In December 1948 the Hessian LDP joined the other liberal parties of the three Western zones and formed the FDP. In Marburg the result of this union was that the party dropped the mild social program it propounded vaguely before. In addition, the campaign speakers revealed an increasingly distinct antioccupation attitude. The FDP candidate who won the Bundestag election in

1949 described his party as a nineteenth-century liberal party that advocated a state governed by laws rather than men, favored a private enterprise economy, and worked for separation of church and state, especially in the matter of education. He said the FDP was dissatisfied with the provisional West German government because it split the Germans. Germans, he said, had been divided enough already: into "old citizens" and "new citizens" because the Allies had cut off German territory and expelled its population; and into "Nazis" and "others" by "the unfortunate effects of denazification which had defamed and discriminated against millions of guiltless citizens."[19]

In 1950 the FDP proposed an end to denazification and "its defamation"; a professional civil service; administrative reform; more self-government; school reform, meaning community schools rather than sectarian schools; a broader refugee assistance program; and an end to the "social experiment in Hessen."[20] The candidates for the FDP/BHE joint ticket enlarged upon the published platform. The FDP candidate advocated re-employment of former Nazi party members and removal of unqualified persons from the civil service, the latter being those who got their positions as a result of denazification. The BHE candidate, speaking on the subject of denazification, said that it was a political device used by Hessian Social Democrats to remain in power.[21]

The platform and the campaign activities of the FDP and its predecessors show that the party supported only the free-enterprise economic policy of military government. Of the major parties it opposed most vigorously reform of the civil service, significant change in the school system of Germany, and denazification. A survey by the Office of Military Government for Hessen in 1949 showed that six of the eleven FDP candidates for the Bundestag were formally chargeable as active Nazis under the Law for Liberation from National Socialism and Militarism and that the candidate for the Marburg district had been in the SS from 1933 on and in the Sturmabteilung (SA) from 1934 on. The party's conservative, nationalist leadership—claiming to be the most *volksbewusst* in Germany—stressed the party's interest in the German

people, including those living outside the borders of the country
(*Grenzlanddeutschen*).[22]

The Christian Democratic Union

The organization of the Christian Democratic Union (CDU)
resembled that of the LDP/FDP at the local level.

The earliest published CDU program in Marburg shows the
broad appeal it made to leftists and rightists, Roman Catholics and
Protestants. It stated that there were no proletarians and capitalists
in postwar Germany. It called for a rehabilitation of Germany according to broad Christian principles. Specifically, the platform
advocated economic unity of Germany; an antimilitaristic development to the point of pacifism; denazification, but also pre-
vention of "dictatorship of the left"; protection of private property and private enterprise, but private property conditioned by a
"true Christian responsibility"; establishment of private schools;
and religious instruction in the schools. The party leaders admitted that the CDU was a catch-all party (*Sammelbecken*) because it appealed to former Centrists, Communists, nationalists,
and liberals. But for this very reason they said the CDU was the
only new party in Germany after 1945.[23]

The diverse character of the CDU makes it difficult to describe
its stand on military government democratization plans. But it is
clear that it opposed the revolutionary effects of denazification. In
Marburg the party was dominated by conservatives who opposed
radical changes in local government that would reduce party
strength. In 1946 a serious split developed within the CDU over
the right of the party leadership to force its city council members
to vote for the party choices for Oberbürgermeister.[24] The party
won, and the members who had opposed resigned.

A few examples of CDU campaign speeches and tactics illustrate
that its local organization was a highly dubious institution for
carrying out military government democratization. As early as
1946 a CDU youth rally featured a speaker who made insidious
allusions to the Allies and to military government. She predicted

that denazification prepared the way for "Bolshevizing" Germany and placed the blame for it upon "emigrants in Allied uniforms."[25] The American intelligence report on the meeting concluded that the speech showed to what degree the CDU followed the old line of Nazi propaganda by "picturing Bolshevism—which is in no way rationally defined—as the arch enemy of Germany and the world," and by its anti-Semitism.

A little more than a year later, on the eve of the ninth anniversary of the burning of the synagogues by the Nazis, the chairman of the Marburg CDU wrote an article on the subject. Referring to statements made in denazification trials and to his observation that large masses of people stood around without saying a word when the synagogue burned in Breslau in 1938, he concluded that there were few Germans who were violently anti-Semitic. Of greatest interest for the present subject, however, is the article's subtle criticism of the occupation. It said that anti-Semitism belongs in general categories of "collective hatred." Obviously referring to the German belief that Americans assumed Germans to be collectively guilty after 1945, the article encouraged Germans to believe that their anti-Semitism under Hitler was no different from American anti-Germanism under the occupation.[26]

In 1949, shortly before the national CDU began to lead the West German Republic to cooperate with the West, local CDU rallies produced violent anti-American speeches and reactions. A speaker at a well-attended rally in Allendorf drew heavy applause when he cited the case of a Bavarian food minister's removal "by a democratic resolution and not by the dictatorship of the Americans." Probably encouraged by the reception of his remarks—and certainly not according to national CDU published principles—the speaker reportedly told his audience that "the sentences imposed at Nuremberg are also a dictatorial measure of the Americans. . . . American aviators, who bombed our cities and murdered women and children, should also be sent to Nuremberg and should be punished. All of them should be hanged anyway." The speech also contained a criticism of dismantlement of peacetime industry:

"The Occupation Forces should not believe that Germany's mental (*geistige*) dismantlement will ever be forgotten. Some day we shall present the bill."[27]

The Communist Party

The highest Communist party (KPD) organization in Marburg was the monthly party convention (*Mitgliederversammlung*). It legislated for the party and elected the executive committee. The ten-man executive committee (*Ortsgruppenleitung*) met once a week to direct party affairs for the entire Kreis. In the villages the party organized local party units (*Ortsgruppen*). Extending its influence over the entire Kreis organization was the Prüfungskommission, consisting of five members elected by the party convention. This committee passed upon new members and received complaints against party leaders and members. It held secret meetings and probably directed the activities of the party completely because of its power to expel members and remove leaders.[28]

The original aim of the Marburg KPD was to destroy national socialism, imperialism, and militarism to prepare for "a democratic Germany." The positive aspect—democratization—was to be achieved by active Communist participation in local affairs and through "propaganda" in speech, writing, and pictures.

Later, during the first election, the KPD published its program. It concentrated upon local problems: housing, food, and social welfare. It called for a home-building program to provide for at least 350 dwellings; extensive use of land, whether it was publicly or privately owned; and the institution of forced agricultural labor service (*Arbeitseinsatz*), with the slogan: "He who fails to work should not eat." The KPD advocated that increased social welfare be made possible by a progressive tax on the wealth of those least affected by the war. It called for extensive denazification, but not of "little Nazis." It was interested rather in those who reaped material benefits from the Nazi regime and in the "intellectuals who should have seen before 1933 what Hitler was striving for."[29]

The Minor Political Parties in Marburg

The National Democratic party (NDP) functioned actively in Marburg from March 1947 until August 1949. In 1949 it joined with the FDP in the Bundestag elections. Military government reports referred to the NDP as "one of the new nationalistic . . . political groups." The party's program called for a union of the West against Communism; a strict free-enterprise economy, demanding the return of the nationalized railways, the post office, and radio to private hands; a German army; local school administration and control; and resettlement of refugees to underdeveloped areas. The party opposed organized labor bitterly. It fought denazification of "little Nazis," and favored a peace settlement that would recognize Germany's 1919 boundaries. It did not recognize the Oder-Neisse line as Germany's eastern boundary and demanded specifically that East Prussia, West Prussia, Pomerania, and Upper Silesia be returned to Germany.[30]

The Bloc of Expellees and Victims of Injustice (BHE) organized locally in March 1952. A refugee party, it demanded better integration of refugees into West Germany, equal rights for all Germans in internal and external politics, and recognition of refugees' claims to their homelands from which they had fled or had been expelled. Fearful that a general treaty would recognize their homelands as non-German territory, the party opposed creation of a German army if it were linked with a general peace treaty. The local party candidate said the party would agree to a German army only after refugees had been housed properly, after war burdens had been equalized (*Lastenausgleich*), and after refugees had been integrated socially. Locally, the party advocated more industry for Marburg.[31]

The Democratic Nonpartisan Community party organized in the city of Marburg in 1948. It concerned itself exclusively with local affairs, demanding a clean administration, a merit system for municipal employees, and popularly elected city councils. It favored public pressure groups for promoting better housing, improving social welfare, food rations, and education. It proposed construction of recuperation and rehabilitation homes for those who could not care for themselves, especially the refugees. And it advocated the death sentence for black-marketeers in food. In 1949 the party changed its name to Demokratische Wirtschafts- und Aufbau-Gemeinschaft Hessen, continuing to campaign for the same broad local program.[32]

A few other minor parties or realignments of older parties appeared in the 1952 elections. One was the Nonpartisan Citizens' Committee of Marburg, consisting of former Democratic Nonpartisan Community party members as well as a number of the less conservative former Free Democrats and Christian Democrats. Its central aim was to promote citizen participation in the Oberbürgermeister elections. The practice had been, and is, for the parties in the city council to agree among themselves who should be the Oberbürgermeister and vote a strict party ticket.[33]

The other splinter parties in the 1952 election were the National Bloc and the Unity and Freedom party. The former was really the remainder of the old NDP with a new name and the latter the Communist party in disguise.[34]

The Political Parties and Democratization

Military government believed that its negative policies of denazification, industrial disarmament, and decentralization were essential to the positive policy of democratization. Other parts of this study, and the political party platforms noted above, show that Marburg's political parties used their democratic structures to oppose and attack military government policy rather than to promote American conceptions of democracy.[35] The parties subverted denazification, opposed industrial disarmament, and approved of military government's inadvertent centralization. German resistance, led by the parties themselves, brought other military government policies to nothing or modified them beyond recognition. American proposals for a unified, single-track school system in Germany met with German resistance, and it was only with extreme difficulty that military government achieved a six-year elementary school in Hessen.* American proposals for civil service reform met the same fate as the school reform proposals. The civil service codes adopted by Land governments were unsatisfactory, and military government eventually dictated civil service regulations to the combined Western zones in 1949.†

The grass-roots political democracy that Americans hoped would result from practice at the local level did not materialize.

* OMGH, Historical Report, 1948, I, Narrative, *passim.* Among other things, the Americans proposed a comprehensive school system for all children and youth below the university level, that all children remain together for six years without segregation according to sex, social class, race, vocational or professional intentions, an increased emphasis upon social studies and cultural subjects, and a corresponding decrease in emphasis upon foreign languages. OMGUS, Monthly Report, No. 16, November 20, 1946, Education and Religious Affairs, pp. 1–2. The German Land governments made proposals for school reform throughout 1947 and 1948. Military government considered them to be unsatisfactory. OMGUS, Monthly Report, No. 31, January 1948, Education and Religious Affairs (Quarterly Review), November 1947–January 1948, pp. 6–7, states: "In no case was the reform plan completely developed. They were therefore given only general approval as reform plans for German education must progressively be rewritten, until all undemocratic aspects be eliminated." See also OMGUS, Monthly Report, No. 44, February 1949, Report of the Military Governor, p. 45; and OMGH, Education and Cultural Relations, to Minister President, Land Hesse: Six Year Elementary School, August 22, 1948, OMGUS Papers.

† OMGUS, Monthly Report, No. 44, February 1949, Legal and Judicial Affairs (Cumulative Review), 1 December 1948–28 February 1949. American proposals for civil service reform in Germany stated that the service should be open to all citizens loyal to democratic principles; promotions were to be based upon merit rather than social antecedents, race, sex, or politics; training in economics and political and social sciences were to be considered adequate background for certain positions rather than legal training alone; the service should be open for new members when positions could not be filled effectively by promotion; all civil servants should have equal rights and retirement benefits rather than make the distinction between officials and employees; public servants should be subordinate to ministers, who are the elected representatives of the people; and civil servants must refrain from political activity. OMGUS, Monthly Report, No. 43, January 1949, Report of the Military Governor, p. 15. In the opinion of military government representatives, the Bavarian law represented "a drastic step backward . . . and seeks to restore the traditional rights and privileges of the German official class within the civil service." They described the Württemberg-Baden law as unsatisfactory and said "the existing drafts in Hesse likewise illustrate the traditional German civil service policies and appear to have been influenced very little by democratic principles in spite of efforts of Military Government representatives." OMGUS, Monthly Report, No. 47, May 1949, Report of the Military Governor, p. 13.

Germans cast their ballots in elections, but that was all.[36] They were not visibly interested in the daily activities of their representatives in the city council, in the Kreistag, in the Landtag, or in the Bundestag. They did not bother to attend city council meetings or Kreistag sessions, except under unusual circumstances. Nor did they form local groups to promote better local government and solve community problems. In fact, the average Marburger was apathetic. He was not interested in politics or public affairs.

Neither did he bother to learn what his rights were under the postwar democratic constitutions.[37] The Office of Military Government for Germany reported that a survey disclosed that over ten thousand homes had been searched without proper warrants in the American Zone in the first half of 1948. Another survey resulted in the conclusion that 85 per cent of all searches conducted in Hesse were not supported by judicial search warrants.[38]

Marburg's political parties worked within the framework of the political apathy of their constituents, doing little to improve the situation. Party membership rolls remained relatively small. The party executive committees prepared slates that they presented to the voters. Important issues before the city council or the Kreistag were debated in party caucuses, and the public knew little of what transpired behind the scenes (hinter den Kulissen). Party groups usually voted according to the decisions made by the party in secret caucus. Grass-roots democracy became, in effect, a contest between party factions that had been chosen on a proportional basis by an apathetic constituency.[39]

In accord with Marburg conditions, the political parties performed a definite benign service for their constituents. The party offices, staffed with permanent secretaries and assistants, helped German citizens meet the everyday problems of life and interceded on their behalf when they were confronted with bureaucrats. Each of the parties had various advisory committees (Beratungs-stellen). They gave free advice on home economics, legal affairs, community affairs, expellee and refugee problems, adoption of children, marriage and family affairs and similar matters. During the serious food shortage between 1946 and 1948 the Marburg CDU even had an advisory committee on cultivation of gardens.

Military government officers at all levels criticized their own efforts at democratization between 1945 and 1948. They admitted that it was difficult to promote anything positive when they engaged in so many punitive measures. They found that institutional democratization lacked vitality. Their own unorganized personal efforts fell far short of the ultimate goal, especially at the Kreis level. As early as 1946 a searching evaluation of the Marburg military government program by an incoming Military Governor produced the observation that "democratization is still in its infancy [and that] . . . we do not have an up-to-date account of what is happening in the Kreis." "Democratically constituted and popularly responsible law-making bodies are an integral part of a democratic form of government," said an OMGUS report in 1947, but "because of the great number and diversity of legislatures at the local level, no systematic Military Government review has been conducted of their activities, and hence no adequate data is available . . . on which to base a general review of the legislative activity of such local bodies." In 1950 the Field Operations Officer for Land Hessen told a group of Kreis officers that the military government reorientation program had meant little in the past.[40]

Reviewing its own work in 1949, the Hessian military government detachment concluded that the democratization program proved inadequate. Democratic structures had been organized, and each major military government section had developed, willy-nilly, a program to reorient the German people in its own particular sphere. The press division had taught democratic journalism; education officers emphasized education for democracy; political affairs officers had tried to influence political leaders; all divisions had negotiated exchanges of persons; some had established film programs; the America Houses had provided libraries, had sponsored lectures, discussion groups, and other activities; and the Army had instituted youth activities programs. But the programs were divided along divisional lines and did not reach down to the grass-roots level. They were rather directed toward the German counterparts of military government officials. In the belief that it had failed before, military government decided in 1948 to reorient the German people themselves. It developed a democratization program that Land Hessen military government officials described as "a long uphill educational battle against the forces of tradition, of political and social apathy, and post-war cynicism."[41]

12

The Grass-Roots Approach

During the third year of occupation Americans began to promote democratic ideas among the German people rather than among the counterparts of military government officers. American representatives continued to meet and influence their civilian counterparts. They continued to promote long-range democratization by negotiating exchanges of persons between Germany and many Western countries. They distributed films and used radio and the press to spread democratic ideas. The Army continued to promote youth activities. But in the local areas, such as Marburg, democratization—which came to be called reorientation—was aimed at the people themselves.

The Office of Military Government for Hessen reported that in 1948 it had seen the "reorientation picture whole and had seen it clear." It believed that the development of a democratic way of life in Germany could not be left to isolated forays, however numerous. Accordingly, the Military Governor reorganized his staff and appointed a reorientation committee to coordinate the efforts of American occupation personnel and those "democratically-minded Germans who worked with them" so that they could reach maximum effectiveness in the democratization program.[1]

Reorientation Begins

A simple and obvious explanation for the change in military government emphasis to reorientation in 1948 was expressed in a Land Hessen military government report written in 1949. The first three years of the occupation, the report said, represented the road back for Germany. Military government had to prevent, destroy, and punish so that Germany might again be brought to a point from which it could develop peaceably. In 1948, with denazification and industrial dismantlement coming to an end and demilitarization completed, military government could concentrate upon the positive long-range plan of democratizing Germany.[2]

But the change in emphasis in 1948 was more than a normal evolution of military government. Americans believed that haphazard personal democratization coupled with the negative policies of the first three years were insufficient for accomplishing their purposes. Moreover, they realized that the institutions they had fostered gave nondemocrats as well as democrats an opportunity to exercise authority. Early in 1948 the Civil Administration Division of the Office of Military Government for Germany reported that previous American attempts to persuade or coerce German Land governments to adopt democratic policies in education, civil service, and public administration had failed. German officials were apparently unwilling to cooperate, and it did not appear likely that military government could command their cooperation. The report concluded that "a positive program must be planned and initiated at once to carry Military Government ideas and principles to the local communities."[3]

A unique form of reorientation activity had germinated in a few military government and information control detachments late in 1947. Press and information officers, and some liaison and security detachment personnel, had begun to carry the American information program to the grass-roots level, chiefly as a supplement to the biweekly Frankfurt radio program. The Press Control Officer in Giessen had organized a German discussion group in December 1947. Others followed suit, going into the Kreise to participate in discussions with Germans on civil liberties, constitutional rights and responsibilities, and various other subjects relating to political democracy.[4]

When he heard of the local experiments, the Military Governor of Hessen urged his detachments to establish similar discussion groups. His decision was probably based upon several factors, among which the desire to promote democratic ideas was one. But it was a well-known fact among military government personnel in Germany that some policy advisers believed the detachments' contributions were not worth their retention. The Military Governor, his Deputy, and his Political Adviser all agreed that there were no military reasons for retaining the detachments, and they believed that the detachments' efforts at democratization with existing personnel would prove negligible. During 1947 and early 1948 an unpublicized controversy regarding the detachments occurred within military government. The Military Government Control Office in Berlin recommended that democratization be conducted from long range rather than from close range through local detachments.[5] The Civil Administration Division, supported by the Land military governors and the detachments in the field, argued that democratization or reorientation must reach the people at the grass roots. The people in turn would influence their elected representatives.

The field offices of military government were hard put to convince their superiors that the detachments contributed measurably to the entire mission of the American forces in Germany. Empire builders that some of them were, they began to press for a reorientation program that would utilize the services of the Kreis personnel. The action of the Hessian Military Governor illustrates the fear of local commanders that their commands would disappear if the detachments were discarded. In July 1948 he instructed all of his detachments to revise their programs so they could carry out the reorientation program at the local level and warned them that their future existence depended upon such reorientation. It was not until the change-over from military to civilian control in Germany that the Kreis detachments were assured of retention for democratization. The minutes of an Office of Military Government for Hessen staff meeting contain the notation: "According to information received, the L&S offices appear to have been accepted by the High Commissioner. There is a likelihood that the Land and Kreis offices will get considerable interest."[6]

The emphasis upon reorientation in 1948 came about also because the Office of Military Government allocated funds specifically for such purposes for the first time. The funds were derived from the sale of American German-language newspapers and from renting motion pictures to licensed theaters. The Office of Military Government for Hessen reported early in 1948 that "numerous projects were being considered by Higher Education largely because of the availability of mark and dollar funds previously lacking," and that it had been possible "to start a number of projects immediately."[7]

The Reorientation Mission

Reorientation constituted a comprehensive, ill-defined program that, if successful, would have caused social, political, and ideological changes in Germany. According to American representatives and official reports, its aims were to make the individual citizen aware of his duties in a democracy, to awaken in the German people and their officials a proper concept of the role of the official in his community ("his first responsibility is to serve his people"), to increase respect for the dignity and the rights of the individual, to emphasize human equality, to create a genuine devotion on the part of adult Germans to democratic ideals, to give the Germans a real and lasting dedication to peaceful objectives, and to develop a living and dynamic program of citizen participation in a democracy, which would be self-sustaining and self-perpetuating.[8]

American representatives emphasized again and again that they were not trying to transplant the American democratic system to Germany. They said that they sought mainly to establish a stable economy and a democratic system adapted to the needs of a future peaceful Germany. Marburg's detachment personnel stressed the "purely German character of the program, emphasizing that a viable tradition of democratic thought is native to Germany."[9]

The Marburg Reorientation Program

From a rather unostentatious beginning, with a town hall–type meeting in the city of Neustadt in July 1948, the Marburg reorientation program grew into a far-reaching, somewhat overlapping series of activities that eventually extended over the entire Landkreis.[10] Between 1948 and 1952 the Marburg Liaison and Security Office, and later the Resident Office, promoted town hall meetings, public forums, youth forums, German-American clubs, seminars and discussion groups, junior chambers of commerce, parent-teacher associations, women's clubs, community councils, student government groups, civil liberties groups, adult education committees, taxpayers' committees, traffic safety councils, welfare councils, and soap-box derbies.

The Marburg Resident Officer described his duties for September 1950 as those of a typical month. He said he had discussed public forum procedure with twenty-five forum committees; approached people in four villages regarding building forums; helped to organize a women's group in Allendorf; and called upon fourteen mayors and discussed with them the possibility of holding town hall meetings, public forums, and public village council meetings. In addition, he reported, he had tried to promote adult high schools in several villages, distributed rules of parliamentary procedure, lectured several mayors on their responsibility to the community, and attended several town hall meetings and forums in the Kreis.[11]

Americans proposed reorientation as a German program, assisted by Americans, that would eventually continue without the aid of military government.[12] But because of German apathy and resistance and because of competition between detachments, American representatives in Marburg pushed reorientation vigorously and actively. Apparently taking into account the pressure his detachments applied upon Germans, the Land Commissioner for Hessen (formerly Director of Military Government for Land Hessen) advised his Resident Officers to refrain from using such words as reorientation, re-education, or their German equivalents, *Umerziehung, Umbildung,* and *Reorientierung,* in describing the program.[13]

But Americans exerted strong pressure upon Germans to promote reorientation activities. Partly because of a peculiar reporting system, detachments found themselves in a vicious competitive struggle in which quantity appeared more significant than quality. They competed in a race for output of reorientation projects. Higher headquarters required that local detachments submit periodic statistical reports. The reports were objective rather than subjective, including chiefly the type of activity, the number of meetings held in the Kreis, and the total number of people who attended. On the basis of such reports Land headquarters compared the detachments with each other. It commended by letter those "doing a good job" and listed in its reports those with "lack of initiative." Recognizing the evil of competition between the various detachments, the Land Commissioner's Office soon abandoned the policy of unfavorable comparison between the Kreise. But competition remained keen. Apparently encouraged by Land headquarters, detachments did their best to promote reorientation activities in quantity. The Land Reorientation Committee cited, with approval, the Marburg detachment's October 1948 report that it had organized 127 town hall meetings for "a complete blanketing of the Kreis." Furthermore, headquarters advised detachments that there were methods that they could use to compel Germans to cooperate in reorientation. Speaking before a Resident Officers' training conference in 1950, the chief of the Hessian Field Operations Division told his audience that "in dealing with Bürgermeisters and Landräte that oppose us or give only 'lip service,' remember that there is a possibility of certain ECA aid being withheld from communities that have such officials."[14]

The fact that Marburgers associated the reorientation program with the permanent office of military government on *Schulstrasse* was sufficient to convince most of them that cooperation was wise. Marburgers invariably referred to American representatives as military government, and they were unable to distinguish the duties of military government as such from the more friendly attempts at democratization by the Liaison and Security Offices and later by the Resident Offices. For example, the Landrat meant to say, in 1954, that the last Resident Officer was well liked, but said instead that "every school-child knew that Mr. Didlo was the military governor." Also, in 1951 a HICOG report on an opinion survey of 1,500 Germans concluded that "the predominant conception the public holds of the Kreis Resident Officer's function—even among those most aware of their existence—is that it is one of control."[15] But the pressure was more real than that. Americans required the Landrat to submit monthly reports on town hall meetings, public forums, and other reorientation activities in the Landkreis. They needed the information for their own reports, but the Landrat assumed that the reports were a basis for surveillance of his activities as a public official. That his assumption was not entirely unwarranted is evident from the detachment's orders, already cited, that town hall meetings be held in 1949 and from the May 1950 report of the Marburg Resident Officer that "the Landrat will insist on only one meeting in each Gemeinde for the summer months. This office plans to encourage citizens to ask for more." If the Landrat tried, in this way, to pass responsibility to military government for what he feared might be an unpopular activity, the Marburg detachment never reprimanded him for doing so. In fact, in 1949 the Landrat received a commendation from the Land Commissioner, at the request of the Marburg Liaison and Security Officer, for outstanding work in the reorientation program.[16]

Materially the Resident Officers carried the full burden of reorientation, thus giving Germans an added reason for believing it to be an American rather than a German program. In Marburg the Resident Officer employed two civilians and charged them with urging, advising, and encouraging forums. He secured most of the speakers and provided money for paying speakers who were brought into the Kreis for special occasions. He provided transportation for speakers to and from the town hall meetings and public forums and for forum leaders to go to Bonn and observe the Bonn parliament in action. He prepared lists of possible discussion topics and had notices printed for posting and provided publicity for forums in the local press. When large auditoriums were required for particular meetings, the Resident Officer paid the rent, or used his influence to get free use of the halls. There was little difficulty in the villages where meetings were often held in local inns, which the innkeepers naturally gave free of charge for the privilege of serving food and refreshments to the participants.

Public Forums and Town Hall Meetings in Action

Public forums and town hall meetings were only one phase of the large-scale reorientation program, but in Land Hessen Americans in the local communities believed them to have been by far the most important.[17]

Responsibility for organizing public forums was placed in the hands of civilian forum committees selected by a military government officer or the Resident Officer. With American advice, encouragement, and material assistance the committees prepared discussion topics, invited speakers, secured the meeting halls, provided publicity, and directed the forums. To promote interest in community affairs, the Marburg Resident Officer tried to convince his forum leaders and the Bürgermeisters that "local affairs were of more immediate importance and value than talk about high-level policy and past and future mistakes of allied strategy."[18] Some Marburgers believed, however, that the topical restriction to local affairs was deliberate for another reason. They thought Americans saw little objection to Germans criticizing local government, which was in German hands exclusively, but they did not want them to criticize national policies, which were partly controlled and directed by the Allied high commissioners. The forums discussed a variety of topics such as "Additional Employment for Marburg," "What Can We Expect from Equalization of Burdens?" "School Reform," "Tourist Attractions," "The City Administration—What Do You Think of It?" "Elections—What Do You Think about Them?" and "The Question of a Public Water System."

Reliable statistics are not available regarding the number of public forums held in Marburg, but the *Marburger Presse* reported that twenty-six villages had held a total of ninety-seven public forums through July 1950. An estimated total of ten thousand persons had attended. The Marburg detachment reports for the period between October 1949 and April 1951 indicate that during that time 248 public forums were held in Marburg with an estimated twenty-six thousand persons in attendance.[19]

The town hall meetings served the same purpose in the villages that the forums served in the larger cities. American representatives or their employees promoted the organization of town hall meetings. They usually asked the Bürgermeister rather than a voluntary committee of private citizens to assume responsibility. The meetings were held chiefly to discuss community affairs. Many of them were nothing more than a report by the Bürgermeister or by other officials upon community projects, the budget, the public water system, or a new school building.

Although the statistics on town hall meetings are also unreliable, the Marburg Resident Officer's reports indicate that between October 1949 and April 1951, 483 meetings were held with an estimated attendance of twenty-three thousand.[20] Late in 1948 the Marburg detachment reported that town hall meetings had been organized in every village of the Landkreis. But many villages held meetings only occasionally or never again after the first meeting.

The public forums and the town hall meetings were not designed to accomplish tangible results, but in Marburg they have been credited with several specific accomplishments. They led to the construction of a schoolhouse in Sterzhausen, new classrooms in Gossfelden, construction of water mains in three villages by cooperative labor of the citizens, the construction of three bridges, road repairs in several villages, the construction of playgrounds in two villages, and wide publicity for the political horse trade in the city council during the Oberbürgermeister election in 1951. In addition forums and town hall meetings passed resolutions of various kinds that they sent to local, regional, and state governments and officials. Some resolutions were answered, a few were acted upon, and most of them remained unanswered.[21]

Marburg's Response to Grass-Roots Reorientation

The response of Marburgers to the reorientation program was indeed sobering. Marburgers apparently misunderstood or ignored the basic objective of the program, which was to awaken public interest in community affairs in preparation for a viable democracy in Germany. Americans who sought to "create an enlightened public, aware of its power and personally interested in the effective exercise of its inherent sovereignty" were sorely disappointed.[22] Despite the large numbers reported in attendance by official American reports, few Marburgers can be found who admit that they or their friends participated actively. An employee of the Resident Office reported that only a small number came, but they came regularly. Only about fifteen people in Marburg participated actively in the discussions, he went on, and they tended to monopolize them.[23] Significantly, in 1951 a public opinion survey seemed to show that about 71 per cent of all Hessians were not even aware of the existence of the Resident Officer in their area. In 1950 only 38 per cent of the Hessians questioned in a poll knew that the American authorities had a program to bring democratic ideas to Germans. Of the 38 per cent, 15 per cent thought the program consisted of press, radio, and public information activities, and only 6 per cent knew them to be forums, town hall meetings, public discussions, and lectures.[24]

The available evidence indicates that those already well informed on America and its culture attended regularly. The Resident Officer, reporting in 1949 on the organization of a German-American club, said that *as usual* the Germans who attended were better prepared to discuss the theme—in this case American Negro writers—than the Americans. A report by an American lecturer who gave a series of America House lectures in twenty-one German cities said that the majority of the clientele of the America Houses must be considered pro-American, and that the meetings "turned out to be rather family affairs." The personal observations of Marburgers support these generalizations. One said he attended two meetings, then stopped because he could not stand to see Germans bending over backward to please the occupation. He thought that the only ones who took part in the discussions were friendly to the occupation. Another reported that he did not attend because the meetings were nothing but a place to "throw bouquets back and forth."[25]

The two civilians upon whom the Marburg detachment depended for promotion of reorientation apparently never appreciated the Americans' purpose. The detachment's civilian reorientation specialist from 1950 to 1952 expressed surprise that only 29 per cent of the Hessian population were aware of the Resident Officers in 1951. He believed, however, that the poll was misleading because it was too representative. "The pollsters should not have asked farm women, nor should they have asked most of the farmers, or the average citizens because they would not know anything about the program anyway." His colleague, in charge of promoting public forums and town hall meetings, said that the reorientation program was basically a scheme worked out by Americans to keep their assignments in Germany and to convince Americans at home that Germans were developing into good allies in the cold war.[26]

Marburg's political party leaders and public officials, outwardly cooperative, secretly believed the reorientation program to be unimportant, superfluous, or downright distasteful. Only Hermann Bauer, the editor of the *Marburger Presse* until 1951, and a member of the Liberal Democratic party until 1948, supported the program sincerely. He lost respect among his kind for doing so. "You have finally cut the knot that had tied you to your political friends," wrote a colleague and friend in 1951. The others participated, to be sure, but the Free Democratic party attacked this "importation of direct democracy from America," and finally threatened to prevent its members from speaking at the meetings. Its members continued, individually, to minimize the significance of the program. The FDP Landtag faction leader from Marburg reportedly told a Resident Office investigator, whom he did not recognize, that "the silly system the Americans are trying to establish here is not used in other countries. . . . The people lack the professional qualifications to survey a political or social situation. Their representatives must . . . represent their requests in the parliament." A member of the FDP county executive committee, writing to his friend about an argument they had had regarding the reorientation program, said he could not take the forum speakers seriously because they were confused and lusted for argument. "It is only too bad," he continued, "that such public forums are considered to have any political value at all." Two of his colleagues in the party expressed similar sentiments: the one that the forums were mutual admiration societies; the other, much more perceptive, said that some Marburgers enjoyed the meetings because they provided diversion and a place to air complaints. He thought the political parties accepted them "understandingly" (condescendingly), but hoped and worked for the day when the parties could again meet the needs of these people.[27]

The Social Democratic party, although it provided more speakers than the other parties, viewed the reorientation program as a stop-gap measure. The Landrat, a leading SPD member, never once included a report of a town hall meeting or a public forum in his political activities reports to the Resident Officers, even though he was specifically required to report political activities from 1947 on and was asked to report them more fully in 1950. He did make regular reorientation reports as required, however, and in May 1949 he prepared a list of specific things that forums and town hall meetings had accomplished. Nevertheless, he concluded that town hall meetings were most fruitful because they helped to "broaden knowledge in various fields. Misunderstandings were corrected by the Bürgermeisters or Community Representatives."[28] Misinterpreting their purpose completely, the Landrat assumed that the meetings should provide the political expert with an opportunity to educate his constituents. Significantly, in 1954 the Landrat suggested that the reason for the current lack of interest in town hall meetings and public forums in Marburg was that political parties were once more functioning properly after the removal of American supervision.

The German response to reorientation at the national and regional levels reflected the local response. The national city-government association (Deutscher Städtetag) circulated a series of questions among its members in 1949 asking their advice on the adoption of a uniform code of behavior toward the forums. It reported that one member city had adopted a policy that no city official should attend a forum, because these officials would not be prepared to give complete information (*erschöpfende Auskunft*) and because members of the city council might be criticized unnecessarily. The Hessian Landtag, reportedly fearing a cabinet crisis, asked Land military government to discontinue or forbid the forums in Hessen in 1949. In May 1949 the Hessian Minister of Interior mimeographed a report that he had received from the Landrat in Usingen and circulated it among the city and county governments of Hessen. The report stated that the forums and town hall meetings were a distinct danger to the existing political system in Germany. They were, the Landrat said, actually a second, extra-legal government, that was not subject to regulation or supervision from above as were the legal local governments. He was concerned especially that "anybody could be elected forum leader," and that many would-be politicians used the forum to wrest political power from the established parties. He also thought the forums provided ex-Nazis with their first postwar political opportunity.[29]

Americans who observed the response of Germans to reorientation concluded that Nazis and conservative public officials were responsible. They judged their own methods to be inadequate, and continually tried to increase the quantity of reorientation projects. They apparently never questioned their assumption that grass-roots political activity is *ipso facto* democratic. "Chief opposition . . . here has crystallized around Nazis and beneficiaries of Nazi regime," the Marburg Resident Officer reported, incorrectly. "Dependence on German officials even for support of the program cannot be counted upon," concluded another report. The suggested remedy was "a program which reaches to the 'grass roots' of the population directly . . . by Military Government . . . over the heads of public officials and party leaders."[30] In effect, Americans wanted to arouse the people in the villages to "exercise their inherent sovereignty" in spite of officials, political parties, Nazis, and Nazi sympathizers. The Marburg Resident Officer set quotas for his civilian employees; he went into the communities himself; he constantly suggested new activities. Where a town hall meeting had achieved some success, Americans tried to promote women's clubs, junior chambers of commerce, youth forums, or other activities in which they could interest a significant number of Germans. Lacking personnel, either American or German civilian, the detachment relied heavily upon Marburgers who had cooperated in the first few activities to organize and promote additional activities. Speakers were in demand several nights a week. It was not unusual for a village teacher to be a member of the forum committee, the youth forum, and a sought-after speaker for other activities. In the larger cities some people participated actively in three or four activities sponsored by the Resident Officer. They spread their energies widely, doing many things, few of them thoroughly. Eventually many ceased to help because they said they were overworked.

In January 1952, when the Resident Office closed in Marburg, reorientation died a sudden death. The latest date on correspondence in the public forum file in the Rathaus is February 9, 1952. The *Oberhessische Presse* never carried a report or a story of a public forum after February 1952. The people I interviewed said the town hall and forum committees had all disbanded.

But reorientation was not completely in vain. Marburgers have taken some of the suggestions of the Americans and fitted them into their own institutions, changing them somewhat. Marburg has an active civil rights committee, composed of approximately thirty persons, mostly lawyers. It probably survived because it is primarily a lawyers' interest group. Its chief activity has been to promote citizen participation in the city council meetings when the Oberbürgermeisters are elected. It is an organization that could promote reforms and ensure respect for the guaranteed rights of German citizens. The Parent-Teacher Association, which had existed prior to the Nazi regime, meets regularly again. Within the city the Oberbürgermeister began in 1954 a practice very similar to the town hall meetings and public forums which were instituted by the Americans in Marburg. In January 1954, Oberbürgermeister Gassmann announced to the press that he would hold periodic meetings in various wards of the city to discuss community problems with any citizens who cared to come.[31]

In the villages the idea of town hall meetings has not disappeared. As in pre-Hitler Germany the village and city councils often call the citizens together to discuss community problems, although the author has never heard of an instance where the meetings were called upon citizens' demands. A particular case is illustrative. In June 1954 the Landrat and the Kreis school superintendent tried to consolidate the schools of two small neighboring villages. The city councils of the two villages, meeting in joint session, could not reach a decision. Thereupon the councils declared the meeting open to the public and asked the local citizens to state their views and vote. They rejected the plan and the schools were not consolidated.

In every way that Marburgers have used the ideas fed them by the occupation they appear to have consciously disassociated their present activities from those promoted by the occupation. The American emphasis upon the common man is forgotten; direction is in the hands of social, political, and economic leaders of the community. The "little people" (*kleine Leute*) are content to leave policy decisions to their "leaders" and to their political parties for which they vote, but to which they do not belong.

13

The Paradox

Americans, educated and conditioned to believe in the American dream and guided by policy statements, worked—crusaded—for an ideal: a peaceful, democratic, free-enterprise Germany. Reaching to the lowest German administrative levels, American detachments ferreted out the people who would deny their purpose. They destroyed institutions and tried to modify or reform others that they believed made peace, democracy, and free enterprise unattainable. They tried to reorient the German people themselves to accept and espouse democratic political and social ideals. In effect, American policy would have transformed Germany. It would have uprooted people and traditions, shattered customs, prejudices, and other nonrationally assumed practices and myths, substituting therefor other people, traditions, customs, prejudices, practices, and myths.[1]

Denazification, which affected approximately one-third of the population, would have eliminated from public life some of the political, social, and economic leaders upon whom Marburgers had always relied faithfully and respectfully for guidance, advice, and education and whom they exhorted their children to emulate. We can ignore industrial disarmament and the transformations it would have achieved, since we have already shown that except for a short time Americans never pushed this policy seriously. But American democratization and reorientation programs would have upset the Marburg sociopolitical structure and toppled a powerful sociopolitical elite. Educational reform sought to transform the German school system to provide mass education beyond the elementary level. As such it would have shattered some of Marburgers' traditional psychological and sociological assumptions and jeopardized an educated elite. Civil service reform would have jeopardized that elite as it transformed a service that Germans praised for its continuity, its devotion to duty, and its strict accountability for corruption, and which Germans apparently defend as vigorously—and irrationally—as Americans defend the two-party political system. In short, former elites were to be replaced by new ones, or if not replaced, they were to be discredited, infiltrated, enlarged, re-educated (any combination of these) to form a new sociopolitical elite sympathetic to democracy as Americans professed it.

The case study of occupied Marburg suggests the conclusion that the transformations that Americans thought their ideal required were never completely achieved. How and why this happened is not simply explained. A recent study suggests that the experiment proceeded without a conscious application of a theory of artificial revolution, and that public ignorance at home, the lack of an extensive and responsible information program overseas, and the lack of positive changes to attract new leaders explain the limited success of the democratic states in Germany and Japan.[2] What happened, in fact, is that American ideals, which were obviously conceived too vaguely ("democracy," with no regard for its absolute essentials) or too pragmatically ("democracy," as symbolized by "how we do it in the States"), and the transformations they seemed to require were left unrealized as Americans focused their attention upon the practical affairs at hand. This development, in effect, suggests that the American ideal was never an ideal with enduring characteristics, but rather a pragmatic program that changed as the conditions in Germany and elsewhere changed.

Obviously the case study provides no data that lends itself directly to a discussion of whether democratic ideals can be translated into doctrine without themselves being destroyed, but it does provide data to suggest the paradoxical effect that such an attempt—no matter how haltingly it was made—produced upon

Germans and Americans alike. Because they operated at the grass-roots level, where American policies and practices converged upon their objects or subjects, the Kreis detachments experienced many of the difficulties inherent in such an attempt.

The most obvious problem the Marburg detachment faced was the natural aversion of Germans to being occupied. Americans could not have erased the fact that they were an army of occupation in a defeated nation—a nation with pride in its history, its culture, and its accomplishments in art, music, literature, and material progress in spite of its recent political past. No matter how astute, careful, and diplomatic the detachment personnel may have been in their daily operations, they bore a stigma that all Germans recognized.

But American military personnel, with some exceptions, were poor examples of the ideal democrat they described to Marburgers. They were crusaders who had apparently lost their faith, but who crusaded nevertheless. Without apparent concern for the similarity of their own ethnocentrism to Nazi racism, Americans regarded Germans as a people not quite equal to themselves. Few Marburgers begrudged the occupation forces adequate and comfortable quarters, once they reconciled themselves to the fact of occupation. But Americans requisitioned homes in which three or four families had lived and gave each of them to one American family. They demanded whole sections of the city for an American enclave. They prohibited the owners from trespassing upon their property or from using the gardens on their property. They refused to permit Germans to live in the unused portions of their homes and they did not always return vacated homes. Americans set aside special trains, or parts of regular trains, for exclusive Allied use. They divided the railway stations, setting up separate waiting rooms, separate ticket offices, and separate facilities of all kinds for the Allied forces and the Germans. Americans rode German trains free of charge, later at a nominal cost. The Army commandeered the best German resorts for American rest and leave camps. Everywhere Germans saw the sign: No trespassing for Germans. In part, the Americans financed their privileges and luxuries with the German taxpayer's money—the same taxpayer that they tried to convince of the ideals of equality and democracy.

Americans apparently observed a different code of justice for Germans than for themselves. Denazification rested upon the doctrine of presumptive guilt. Germans had to prove their innocence, and there are Marburgers who believed, as late at 1954, that the American legal system rests upon that premise. Early in the occupation, German civilians and the German police were severely punished for even defending themselves against personal attack by American troops. At the same time Americans who attacked Germans often received little or no punishment. Military government officers sentenced Germans to prison for black-market activities, but Americans supplied the basic medium of exchange on the black market in such quantities that Marburgers naturally assumed that Americans were not punished for selling cigarettes, coffee, and other items.

In their personal social relationships with Marburgers Americans helped to undermine their own basic ideals. Nonfraternization was basic policy even though it failed. Although not wholly of their own volition, Marburg's military government officers and men made few inroads into Marburg's social circles. The social functions they did attend were usually arranged by themselves or by Germans as social counterparts of their more official intercourse. Thus, Americans in Marburg associated socially almost exclusively with the upper social, economic, and political groups —the very people that had most to lose from the transformations military government tried to promote. Whether this had any direct influence upon American policies must remain for the moment an open question, but it is significant that Marburgers were encouraged to think that Americans' personal sympathies lay with those who opposed military government policies rather than with those who supported them.

Military government organization and military personnel and rotation policies lay behind many of the serious difficulties of the Kreis detachment. The Marburg detachment's personnel, consisting mainly of upper-middle-class Americans who possessed professional training and experience, was not particularly suited or trained for military government administration.[3] The training it did have was for supervision and control rather than actual government. Later, when the detachment's duties changed to observing and reporting on the local situation, the American program in Germany had mushroomed and the small detachment could not possibly have observed and reported intelligently the effect of all policies, even if it had kept its original staff. But the staff changed often. The new detachment members usually knew little about what had happened in Marburg before their arrival. They depended upon their civilian employees and upon civil officials, often deciding issues contrary to the decisions of their predecessors and often submitting faulty intelligence reports to higher headquarters about denazification, political activity, and reorientation. Furthermore, detachment officers, lacking sufficient military rank, sometimes could not carry out their mission because higher-ranking officers, who were automatically area commanders, demanded services and facilities that military government could not supply without overstepping its authority or without using constraint upon civil officials.

The Marburg detachment reduced its potential effectiveness by remaining politically neutral. Deliberately refusing to take political sides except in specific instances, Americans led Marburgers to believe Americans to be politically naïve—which some of them apparently were. The detachment chose its employees and Marburg's civil officials without apparent regard for their political connections, concentrating rather upon a clean record during the Nazi regime. It appointed democrats, Communists, Socialists, nationalists, and opportunists and expected them to work together because they had in common anti-Nazi or non-Nazi records. In its desire to stand above party differences and allow the "other Germans" (i.e., anti-Nazis) a free hand, the Marburg detachment ignored the fact that the German political party, on the local level especially, is an educational, welfare, and social organization as well as a political machine and a representative of special interests. Instead of using the party as an agency for pro-

moting their policies, especially democratization and reorientation, Americans expected and encouraged Marburgers to form
voluntary associations, such as civil rights groups and women's
groups, so common to America but not to Germany, to take the
place of the party in the local community. Marburgers believed
that the detachment's political neutrality was a design to revolu-
tionize political activity at the local level as part of its attempt to
transform Germany completely.

American policy changes, some of which were the result of a
normal development and some of which took into account the
changes in the international situation, often made the detachment
officers appear naïve and vacillating. American economic policy
changed from deindustrialization to reindustrialization between
1945 and 1950. Denazification ended in Marburg at about the
same time that the Russians blockaded Berlin and Marshall Plan
aid began to arrive. Americans dropped their demands for decentralization and intensified democratization through the reorientation program at about the time they began to woo the
Germans to cooperate with the West. Demilitarization eventually
changed to rearmament. To Marburgers who looked on from the
local level, the detachment represented a nation that professed an
ideal, but acted out of purely selfish interests.

As policies and emphases changed, the Marburg detachment
tried unsuccessfully to reinterpret American policies in terms of
their ideal. But Marburgers were not easily convinced that Americans were concerned about the welfare of Germans or that Americans promoted peace and democracy by making policy changes.
Nor did Marburgers think they would benefit, except as Americans
benefited also. While Americans shipped food, pushed German
economic recovery, and discussed the desirability of a West German military force, Germans remembered the theory of collective guilt, demilitarization, denazification, and the Morgenthau
Plan, which had received so much publicity and so little support.
Moreover, they saw Americans bore holes in the Lahn bridge abutments so that it could be demolished if Americans retreated west-
ward, and they honestly believed that American troop maneuvers

in Germany constituted evacuation drills. Marburgers talked freely about ensurance against Russian attack. Some of them refrained from using the America House library reportedly because they did not want their names in the records. Young men said they did not want to serve in a West German army. Some of them said they would join the Russians in the event of war so that they could surrender to the Americans at their first opportunity. They would rather spend the duration of the war in an American prisoner-of-war camp than fight a war they believed would be for America's benefit. Although it was not true in Marburg, some German firms advertised in Communist newspapers, hoping thereby to ensure themselves favorable treatment if the Americans left and the Russians came. Marburgers seemed convinced that Americans would desert Germany if they found it convenient to do so to achieve their own purposes.

The Marburg detachment's democratization and reorientation programs produced perplexing results. We have seen that the political parties that had been authorized at the local level to provide experience and practice in democracy found it convenient and expedient to criticize the American occupation. American desires for more responsible politicians and officials achieved similar results. After they had been induced by American persuasion and example to hold press conferences and to issue statements to the press, German officials and agencies responded with paradoxical effect. The Landrat said that Marburg's officials had saved the Allendorf industries from complete destruction at the hands of military government. In another press release the Landrat credited Germans with promoting economic recovery in spite of military government policy. A military government decree of 1948 which demanded that German trades operate on a free-enterprise basis would have checked the German economy, the Landrat said, and it was only through constant efforts of responsible German "lawgivers" and scrutiny of details by administrative officials that trades were brought back into a planned and ordered system once more. The problems of overproduction and lack of markets, he implied, were solved by German action that subverted the intent of military government.[4]

The reorientation program produced similar paradoxical results in Marburg. The program is discussed in detail in an earlier chapter, but its significance for the success of the American mission in Marburg merits special emphasis. The fact of the matter is that free discussions, especially in the village council meetings, gave those people who had been denied political rights under denazification laws an opportunity to express themselves and in some cases to dominate the activities of the local administration. Men who had been mayors, teachers, or officials under the monarchy, the republic, and the Nazi regime because they enjoyed local prestige, wealth, and family connections did not pass into limbo by denazification. They attended the council meetings and the town hall meetings to watch if not to speak. The impact that their presence made upon the councils is probably best illustrated by the comment of the mayor of one of the villages to the Landrat in 1946. He wrote: "In the city many a man will go under and be forgotten, but out here in the country people do not forget."[5] In the final analysis the pseudo-direct democracy that military government desired made it possible for those they wanted to exclude from political activity to continue actively though not officially. But as German denazification tribunals cleared many of those whom military government had dismissed and they returned to office, the village councils became more and more independent of military government supervision and of public opinion.*

The paradoxes that military government produced in its operations at the Kreis level, although highly significant, only suggest the fundamental problem inherent in military government's entire German program: the contradictions of the program itself.

---

* There is no evidence upon which to assume a cause-effect relationship between these three developments. There were many causes, not the least of which were that Marburgers wanted to rid themselves of everything imported by the occupation, and that military government left the villages without supervision after it gave up its decentralization emphasis and withdrew most of the detachment's personnel.

Looking back upon the occupation with some perspective, Marburgers argued in 1954 that the detachment tried deliberately to continue the chaos and confusion that resulted from the war. Detachment officers, on the other hand, said they had been helpless because their orders were vague and vacillating, because the army chain of command was cumbersome, because they did not possess adequate staff, because four-power control brought top-level disagreements, and because the Germans would not cooperate.

But the problem originated, not in the details of administration, but in the fact that American policies reflect two contradictory interpretations of Nazi Germany and German society and thus, also, two contradictory interpretations of how to achieve the reconstruction of Germany. American policy rested at once upon the assumption that the Nazi state existed by force and that it was a corporate body—an organic unit such as the Nazis claimed it was. According to the latter, reconstruction would involve widespread punitive measures and widespread reform-and-reorientation activities to force Germans to be free. According to the former, punitive measures would destroy the Nazi elite and make room for the "other Germans," who with some education and encouragement would follow their natural inclinations to reconstruct a peaceful, democratic (and free-enterprise?) Germany.

A backward look at the occupation may lead to the conclusion that American policy was a combination of the two apparently contradictory policies noted above: that it was punitive in the sense that it removed the Nazi elite and permissive in the sense that it created reformed institutions—using its superior authority—within which a new elite would function, even if that elite had to be created by the occupation. By this more subtle method Germans would be forced to be free. Whatever the reasons may have been, this policy was never consciously applied at the local level, and can be construed as a policy only by minimizing the *intended* scope of denazification (by looking backward to actual practice) and by ignoring the chronology of the occupation in which punitive and negative policies were pushed first and reform and positive policies were pushed last, but which were hardly pushed together except in the most haphazard way.

Returning to the contradictions: Denazification, resting on its theory of presumptive guilt, punished individuals for crimes committed by the organizations in which they held membership. They were not punished as individuals, but as parts of a corporate body (an organism), regardless of their function within that body. Demilitarization and deindustrialization, in part, rested upon a similar interpretation. They would have reduced the military and industrial potential of the whole nation, assuming that this potential in the hands of any Germans or the corporate (organic) German state constituted a danger to the peace.

Democratization, reorientation, decentralization, and other reform programs rested, in part, on the assumption that the Nazis arose and maintained themselves by force. Denazification can be, and has been, regarded as a purge of the elite who had forced the "other Germans" into subjection. But the attitude of Americans toward the task and denazification's intended scope belie this argument. These policies were designed to remove or reform the institutions that had permitted the Nazis to capture the nation and keep it in submission. Americans established political structures, permitted elections, and authorized political parties to form to give the German people an opportunity to exercise their sovereignty. They assumed that, if given freedom of choice and expression, Germans would naturally defend their natural rights to life, liberty, and equal treatment that they had lost during the Nazi regime. Americans wanted to decentralize to prohibit a captive central government from forcing the people into submission once again. When, after 1948, the German response to permissive democratization appeared too feeble, Americans, seeing the "reorientation picture whole and clear," developed a grass-roots reorientation program—inefficient and misdirected as it may have been locally—to force Germans to be free.

The combined effects of denazification, deindustrialization, decentralization, democratization, and reorientation upon Marburg produced the result described throughout this study. Prominent Marburg politicians who claimed to be democrats could not swallow the bitter pill of presumptive guilt and collective guilt, and some could not understand why denazification ended when it did.

Marburgers who could have accepted democratization and decentralization were vexed by early denazification and deindustrialization. Those who could have accepted denazification and industrial disarmament (not deindustrialization, but a new industrial order) could not support the other three programs because they were themselves Communists and left-wing Socialists who favored centralization and whose conceptions of democracy were different from those of Americans. Nazis by conviction could not accept any of the policies. Thus the Marburgers who opposed American policies for reasons unrelated to Nazism found themselves in agreement with the Nazis. American policies seemingly provided something for everybody—to criticize. The mutual complaints of Marburg's democrats, nondemocrats, *"ohne mich"* Germans, and Nazis tended to draw them together into a community of opposition against anything imported by the occupation. Those who were not drawn into the community of opposition remained outside as potential revolutionaries, cynics, and nihilists.

The Positive Impact

American representatives left what appears to be a lasting impression of their personal characteristics. Marburgers think Americans are energetic. They approached their duties with a zeal that could have been based only upon hope of realizing a high ideal. They provided an example of efficiency and practical know-how by their reconstruction work during the early phase of the occupation, thus verifying for Marburgers the fact that Germany had lost the war and had not been sabotaged from within. American officers and men gave a practical lesson in equality by their familiarity with each other and by their mutual respect. They impressed the Marburgers by their individualism, both in acts of kindness and in crime and corruption. Above all, Americans seemed to get things done. They kept their desks clean. They cleaned up the city. They put public utilities into working order. They provided emergency food supplies when famine and disease threatened. They attacked problems as they arose and solved them without delaying to achieve perfection. Americans, Marburgers think, are practical, energetic, kind, and likable people.

Some American policies made a positive impact upon Marburgers. The America House, which remains in Marburg as a
permanent establishment, provided a place where Marburgers
might inform themselves about America and its culture, attend
language classes, hear lectures and music, and participate in discussion groups. The reorientation program did affect Marburgers,
even though Marburgers modified or discarded most of the institutions imported by American representatives. The example
of military government officers holding press conferences and giving press interviews left a lasting imprint. The American press
and radio information programs set an example of free exchange
of information that appealed to many Marburgers. Some were first
astounded by the fact that they could continue to listen to the
German radio while the war still raged. Later, they took it for
granted that they were free to hear any broadcast or read any
literature without fear of repercussion.

Military government accomplished a positive aim by deindustrialization. It changed the Allendorf industries from military
to civilian production.

Most of all, the American occupation of Marburg gave many
Marburgers an understanding of America. Confusing though it
was to them, many understood that American policies were based
upon a mixture of realism and idealism—a realism that became
obvious as the occupation went on, but an idealism that was real
to Americans. Americans were generous in their economic aid, but
they expected German cooperation with the West in return. Americans talked of peace but remained armed. Americans wanted
Germany to be a partner of the West, but they bored holes into the
Lahn bridge abutments. Americans kept large forces in Germany,
but Marburgers believed their maneuvers consisted chiefly of stra-
tegic withdrawals behind the Rhine.

The Negative Impact

The American occupation of Marburg failed to accomplish
much of what it set out to do. In failing it brought upon itself a
great deal of criticism and vituperation from Marburgers. Denazification did not accomplish its aim of eliminating Nazis from

public life, but it aroused Marburgers against American policies. Deindustrialization, which Americans abandoned early, caused Marburgers to believe America capable of allowing Germans to starve. Democratization succeeded in part, but it irked Marburgers to think that Americans believed they had the only viable political system in the world. Civil service reform proposals only tended to crystallize German opposition to all American reform. School reform proposals left little imprint upon the German school system, except for a few curricular revisions; and American insistence that the system be changed—even that the school year begin in September rather than April—proved fruitless. In short, most of what Americans tried to promote as positive programs in Marburg produced negative effects that far outweighed their positive results.

The Cathartic Effect of Marburg's Occupation

The American occupation of Marburg left almost universal agreement among Marburgers that the individual American, with a few understandable and perhaps forgivable exceptions, made a lasting favorable impression upon the community. On the other hand, Marburgers agree that American policy made a lasting unfavorable impact upon the community.

The combination of the respect Marburgers feel for the individual American and the dislike they feel for occupation policies has provided Marburgers with a most convenient argument for self-justification of their individual actions, or inaction, under the Nazi regime. They honestly believe that American soldiers did not sympathize with denazification, deindustrialization, and other features of American policy, which Marburgers thought to have been extremely harsh. But, they argue, individual Americans did nothing to change that policy. They did not resist that policy. They did not refuse to denazify. When they did, as General Patton did, they suffered the consequences of their refusal. In fact, as good American patriots many carried out the policies to the best of their ability. Marburgers believe—correctly in many instances—that those who objected in spirit either kept quiet or did what they could to modify the effects of the policies, or they accepted demobilization or transfer rather than carry out such policy, while others continued silently as military government representatives in order to keep their jobs and enjoy the benefits of occupation life.

Marburgers think the relationship between the individual American soldier and the occupation policies mirrored exactly their own relationship to the Nazi state. In the American soldier who did not sympathize with American policies they saw the German who did not sympathize with Nazism. In the American soldier who did nothing to change that policy they saw the *"ohne mich"* German—the "little man." In the soldier who did not resist that policy they saw the German who did not resist Nazism. In the soldier who did not refuse to denazify they saw the German who did not refuse to carry out Nazi orders. In the American soldier who resisted and suffered the consequences they saw the German who resisted and went to the concentration camp. In the good American patriot they saw the good German patriot. In the American soldier who objected in spirit and kept quiet or withdrew himself they saw the German who kept quiet or withdrew into private life under the Nazi regime. In the American soldier who continued silently as a military government representative in order to keep his job and enjoy the benefits of occupation life they saw the German who joined the Nazi party to keep his job or get a better one. And in the American who tried to modify military government policy from within they saw the German who joined the Nazi party hoping to reform it.

Marburgers who reflect honestly recognize the difference between a German who supported or did not oppose Nazi policies and an American who supported or did not oppose American policies. But most Marburgers convinced themselves, by the object lesson of American occupation, that Americans confronted with the choices open to Germans under Hitler would have chosen much as Germans did. Therein lies the catharsis.

Notes

Chapter 2

1. See *Marburger Presse*, March 29, 1946, p. 5. Rudolph Bultmann, "Bericht über unser Ergehen in Marburg seit dem 28.März 1945," n.d.; a typewritten copy is in the collection of papers left in the Marburg America House by E. Y. Hartshorne (the collection is hereafter cited as Hartshorne Papers). "Zeckey über Siebecke und über die KPD und SPD" [March 11, 1946], copy in Eugen Siebecke Papers (in Siebecke's possession, Marburg, Germany). Eugen Siebecke to Oberst B. A. Dickson, G2, 1st Army, through CIC, Marburg, April 27, 1945, Siebecke Papers. "Stenogrammdiktat nach dem Gedächtnis," n.d., a report dictated about a year after Marburg's capture by Oberbürgermeister a. D. Voss, the former Nazi lord mayor of Marburg, copy in Hermann Bauer Papers (in Bauer's possession, Marburg). Hermann Bauer to Schulrat Tilgner, March 30, 1945, Bauer Papers. Polizei Tagebuch, #102/45 IV, Marburg Police Department, Miscellaneous Reports and Papers, Polizeiamt Marburg (hereafter cited as Police Reports and Papers). Various reports and journals of the detachment found in the Office of Military Government for Germany (OMGUS) Papers (in Kansas City Army Records Center, Kansas City, Missouri).

2. Quoted in J. F. J. Gillen, *State and Local Government in West Germany, 1945–1953, with Special Reference to the U.S. Zone and Bremen* (Mehlem: Office of the United States High Commissioner for Germany, 1953), p. 3.

3. See Howard Becker, "Constructive Typology in the Social Sciences," *American Sociological Review,* V (February 1940), 40–55.

4. Milton Mayer, *They Thought They Were Free: The Germans, 1933–45* (Chicago: University of Chicago Press, 1955); Mayer, "The Germans: Their Cause and Cure, Part I. My Ten Nazis," *Harper's Magazine,* CCVII (December 1953), 23–31.

5. Richard Ebel and Willi Emrich, *Hessische Gemeindeordnung v. 25.2.1952 und Hessische Landkreisordnung v. 25.2.1952: Textausgabe mit Erläuterungen und Stichwortverzeichnis* (Frankfurt: Wilhelm Lem-

pert-Verlag, 1953), Gemeindeordnung, pars. 137–41; Kreisordnung, par. 35.

6. Franz Borkenau, "Marburg," February 17, 1946, OMGUS Papers; Dietrich Dern and others, *1923-1925-1935, NSDAP Marburg: Festschrift zum 10 (12) jährigen Bestehen der NSDAP in Marburg, verbunden mit Aufmarsch aller Gliederungen im Kreis Marburg und Einweihung des Heinrich-Abel Hauses* (Marburg: Oberhessische Zeitung, n.d.), p. 5.

7. Hessisches Statistisches Landesamt (hereafter HSL) to author: Ergebnisse der Reichstagswahlen, 1920–1933, May 31, 1954. HSL, Beiträge zur Statistik Hessens, Nr. 3, 12, 29, 39 (Wiesbaden: HSL, 1948–50).

8. Dern and others, *NSDAP Marburg, passim*; HSL to author, May 31, 1954.

9. See Gerhard Isenberg, "Zur Typologie der Deutschen Landkreise," *Raumforschung und Raumordnung, Organ der Akademie für Raumforschung und Landesplanung* (Bonn), X (2.Quartal, 1950), 44–45, for a classification of German Landkreise and a description of a backward small-farm Landkreis.

10. HSL, *Hessische Gemeindestatistik, 1950,* Beiträge zur Statistik Hessens, Nr. 48 (Wiesbaden: HSL, 1952), I, especially pp. 34, 62–66, II, IV; Statistisches Bundesamt, *Statistisches Jahrbuch für die Bundesrepublik Deutschland, 1952* (Stuttgart-Cologne: Verlag W. Kohlhammer, 1952), table IX, pp. 98–99. The per cent of farms in the various size ranges in selected Länder and the Federal Republic is as follows:

	Size Range of Farms			
Area	0.5 to 2 Hectares	2 to 5 Hectares	5 to 20 Hectares	20 and over Hectares
Landkreis Marburg	36%	31%	29%	4%
Land Hessen	39	30	27	4
Land Bavaria	18	23	46	13
Land Lower Saxony	28	22	34	16
Federal Republic	29	26	34	11

11. Statistics provided by the Industrie und Handelskammer, Marburg and HSL, *Die Volks- und Berufszählung vom 29.Oktober 1946 in Hessen (Endgültige Ergebnisse),* Beiträge zur Statistik Hessens, Nr. 18 (Wiesbaden: HSL, 1948), p. 31. Total population figures in October 1946 were: Stadtkreis 37,382; Landkreis, 92,991.

12. Karl Apel, "Mardorf, Kreis Marburg, das Trachtendorf in der Krise," *Schriften des Instituts für Kultur- und Sozialforschung* (Munich), I (1950), 152–68.

13. OMGUS, Monthly Report of the Military Governor, Report No. 7, February 20, 1947, Explosives Industry. OMG, Marburg, to OMGH: Report of Behringwerke, February 5, 1948, OMGUS Papers. "Industriebetriebe der Kreise Marburg-Stadt und -Land mit etwa 20 und mehr Beschäftigten," prepared by Industrie und Handelskammer Marburg, n.d.

14. Detachment F1C2, Subject: Summary of Public Health and Welfare Activities, July 6, 1945, Hartshorne Papers. "January Gemeinde

Elections Statement No. 1," copy in Landkreis Marburg Papers (in Landratsamt, Marburg). Wohnungsamt Marburg to Oberbürgermeister: Memorandum, November 10, 1948, Stadtkreis Marburg Papers (in Rathaus, Marburg). "Nachweisung über die im Landkreis Marburg/Lahn vorhandenden Kriegsschäden und deren Wiederaufbau," n.d., copy in Bauer Papers. *Marburger Presse*, February 21, 1947, p. 3. "Marburg im Bombenkrieg," a statistical compilation of bomb damage in Marburg and Landkreis Marburg, copy in Bauer Papers.

15. HSL, *Die Volks- und Berufszählung vom 29.Oktober 1946 in Hessen*, pp. 38–39.

16. OMGUS, Monthly Report, No. 10, May 1946, Manpower, Trade Unions and Working Conditions, p. 5.

17. Landrat to MG-CIC, Marburg: Wochenbericht vom 28.2 bis 6.3. 1947, March 6, 1947, Landkreis Marburg Papers.

18. Howard Becker, "German Families Today," in Hans J. Morgenthau, ed., *Germany and the Future of Europe*, The Norman Wait Harris Memorial Foundation Lectures, The Twenty-sixth Institute, May 28–June 1, 1950 (Chicago: University of Chicago Press, 1951), p. 16.

19. OMGUS, Monthly Report, No. 21, March 1947, Report of the Military Governor, p. 25; Senior District Resident Officer, Marburg, Annex to U.S. Resident Officer Position Description, October 27, 1949, Office of the U.S. High Commissioner for Germany Papers (hereafter cited as HICOG Papers).

Chapter 3

1. Harold Zink, *American Military Government in Germany* (New York: The Macmillan Company, 1947), p. 133. See also Zink, *The United States in Germany, 1944–1955* (Princeton: D. Van Nostrand Company, Inc., 1957), especially chaps. 2, 3, 6; Walter Dorn, "Debate over American Occupation Policy in Germany in 1944–1945," *Political Science Quarterly*, LXXII (December 1957), 481–501; John L. Snell, *Wartime Origins of the East-West Dilemma over Germany* (New Orleans: The Hauser Press, 1959); Dale Clark, "Conflicts Over Planning at Staff Headquarters," in Carl J. Friedrich and others, *American Experiences in Military Government in World War II, American Government in Action* (New York: Rinehart and Company, Inc., 1948), pp. 211–37; Hajo Holborn, *American Military Government: Its Organization and Policies* (Washington: Infantry Journal Press, 1947); and Eugene Davidson, *The Death and Life of Germany* (New York, Alfred A. Knopf, 1959), chaps. 1, 2.

2. Dexter L. Freeman, ed., *Hesse, A New German State*, with a foreword by James R. Newman (Frankfurt: Druck- und Verlagshaus Frankfurt a.M. GmbH., 1948), p. 27.

3. Zink, *American Military Government*, pp. 137–38. But see his *The United States in Germany*, chap. 6, for a moderate account of the "Thorny Problem of Policy."

4. Detachment F1C2 to CO, Company C, 2nd ECA Regt.: History of Detachment F1C2—July 1945, n.d., OMGUS Papers.

5. Drew Middleton, *The Struggle for Germany* (Indianapolis: The Bobbs-Merrill Company, Inc., 1949), pp. 33–34.

6. USFET: Reorganization of Military Government Control Channels in Order to Develop German Responsibility for Self-Government, October 5, 1945, quoted in R. A. Irving, comp., "Chronology, M. G. Det. E1A2 (E-5), Office of Military Government for Hesse and Office of the Land Commissioner for Hesse, 1944–1950" (Wiesbaden: OLCH, n.d.), app., 5 (typewritten), HICOG Papers. OMGH, Historical Report, October 1945 through June 1946, I, 7 (mimeographed), OMGUS Papers.

7. Protocol about the conference with Colonel Kilgore which took place September 19, 1946, with Oberbürgermeister Müller, n.d. (trans. by Bürgermeister's staff); Niederschrift über eine Besprechung am 29. Oktober 1946, Stadtkreis Marburg Papers.

8. *Kreisblatt für den Landkreis Marburg an der Lahn*, Number 1, January 6, 1949, p. 1; Number 18, May 5, 1949, p. 3; Samuel R. Combs, "Our Reorientation Mission," a speech delivered at the opening session of the Hesse Reorientation Training Conference, Haus Schwalbach, on Monday, January 23, 1950 (mimeographed), HICOG Papers.

9. OMG, Regierungsbezirk Oberfranken and Mittelfranken: Intelligence Report, May 26, 1946, OMGUS Papers.

10. OMGUS, Standing Operating Procedure, Liaison and Security Offices and Administrative Units (Berlin: March 31, 1947, lithographed), HICOG Papers.

11. HICOG, The Kreis Resident Officer, prepared by the Chief, Personnel Division, David Wilken; Chief, Classification and Wage Branch, Idar Rimestad; Classification Standards Analyst, C. F. Blackman (Frankfurt: July 1950, lithographed). HICOG, U.S. Resident Officer's Handbook (Frankfurt: July 1951, lithographed), HICOG Papers.

12. Draft prepared by KRO, Marburg, 1951 (typewritten), HICOG Papers.

13. Zink, *American Military Government*, p. 23; chap. iii, *passim*.

14. Zink, *American Military Government*, p. 59, states that "as the detachments doubled and tripled in size after V-E Day, the general level deteriorated because of the use of tactical officers and others with little or no specialized military government training, but even so professional expertness remained at a reasonably high level."

15. Richard J. Eaton to author, January 27, 1955.

16. Zink, *American Military Government*, pp. 36–37. See Julian Bach, *America's Germany, An Account of the Occupation* (New York: Random House, 1946), p. 51, for a discussion of the desire of Americans to get home.

17. OMGH, Historical Report, July 1946 through December 1946, I, 1 (mimeographed), OMGUS Papers.

18. *Marburger Presse*, October 3, 1949, p. 1.

19. I made the study by selecting randomly the names of fifteen office employees from the payroll lists in the Besatzungskostenamt (Occupation Costs Office) in Marburg. The eleven investigators' names I selected de-

liberately, because they were hired specifically for intelligence work. I checked the names against the police files and the Marburg registration lists (every resident must register), and I interviewed all persons whose names I had found who still lived in Marburg.

20. Detachment F1C2, Daily Journal, September 5 to September 6, 1945, OMGUS Papers (hereafter cited as Daily Journal). Robert Treut was the same man who was removed two months later for being a Nazi.

21. "Ein Versehen meines Botenjungen wird schuld daran sein, dass dieser Bericht an die CIC gelangte. Dies war keinesfalls meine Absicht gewesen." Hans Frese to Ludwig Mütze, June 13, 1945, Stadtkreis Marburg Papers.

22. William W. Lechner, Field Adviser, to OMGH: Cooperation and the Landrat of Marburg, August 21, 1947, OMGUS Papers.

23. Landrat to CIC and Militärregierung: Bericht auf Grund der dortigen Verfügung vom 24. April 1946, April 27, 1946, Landkreis Marburg Papers.

Chapter 4

1. *Hessische Post*, May 12, 1945, p. 2; Daily Journal, July 1945 to October 1945, *passim*, OMGUS Papers. The Oberbürgermeister wrote to the Military Governor, ostensibly to excuse Germans for violating curfew regulations, but obviously to criticize the activities of the occupation troops. He requested that curfew hours be signaled by a short blast of the old air-raid siren, because "the civilian population is no longer in possession of its watches." Oberbürgermeister Siebecke to Militärregierung, August 27, 1945, Stadtkreis Marburg Papers.

2. Polizeidirektor Kroll, Supplement to the report for Herrn Ober-Präsident in Kassel about the Police of Marburg/L (trans. by Kroll's staff), June 22, 1945, Police Reports and Papers; Richard J. Eaton to author, January 27, 1955.

3. Polizeidirektor Kroll to Oberbürgermeister Siebecke, May 7, 1945. Gustav Zeckey, Beauftragter für politische Angelegenheiten beim Stadtkommissar: Tätigkeitsbericht, December 17, 1945, Stadtkreis Marburg Papers.

4. OMGUS, Monthly Report, No. 1, August 20, 1945, Denazification, pp. 2, 13.

5. Walker Hancock to author, December 16, 1954, said that "American regulations against public gatherings made theatrical performances, concerts, and art exhibitions impossible long after the Germans in other zones were enjoying these" and that "musical recitals which were allowed in churches, if accompanied by prayers and benedictions, were always packed, but only served to accentuate the ridiculous situation." Walker Hancock was the detachment's Monuments, Fine Arts and Archives Officer.

6. OMGUS, Monthly Report, No. 1, August 20, 1945, p. 4.

7. Stadtkommissar [Erich Kroll] to Regierungspräsident Kassel: Lagebericht, September 7, 1945, Police Reports and Papers.

8. Hermann Bauer to Herrn [Samson B.] Knoll: Wie man heute über die amerikanische Besatzung denkt, August 10, 1945, copy in Bauer Papers. "Die Lockerung des Fraternisierungsverbotes kam nur kleinen Mädchen zugute; wir, die wir uns Ihnen innerlich als Bundesgenossen verbunden fühlten, geniessen heute noch das gleiche Misstrauen wie zu Anfang der Besetzung!"

9. "Report of Captain Lansberry," OMGUS Papers; Der kommissarische Oberbürgermeister to Hagenbach, March 30, 1945; Kurator, Universität, to Oberbürgermeister, April 8, 1945, Stadtkreis Marburg Papers.

10. Staatspolitischer Ausschuss, Gründe des Anwachsens der Abneigung gegen die amerikanische Militär-Regierung (Streng Geheim), November 7, 1945, Stadtkreis Marburg Papers; "Relief of Occupation Pressure in Town of Marburg," Draft Staff Study, n.d., Hartshorne Papers. (The Staatspolitischer Ausschuss is hereafter abbreviated SPA).

11. Walker K. Hancock to CO, Detachment G-39, Subject: Defacement of Cultural Building, September 20, 1945, OMGUS Papers; Richard J. Eaton to author, February 5, 1955; Bürgermeister, Anordnung, Anschlag 10x, March 30, 1945, Stadtkreis Marburg Papers; Hermann Bauer, interview, June 22, 1954. Bauer recalled this incident in his attempt to prove to me that the Marburg detachment was extremely lax in its enforcement of policy; that the detachment officers were too easygoing; that they were much more concerned with their own personal matters than with carrying out the wishes and desires of their government. Although Bauer was never a Nazi, there is a surprising similarity between Bauer's desire to blame military government for his own violation of the law and the Nazi proclivity, after 1945, to blame other nations for the rise of Hitler.

12. See, for example, Karl H. Knappstein, "Die versäumte Revolution," Die Wandlung (Heidelberg), II (November 1947), 663–67; Howard Becker, German Youth: Bond or Free, International Library of Sociology and Social Reconstruction, Karl Mannheim, ed. (London: Kegan Paul, Trench, Trubner and Company, Ltd., 1946); Gustav Stolper, German Realities (New York: Reynal and Hitchcock, 1949); James P. Warburg, "Germany and World Peace," Morgenthau, ed., Germany and the Future of Europe, pp. 142–62; William Ebenstein, The German Record, A Political Portrait (New York: Farrar and Rinehart, Inc., 1945); and "Die versäumte Evolution," Der Ruf, Unabhängige Blätter der Jungen Generation (Munich), II (January 15, 1947), 1–2.

13. Becker, German Youth, p. 228; Stolper, German Realities, p. 58; Warburg, "Germany and World Peace," p. 147.

14. See, for example, Allen W. Dulles, Germany's Underground (New York: The Macmillan Company, 1947); Hans Rothfels, The German Opposition to Hitler (Hinsdale: Henry Regnery Company, 1948); Gerhard Ritter, The German Resistance: Carl Gördeler's Struggle against

Tyranny, trans. by R. T. Clark (New York: Frederick A. Praeger, 1958); and Paul Kluke, "Der deutsche Widerstand, Eine kritische Literaturübersicht," *Historische Zeitschrift* (Munich), CLXIX (April 1949), 136–61.

15. OMGUS, Monthly Report, No. 1, August 20, 1945, pp. 1, 3, 17; C. J. Friedrich, "The Three Phases of Field Operations in Germany, 1945–1946," Friedrich and others, *American Experiences in Military Government,* p. 246.

16. OMGUS, Monthly Report, No. 1, August 20, 1945, p. 1.

17. See *Marburger Presse,* September 27, 1946, p. 2. Richard Bromm, interview, May 24, 1954, said, "military government protected Germany against radicalism."

18. Daily Journal, July 27 to July 28, 1945; September 13 to September 14, 1945, OMGUS Papers; Hermann Bauer to Willi Junker, September 1945, Bauer Papers; SPA, Bericht über die politische Lage in Marburg, October 11, 1945, Stadtkreis Marburg Papers.

19. Hermann Bauer to Herrn Knoll: Wie man heute über die amerikanische Besatzung denkt, August 10, 1945, copy in Bauer Papers.

20. The man was Theo Abel. He had served on the political committee from April to December 1945. Three members of the committee volunteered this information during interviews.

21. Daily Journal, April 14 to April 15, 1945; Walker K. Hancock to CO, Detachment G-39, September 20, 1945, OMGUS Papers.

22. Eugen Siebecke, interview, July 23, 1954; Hermann Bauer, interview, June 30, 1954. Marburgers often tell a humorous story about this officer. He did not speak German well and apparently always became confused regarding the use of the formal "Sie" and the informal "Du" in addressing people. He reportedly addressed his dog "Sie" and German visitors to his office "Du." Some have suggested that he knew enough German to distinguish between the two uses.

23. Oberbürgermeister Siebecke to Herrn Zachau, May 3, 1945. Memorandum to Oberbürgermeister, May 8, 1945. OMG, Marburg, to Bürgermeister: Kitchen and Dining Room Supplies, April 25, 1945, Stadtkreis Marburg Papers. The detachment's strength on March 15, 1945, was fourteen officers and eighteen enlisted men.

24. Hermann Bauer, interview, June 16, 1954; Heinrich Laubach, interview, July 14, 1954. Laubach is the chairman of the *Notverband für Besatzungsverdrängte* (Emergency Union of Those Displaced by the Occupation). He permitted me to read the correspondence and the reports of the organization in Marburg.

25. Headquarters, 6871st District Information Services Control Command to University Officer, Land Greater Hesse, December 26, 1946, Hartshorne Papers.

26. Daily Journal, April 7 to April 8, 1945, OMGUS Papers. *Hessische Post,* June 2, 1945, p. 2. Detachment F1C2 to CO, Company C, 2nd ECA Regt.: History of Detachment F1C2—July 1945, n.d., OMGUS Papers. Nathaniel Cooper, Detachment F1C2: Summary of Public Health and Welfare Activities, July 6, 1945, Hartshorne Papers.

27. Wohlfahrtsamt to Oberbürgermeister: Richtlinien der Stadtverwaltung Marburg–Lahn für den Arbeitseinsatz weiblicher Arbeitskräfte, April 13, 1945, Stadtkreis Marburg Papers.

28. Oberbürgermeister, Bekanntmachung, April 27, 1945; Oberbürgermeister to Militärregierung, May 5, 1945, Stadtkreis Marburg Papers.

29. SPA, Minutes, June 15, 1945, and September 4, 1945; SPA to Oberbürgermeister, June 16, 1945, and August 31, 1945; Oberbürgermeister to addressees, June 21, 1945, Stadtkreis Marburg Papers; and Aktenvermerk, October 30, 1945, Police Reports and Papers.

30. OMGUS, Monthly Report, No. 11, June 20, 1946, p. 1.

31. Daily Journal, April 24 to April 25, 1945, OMGUS Papers; Stadtkommissar to Regierungspräsident, September 7, 1945, Police Reports and Papers; Richard J. Eaton to author, January 27, 1955.

32. "Zeckey über Siebecke und über die KPD und SPD," [March 11, 1946], copy in Siebecke Papers. It was later discovered that this man had a police record dating back to the Weimar Republic. No evidence of his record was available to the detachment in Marburg because the man had lived in Bavaria prior to the capitulation. Landrat to Militärregierung, April 12, 1945, Landkreis Marburg Papers; Jakob Römer, interview, April 15, 1954; OMGUS, Biological Products Division, Public Health Branch: Memorandum, with enclosure: Auskunft aus dem Strafregister der Staatsanwaltschaft zu Altgötting/Obb, February 27, 1947, OMGUS Papers.

33. OMG, Marburg, to Oberbürgermeister, August 16, 1945; Stadtbaurat to Vorsteher des Finanzamtes, April 1, 1945; Oberbürgermeister to Postamt, March 30, 1945, Stadtkreis Marburg Papers; Oberbürgermeister to Major Eaton, April 4, 1945, Stadtkreis Marburg Papers; Daily Journal, April 4 to April 5, 1945, OMGUS Papers; Richard J. Eaton to author, January 27, 1955.

34. Freeman, ed., *Hesse, A New German State,* p. 29.

35. For an indication of the confusion among Marburgers see SPA, Minutes, May 1945 to December 1945, *passim,* Stadtkreis Marburg Papers.

36. OMG, Marburg, to OMGH: Special Report, Denazification, November 8, 1945, OMGUS Papers; George D. Fexy to author, March 24, 1955.

37. Landrat von Boxberger to Bürgermeister, April 16, 1945, Landkreis Marburg Papers.

38. OMG, Marburg, to CG, Western Military District: Weekly Military Government Report, October 14, 1945, OMGUS Papers, contains report that twenty Bürgermeisters were removed in one week and that military government cleared the replacements.

39. Landrat to Bürgermeisters, December 6, 1945, Landkreis Marburg Papers.

Chapter 5

1. Francis Sheehan, interview, July 21, 1954.

2. Ludwig Mütze to Mr. Bernard, June 19, 1945, Mütze Papers (in

Mütze's possession, Marburg, Germany); Report of an interview with Bürgermeister Dickman in OMGUS, ICD, Marburg, to OMGH: Reaction in Marburg to One Year of American Occupation, June 27, 1946, HICOG Papers.

3. Polizei Tagebuch, #102/45 IV, Police Reports and Papers.

4. Richard J. Eaton to author, January 27, 1955.

5. Superintendent Schmidman, Memorandum of the Protestant Church of Marburg for the Allied Military Government, April 1945; Superintendent Schmidman to the Theologische Fakultät of the Philipps-Universität, April 28, 1945, Hartshorne Papers.

6. Wilfred Müller-Broadman to Bürgerrat der Stadt Marburg, February 5, 1946; Heinz-Hello Wagener to Bürgerrat, February 5, 1946, Stadtkreis Marburg Papers; Rector of the University to Area Commander, January 28, 1946; OMG, U.S. Zone, ICD Survey Section, Marburg, to Dr. Hartshorne, April 2, 1946; Professor Balla, Dean of the Theological Faculty, to the Rector, Philipps-Universität, January 30, 1946, Hartshorne Papers. In addition to these there is a large file of incident reports in the Hartshorne Papers. E. Y. Hartshorne, the University Officer, collected the reports late in 1945 in order to support a recommendation he made to reduce the number of troops in Marburg.

7. Liberally translated and paraphrased from: "Unter der Bevölkerung Marburg's sind diese Ueberfälle Tagesgespräche; man wagt sich nicht mehr abends auf die Strasse und fühlt sich schutzlos roher Willkür ausgeliefert. Der letzte, kümmerliche Rest von gutem Einvernehmen mit der Besatzungsmacht schwindet und die uns am Herzen liegende Sache der Demokratie erhält dadurch einen weiteren schweren Stoss. Jederman ist sich darüber klar, dass diese Vorgänge Wasser auf die Mühle der Nazis sind und unsere ohnehin schon schwierige Arbeit der politischen Erziehung auf das Schwerste nimmt." Otto Roppel to Dr. Hartshorne, February 9, 1946, Hartshorne Papers.

8. OMGUS, Monthly Report, No. 2, September 20, 1945, p. 4.

9. The file is in the OMGUS Papers.

10. Kreis Resident Office (KRO), Marburg, to Office of Land Commissioner for Hessen (OLCH): Monthly Reorientation Statistical Report, March 4, 1950, HICOG Papers.

11. Professor Werner Krauss, Romanisches Seminar, to University Officer, Marburg, February 20, 1946, Hartshorne Papers; Ernst Sangmeister to Ludwig Mütze, July 2, 1946, Mütze Papers; Wilhelm Büchner to Oberbürgermeister, May 14, 1945, Stadtkreis Marburg Papers; Hans A. Rümelin, ed., So Lebten Wir: Ein Querschnitt durch 1947 (Willsbach, Württemberg: Scherer-Verlag, 1947), p. 4.

12. Eugen Siebecke, interview, July 22, 1954; Trial Record, Intermediate Military Court. Accused: Eugen Siebecke, male, 55, Marburg/Lahn, Bismarckstr., 11, charged with violation of Ordinance No. 1. Article II, Par. 33 . . . [March 12–14, 1946], Siebecke Papers (hereafter cited as Siebecke Trial Record).

13. Daily Journal, July 27 to July 28, 1945, OMGUS Papers.

14. Oberbürgermeister to Militärregierung, May 28, 1945, Stadtkreis Marburg Papers. The Oberbürgermeister wrote that he had three lawyers who would gladly do the job.

15. Gendarmerieposten, Cappel, to Landrat, May 18, 1945, Landkreis Marburg Papers.

16. Landrat to Militärregierung and CIC, August 19, 1948, Landkreis Marburg Papers.

17. Ludwig Mütze, interview, July 2, 1954. Mütze said there were about five whom he would have beaten personally.

18. Ludwig Mütze to Mr. Bernard, June 19, 1945, Mütze Papers.

19. Richard J. Eaton to author, January 27, 1955.

20. Hermann Bauer to Herrn Knoll, August 10, 1945, Bauer Papers.

21. Paraphrased and liberally translated from: "Nein, sehr verehrter Herr Noll, *so* hatten wir uns Ihren Kampf gegen den Nationalsozialismus *nicht* vorgestellt! . . . Wir [wurden] durch die Praktiken Ihrer Instanzen schwer enttäuscht. . . . Wir hatten gewünscht, bei der Ausmerzung der Nationalsozialisten aus dem Verwaltungs- und Wirtschaftsleben zu Rate gezogen zu werden, da nur so schnelle und gründliche Arbeit möglich war, doch selbstherrlich ging man von amerikanischer Seite vor, und uns deutschen Hitler-Gegnern blieb nur die undankbare Aufgabe, Fehlentscheide unter Umständen zu berichten."

22. SPA, Gründe des Anwachsens der Abneigung gegen die amerikanische Militär-Regierung (Streng Geheim), November 7, 1945, Stadtkreis Marburg Papers.

23. "Verständnislos und verbittert standen die Marburger dabei und sahen ihre letzten Habseligkeiten einer sinnlosen Zerstörung preisgegeben, nachdem die alliierten Waffen längst den völligen Sieg erfochten hatten." The two cafés in question were, and are, the pride of upper-middle-class Marburgers.

24. A classified report by the Marburg military government team on the prisoner-of-war camp in Marburg stated that some beatings had occurred, but that they were administered by the German camp commanders.

25. Richard J. Eaton to author, January 27, 1955, volunteered the conclusion that controlling displaced persons was one of the biggest jobs ("and headaches") of military government. Late in 1945 and in 1946 the *Marburger Presse* reported in almost every issue robberies and attacks by armed displaced persons. The Hartshorne Papers also contain a file of reports on such incidents.

26. Hermann Bauer to [Shepard] Stone, December 17, 1946, Bauer Papers.

27. Hermann Bauer, interview, June 22, 1954, described the impression that was made upon him by the unconcern of Americans that Germans continued to listen to the German radio even though the war was not yet over when Marburg was occupied.

28. The head of the criminal police in Marburg analyzed the benefits

as follows: each American kitchen had about ten German employees; each worker had a family and friends to support. Therefore each American kitchen probably helped feed about fifty people.

29. Daily Journal, May to July, 1945, *passim*, OMGUS Papers.

30. Jakob Römer to Ludwig Mütze, June 19, 1945, Stadtkreis Marburg Papers. The German reads "[Die Amerikaner], die in der Personalpolitik oft eine unglückliche Hand haben."

31. OMGUS, ICD, Marburg, to OMGH: Reaction in Marburg to One Year of American Occupation, June 27, 1946, HICOG Papers.

32. Karl Menkel, interview, July 8, 1954.

Chapter 6

1. Hermann Bauer to Schulrat Tilgner, March 30, 1945, Bauer Papers. SPA to Mr. Knoll: Entstehung, Entwicklung und Arbeitsgebiete des Staatspolitischen Ausschusses der Stadt, Marburg a/Lahn, August 10, 1945, Siebecke Papers. "Für Ordnung und Sauberkeit!" n.d., a ms. found in the Bauer Papers. It bears fourteen signatures. It was revised on April 18, 1945, and again on April 20, 1945. On the latter date it was printed for posting in public places.

2. Staatspolitischer Referent to Militärregierung, May 17, 1945, Stadtkreis Marburg Papers.

3. SPA to Mr. Knoll, August 10, 1945, Siebecke Papers; Hermann Bauer to Mr. Seaman, Militärregierung, April 22, 1945, Bauer Papers; Hermann Bauer, interview, June 14, 1954. Bauer spoke from penciled notes he had kept in 1945.

4. Ernst Sangmeister to Herrn Kombächer, April 21, 1945; Ludwig Mütze to Hermann Bauer, April 26, 1945, Bauer Papers; SPA to Mr. Knoll, August 10, 1945, Siebecke Papers.

5. SPA, Minutes, May 26, 1945, Stadtkreis Marburg Papers.

6. SPA, Minutes, May 26, 1945; Oberbürgermeister to Militärregierung, May 19, 1945, Stadtkreis Marburg Papers.

7. Hermann Bauer to Schulrat Tilgner, March 30, 1945; Ludwig Mütze to Hermann Bauer, March 10, 1952; Mütze to Bauer, March 21, 1952; Bauer to Mütze, July 4, 1950; Mütze to Bauer, July 7, 1950, Bauer Papers.

8. Hans Frese to Erich Kroll, April 30, 1945; May 15, 1945, Stadtkreis Marburg Papers.

9. Otto Dula, interview, June 12, 1954.

10. Hans Frese to Erich Kroll, April 30, 1945.

11. SPA, Minutes, June 5, 1945; Hans Frese to Ludwig Mütze, June 13, 1945; Aktenvermerk [memorandum for files of SPA], June 18, 1945, Stadtkreis Marburg Papers; Ludwig Mütze, interview, June 12, 1954; Eugen Siebecke, interview, July 22, 1954; Hans Frese, interview, July 3, 1954.

12. SPA, Minutes, June 5, 1945; Daily Journal, June 9 to 10, 1945, OMGUS Papers.

13. Ludwig Mütze to Oberbürgermeister, May 28, 1945, with enclosure: Richtlinien, nach denen die Säuberung der deutschen kommunalen und staatlichen Verwaltungszweige von Nazis durchgeführt werden könnte; SPA to Haupt- und Personalamt, Stadtverwaltung, August 1, 1945; File 046, subdivision 0460; Staatspolitischer Referent to Wilhelm Weis, June 29, 1945; SPA to Oberbürgermeister, June 16, 1945; August 16, 1945; SPA to Militärregierung, August 11, 1945; SPA to Ludwig Mütze, May 29, 1945; SPA, Minutes, June 15, 1945, Stadtkreis Marburg Papers.

14. SPA, Minutes, May 8, 1945; June 19, 1945.

15. SPA to Mr. Knoll, August 10, 1945, Siebecke Papers.

16. Robert Treut to Oberbürgermeister, September 19, 1945; Staatspolitischer Referent to Oberbürgermeister, May 11, 1945; June 16, 1945; SPA to Oberbürgermeister, June 16, 1945; June 21, 1945; August 26, 1945, Stadtkreis Marburg Papers.

17. A spurious tale is often repeated in Marburg to illustrate this point. It is usually similar in three factors: a man who changed his name, signed his own death certificate, and married his widow. See John H. Herz, "The Fiasco of Denazification in Germany," *Political Science Quarterly*, LXIII (December 1948), 586, who wrote that it appeared first in the *Berliner Zeitung* on February 15, 1948.

18. SPA, Minutes, June 1945 to December 1945, *passim*; SPA, Memorandum of Activities, October 29, 1945; SPA to Oberbürgermeister, October 17, 1945; SPA, Bericht über die politische Lage in Marburg, October 11, 1945, Stadtkreis Marburg Papers.

19. SPA, Minutes, May 11, 1945; May 26, 1945, Stadtkreis Marburg Papers; Daily Journal, August 9 to August 10, 1945; August 10 to August 11, 1945, OMGUS Papers. The official was not reinstated.

20. Staatspolitischer Referent to Militärregierung, June 1, 1945, Stadtkreis Marburg Papers.

21. SPA to Oberbürgermeister, August 16, 1945, Stadtkreis Marburg Papers.

22. See C. J. Friedrich, "The Three Phases of Field Operations in Germany, 1945–1946," Friedrich and others, *American Experiences in Military Government*, p. 246.

23. OMGUS, Monthly Report, No. 1, August 20, 1945, The Political Situation, p. 1; German Governmental Organization and Civil Administration, p. 1.

24. Daily Journal, September 15 to September 17, 1945, OMGUS Papers; Captain Eugene Tedick to Oberbürgermeister, December 5, 1945, Stadtkreis Marburg Papers.

25. Daily Journal, July 25 to July 26, 1945, OMGUS Papers; SPA, Minutes, August 21, 1945, Stadtkreis Marburg Papers. Bauer's statement to the committee reads, in part: "Zumindest glaubt der Herr Oberbürgermeister den Ausschuss mit einem Lächeln abtun zu können: "Der Ausschuss mag da oben tagen, doch anerkannt ist er nicht; bestimmen werde ich, nur ich allein!' "

26. SPA to Oberbürgermeister, November 23, 1945; Captain Eugene Tedick to Oberbürgermeister, December 5, 1945, Stadtkreis Marburg Papers.

27. SPA to Militärregierung, August 11, 1945; SPA to Oberbürgermeister, August 16, 1945; SPA, Minutes, June 15, 1945; SPA to Haupt- und Personalamt, Stadtverwaltung, August 1, 1945, Stadtkreis Marburg Papers; *Marburger Presse,* September 25, 1945, p. 3.

28. SPA to Oberbürgermeister, August 10, 1945; August 26, 1945; SPA, Bericht über die politische Lage in Marburg, October 11, 1945, Stadtkreis Marburg Papers.

29. Ernst Sangmeister to Ludwig Mütze, July 2, 1945, Mütze Papers.

30. SPA, Minutes, October 29, 1945.

31. Bach, *America's Germany,* p. 243.

32. *Marburger Presse,* May 17, 1946, p. 6; May 28, 1946, p. 4.

33. Daily Journal, May 10 to May 11, 1945; OMGH to CO, Detachment G-39: Employees, Public Safety, February 25, 1946, OMGUS Papers.

34. Robert Treut to Oberbürgermeister, January 10, 1946; SPA, Bericht über die politische Lage in Marburg, October 11, 1945, Stadtkreis Marburg Papers; Otto Dula, interview, June 12, 1954; Margarete Treviranus, interview, June 5, 1954; *Marburger Presse,* October 16, 1945, p. 3.

35. Robert Treut to Oberbürgermeister, October 16, 1945, Stadtkreis Marburg Papers.

36. SPA to Oberbürgermeister, October 31, 1945, Stadtkreis Marburg Papers. Treut had assumed the chairmanship of the committee because Mütze was often away, working on the problem of reopening the schools. The German reads: "Da drüben platzt in diesen Tagen sowieso die Bombe. Der Ausschuss fliegt auf. . . . Besonders der Herr Treut wird entlassen."

37. William E. Griffith, "The Denazification Program in the United States Zone of Germany," unpublished Ph.D. dissertation, Harvard University, 1950, pp. 63 ff.

38. Donald B. Robinson, "Why Denazification Is Lagging," *The American Mercury,* LXII (May 1946), 568.

39. Oberbürgermeister to Captain Eugene Tedick, October 26, 1945, Stadtkreis Marburg Papers.

40. Siebecke Trial Record; Ludwig Mütze, interview, June 12, 1954; Eugen Siebecke, interview, July 22, 1954; Marion Collier to author, n.d., received January 29, 1955.

41. OMG, Marburg, to OMGH: Weekly Denazification Report (Corrected Copy) for period from 5 December to 12 December 1945, December 13, 1945, OMGUS Papers. Mütze had resigned from the committee and Robert Treut, the former secretary and interpreter, was the chairman in question. He was cleared a month later.

42. SPA to Oberbürgermeister, December 12, 1945, Stadtkreis Marburg Papers.

43. Bürgerrat, Minutes, February 8, 1946; February 11, 1946; February 22, 1946; May 1, 1946, Stadtkreis Marburg Papers.

Chapter 7

1. Directive to the Commander in Chief of the United States Forces of Occupation Regarding the Military Government of Germany [JCS 1067], printed in *Germany, 1947–1949*, pp. 21–33. (The directive is hereafter cited as JCS 1067.)

2. Even though the Morgenthau Plan received wide publicity in the American press after Germany's defeat, it never became the basis for American industrial policy in Germany. See especially Holborn, *American Military Government*, pp. 40–41; Alvin Johnson and Ernest Hamburger, "The Economic Problem of Germany," *Social Research*, XIII (June 1946), 135–82; Ferdinand A. Hermens, "The Economics of Potsdam," *The Review of Politics*, VIII (July 1946), 381–403; Eugene Davidson, *The Death and Life of Germany, An Account of the American Occupation* (New York: Alfred A. Knopf, 1959), pp. 37–40, 143, 191; and B. U. Ratchford and W. D. Ross, *Berlin Reparations Assignment, Round One of the German Peace Settlement* (Chapel Hill: The University of North Carolina Press, 1947), p. 34, for the argument that early plans, such as the Morgenthau Plan and the recommendations made by the Foreign Economic Administration, proved to be unworkable because the assumptions upon which both plans rested did not apply to Germany after defeat.

3. Policy Statement on Reparations by the Department of State, December 12, 1945, printed in Ratchford and Ross, *Berlin Reparations Assignment*, app. D, pp. 214–21; *Germany, 1947–1949*, pp. 3–8, 356–71.

4. OMGUS, Monthly Report, No. 1, August 20, 1945, p. 4.

5. For detailed reports see OMGUS, Economic Data on Potsdam Germany, Special Report of the Military Governor, September 1947; OMGUS and Control Commission for Germany (British Element), The European Recovery Program, US/UK Occupied Areas of Germany, 1 April 1948–30 September 1948, Joint Report of the United States and United Kingdom Military Governors, September 1948; and OMGUS, Three Years of Reparations, Progress of Reparations from Germany in the Form of Capital Industrial Equipment, Special Report of the Military Governor, November 1948.

6. OMG, Marburg, to OMGH: Report of Behringwerke, February 5, 1948, OMGUS Papers.

7. OMGUS, Monthly Report, No. 1, August 20, 1945, Medical and Health Affairs, p. 4; No. 2, September 20, 1945, p. 10; No. 36, June 20, 1948, Statistical Annex, table 1, p. 32.

8. The apparent inability of American officers, especially engineers, to think in terms of control rather than in terms of production and efficiency is adequately discussed in Ratchford and Ross, *Berlin Reparations Assignment*; Hans Habe (pseud.), *Our Love Affair with Germany* (New York: G. P. Putnam's Sons, 1953); Engler, "The Individual Soldier and the Occupation"; and it is probably most apparent in the work of the Military Governor himself: Clay, *Decision in Germany*. See William H.

Hale, "Our Failure in Germany," *Harper's Magazine*, CXCI (December 1945), 517, for the statement that military government control officers had a War Production Board mentality.

9. OMGUS, Monthly Report, No. 2, September 20, 1945, Medical and Health Affairs, p. 7; OMG, Marburg, to OMGH: Report of Behringwerke, February 5, 1948, OMGUS Papers.

10. OMGUS, Monthly Report, No. 2, September 20, 1945, p. 10.

11. OMG, Marburg, to OMGH: Report of Behringwerke, February 5, 1948, OMGUS Papers.

12. OMGH, Property Control Division, to OMGH, Property Control, Civilian Agencies Section: Field Inspection Report, Marburg–LK Marburg, March 11, 1947; OMGUS, Monthly Report, No. 7, February 20, 1946, Reparations and Restitutions, p. 3; OMG, Marburg, to CO, Detachment E-4, 2nd MG Bn (Sep), December 10, 1945, OMGUS Papers.

13. OMGH, Property Control Division, to OMGH, Property Control, Civilian Agencies Section: Field Inspection Report, Marburg–LK Marburg, March 11, 1947, OMGUS Papers; OMG, Marburg, to OMGH, Information Report No. 351—Political, December 7, 1948, HICOG Papers; OMGUS, Monthly Report, No. 39, September 20, 1948, Reparations and Restitutions (Quarterly Review), July–September 1948, p. 17; *Marburger Presse*, April 7, 1949, p. 2.

14. Landrat to Militärregierung, Marburg, February 27, 1947, Landkreis Marburg Papers; OMG, Marburg, to OMGH: Periodic Report for Week Ending 2400 hours, 19 February 1947, February 20, 1947, OMGUS Papers.

15. *Marburger Presse*, March 22, 1946, p. 3; March 2, 1949, p. 2; OMG, Marburg, to OMGH: Information Report, No. 319, Economics: Settlement of German Peace Industry at the Former DAG and WASAG Territory in Allendorf, Kreis/Marburg, November 19, 1948, HICOG Papers.

16. *Marburger Presse*, June 18, 1946, p. 5. The coalition was made up of Social Democrats, Christian Democrats, and Liberal Democrats.

17. *Marburger Presse*, December 21, 1945, p. 1.

18. Landrat to Regierungspräsident, Kassel, March 13, 1946, Landkreis Marburg Papers. Twenty-five hundred refugees had arrived in Marburg in February 1946.

19. OMGH, Economics Division, Reparations Field Office (Kassel), to Chief, Reparations Section, OMGH: Removal of Camouflage from Fabrik Allendorf, June 18, 1947, OMGUS Papers.

20. *Marburger Presse*, March 22, 1946, p. 3.

21. Speech by Oberbürgermeister Karl Theodor Bleek, printed in *Marburger Presse*, November 10, 1947, p. 1; Ausführungen der kommunalen Verwaltung zum Pressebericht, January 14, 1949, Landkreis Marburg Papers.

22. *Marburger Presse* (editorial), July 19, 1949, p. 2.

23. The speech by Oberbürgermeister Bleek is printed in the *Marburger Presse*, November 10, 1947, p. 1. Emphasizing what he believed

to be an unreasonable position of American policy makers on the subject he said: "Wir wissen aus der Natur, welche Einwirkungen und welche Wirkung das Sonnenlicht auf den Morgentau hat."

24. OMGUS, Monthly Report, No. 19, January 20, 1947, p. 27.

25. Landrat to Militärregierung and CIC, Marburg, April 27, 1946, Landkreis Marburg Papers.

26. HSL, *Die Wohnungszählung vom 29.Oktober 1946 in Hessen (Endgültige Ergebnisse)*, Beiträge zur Statistik Hessens, Nr. 1 (Wiesbaden: HSL, 1948), p. 16; OMGUS, Monthly Report, No. 31, January 20, 1948, table xiii, figs. 1a and 1b.

27. Landrat to Militärregierung and CIC, November 27, 1947, Landkreis Marburg Papers.

28. *Marburger Presse*, January 14, 1950, p. 2; February 16, 1950, p. 4.

29. OMGH, Economics Division, Reparations Field Office, Kassel: Letter of Instruction to Reparations Supervisor Fabrik Allendorf, March 25, 1947; to Chief, Reparations Section, OMGH: Removal of Camouflage from Fabrik Allendorf, June 18, 1947, OMGUS Papers.

30. Habe, *Our Love Affair with Germany*, p. 15. The author was the former American supervisor of eighteen American Army German-language newspapers in 1945. He returned to Munich as a civilian in 1949 to become the only American editor of a German weekly, the *Münchner Illustrierte* and later the *Echo der Woche*.

31. *Marburger Presse*, April 23, 1948, p. 4; OMGH, ICD, Marburg Outpost, to OMGH: Public Opinion Report, April 20, 1948, HICOG Papers.

32. OMGUS, Monthly Report, No. 30, December 1947, Information Control (Quarterly Review), October–December 1947, pp. 1–2; Clay, *Decision in Germany*, p. 158.

33. OMG, Marburg, to OMGH: Information Report No. 85–Political, March 9, 1949, HICOG Papers; Otto Dula, interview, June 12, 1954; Hans Frese, interview, July 3, 1954; Heinrich Dreher, interview, June 6, 1954.

34. Quoted in Ratchford and Ross, *Berlin Reparations Assignment*, p. 189.

Chapter 8

1. JCS 1067, April 1945, printed in *Germany, 1947–1949*, pp. 22–23.

2. Directive to Comamnder in Chief of United States Forces of Occupation Regarding the Military Government of Germany [JCS 1779], July 11, 1947, printed in *Germany, 1947–1949*, p. 35. (The directive is hereafter cited as JCS 1779.)

3. Detailed studies include: Hans Meyerhoff, "The Reconstruction of Governmental Administration," in Gabriel Almond, ed., *The Struggle for Democracy in Germany* (Chapel Hill: The University of North Carolina Press, 1949), pp. 185–220; Roger Wells, "Local Government" and

"State Government," in E. H. Litchfield and associates, *Governing Postwar Germany* (Ithaca: Cornell University Press, 1953), pp. 57–83, 84–116; Rodney L. Mott, "Public Finance," *ibid.*, pp. 326–58.

4. OMGUS, Monthly Report, No. 6, January 20, 1946, Political Activity, p. 3.

5. Kreis Resident Office (KRO), Marburg, to Office of Land Commissioner for Hessen (OLCH): Monthly Reorientation Report, September 4, 1950, HICOG Papers.

6. Zink, *American Military Government*, p. 63.

7. Headquarters, USFET: Reorganization of Military Government Control Channels in Order to Develop German Responsibility for Self-Government, October 5, 1945, quoted in Irving, comp., Chronology, app. p. 5, HICOG Papers.

8. OMG for Regierungsbezirk Oberfranken and Mittelfranken: Intelligence Report, May 28, 1946, OMGUS Papers.

9. Two examples among many are: Kenneth Dayton, Acting Director, CAD, to Control Officer, OMGUS, Memorandum for Discussion: Program for Improving MG Operations at Local Level, November 1947; OMGUS, Control Office and CAD, to Chief of Staff: Reduction of Liaison and Security Detachments, November 29, 1947, OMGUS Papers.

10. Zink, *American Military Government*, p. 64. For a German viewpoint see Hedwig Maier and Gustav von Schmoller, *Das Besatzungsregime in den drei westlichen Besatzungszonen, Eine kritische Untersuchung der Praxis der Besatzungsmächte in den Jahren 1945–1948, Erster Teil: Die Beschränkungen der staatlichen Hoheitsgewalt und der Grundrechte* (Stuttgart: Deutsches Büro Für Friedensfragen, 1948).

11. Oberbürgermeister Bleek to Regierungspräsident, Kassel, May 22, 1947; June 23, 1947; February 14, 1949, Stadtkreis Marburg Papers.

12. OMGUS, Monthly Report, No. 2, September 20, 1945, German Governmental Organization and Civil Administration, p. 4.

13. For discussion of German resistance to local government reform see Mott, "Public Finance," and Brecht, "Personnel Management," in Litchfield and associates, *Governing Postwar Germany*, pp. 326–58, 263–93.

14. OMGUS, Monthly Report, No. 30, December 1947, German Governmental Organization and Civil Administration (Cumulative Review), 1 December 1946–31 December 1947, p. 2.

15. Report of an interview with Karl Theodor Bleek in *Marburger Presse*, May 31, 1946, p. 2.

16. Memorandum from HICOG, Political Affairs Division, to HICOG, Legal Affairs Division: Law Concerning Amendment to the Gemeindeordnung for Land Hesse, June 20, 1950, HICOG Papers.

17. Ebel and Emrich, *Hessische Gemeindeordnung*. See also Gillen, *State and Local Government in West Germany*, and Wells, "Local Government" and "State Government," in Litchfield and associates, *Governing Postwar Germany*, pp. 57–83, 84–116.

Chapter 9

1. Except where otherwise cited, the sources I used to describe the denazification program are C. J. Friedrich, "Denazification, 1944–1946," in Friedrich and others, *American Experiences in Military Government* (New York, 1948), pp. 253–75; William E. Griffith, "The Denazification Program in the United States Zone of Germany" (unpublished Ph.D. dissertation, Harvard University, 1950); John H. Herz, "The Fiasco of Denazification in Germany," *Political Science Quarterly*, LXIII (December 1948), 569–94; John G. Kormann, "U.S. Denazification Policy in Germany, 1944–1950" (Mehlem: Office of U.S. High Commissioner for Germany, 1952, mimeographed); J. K. Pollock, J. H. Meisel, and H. L. Bretton, *Germany Under Occupation, Illustrative Materials and Documents*, rev. ed. (Ann Arbor, 1949); Harold Zink, "The American Denazification Program in Germany," *Journal of Central European Affairs*, VI (October 1946), 227–40; OMGUS, Monthly Report, No. 34, April 1948, Denazification (Cumulative Review), 1 April 1947–30 April 1948; and *Germany, 1947–1949*.

2. OMG, Marburg, to OMGUS: Weekly Intelligence Report, March 23, 1946, HICOG Papers; Griffith, p. 105, states, "In general . . . Law No. 8 threw the denazification program into a state of confusion, uncertainty and flooding with work from which it never really recovered."

3. OMGUS, Monthly Report, No. 9, April 20, 1946, Denazification and Public Safety, table 1, p. 8; OMG, Marburg, to OMGH: Weekly Denazification Report, December 7, 1945; OMG, Marburg, to OMGH: Information Report No. 360—Political. Denazification or Renazification in LK-SK Marburg, December 14, 1948, OMGUS Papers.

4. OMGUS, ICD, AMZON Views Its Civil Service, [Number] 3, Prestige Value of Government Work, Opinion Surveys Report No. 164, April 2, 1949, OMGUS Papers. See also Arnold Brecht, "Personnel Management," in Litchfield and associates, *Governing Postwar Germany*, pp. 263–93, for a discussion of the "vested rights" German civil servants enjoy and demand.

5. Landrat to Oberpräsident, Kassel, June 29, 1945, Landkreis Marburg Papers.

6. Interviews with two former Landkreis political committee members, June 15, 1954, and May 21, 1954; letter from former political committee member, September 13, 1958, in possession of author.

7. Interview with subject, June 5, 1954; letters, September 16 and October 13, 1958, in possession of author.

8. Oberbürgermeister, Aktenvermerk, November 9, 1945, Stadtkreis Marburg Papers.

9. Interviews with two of the removed officials who worked in the tax office, June 4 and June 6, 1954; letters, September 16 and October 13, 1958, in possession of author. Both men gave essentially the same account.

10. OMGUS, Monthly Report, No. 3, October 20, 1945, Trade and Commerce, p. 1.

11. OMGUS, Monthly Report, No. 7, February 20, 1946, Manpower, Trade Unions and Working Conditions, p. 2; No. 20, February 1947, Manpower, Trade Unions and Working Conditions (Cumulative Review), 8 May 1945–28 February 1947, p. 3; Landrat to CIC, Marburg, May 18, 1946, Landkreis Marburg Papers.

12. There were, of course, many other ways to acquire cigarettes and other items from American soldiers. Germans traded their cameras, their jewelry, alcohol, and other things directly to soldiers or intermediaries for post-exchange commodities. Black-market prices in 1945 ranged from RM 50 to 150 for twenty cigarettes, and RM 700 to 1,200 for a pound of coffee. In 1947 they ranged from RM 90 to 120 for twenty cigarettes, RM 20,000 to 50,000 for a Leica camera, RM 30 to 35 for a bar of soap, and RM 150 to 300 for an American dollar bill. OMGUS, Monthly Report, No. 2, September 20, 1945, Trade and Commerce, p. 6; No. 27, September 1947, Trade and Commerce, August–September 1947, p. 10. The lowest and highest monthly salaries on April 1, 1948, were: for officials (Beamte), RM 137.58 and 1,164.92; for employees (Angestellte), RM 89.09 and 886.68. Statistisches Jahrbuch für die Bundesrepublik Deutschland, 1952, pp. 444–45.

13. Arbeitsamt to SPA, June 12, 1945, Stadtkreis Marburg Papers; Paul Günther to author, September 30, 1958, said: "Important and influential officials during the Nazi regime who were dismissed by the occupation forces and then ordered to work in minor positions or to do physical labor obtained statements from reputable doctors that they were incapable of this form of labor." Günther was a military government employee from 1945 to 1949.

14. Ludwig Mütze to Mr. Bernard, June 19, 1945, Mütze Papers; Hermann Bauer to Herrn Knoll, August 10, 1945, Bauer Papers; SPA, Gründe des Anwachsens der Abneigung gegen die amerikanische Militär-Regierung (Streng Geheim), November 7, 1945, Stadtkreis Marburg Papers.

15. Thesen zur "Entnazifizierung," October 25, 1945, Stadtkreis Marburg Papers. The SPA endorsed the theses on November 9 and resolved to forward them to German and American higher authorities. SPA, Minutes, November 9, 1945.

16. See Gabriel A. Almond and Wolfgang H. Kraus, "The Social Composition of the German Resistance," in Gabriel A. Almond, ed., The Struggle for Democracy in Germany, pp. 64–107, for a discussion of the conservative opposition to Hitler.

17. Hans Frese to Erich Kroll, April 30, 1945, Stadtkreis Marburg Papers. Frese admitted to me that he used "severe tactics" in gathering his information. He said the SPA finally had him removed from his position chiefly because he was too "active" (rührig). Hans Frese, interview, July 3, 1954. Although Mr. Frese does not consider himself to be a radical (letter to author, October 7, 1958), his independent political and social views place him considerably to the left on the Marburg political continuum.

18. Interview with subject, Marburg, Germany, June 12, 1954.

19. SPA, Gründe des Anwachsens der Abneigung gegen die amerikanische Militär-Regierung (Streng Geheim), November 7, 1945, Stadtkreis Marburg Papers.

Chapter 10

1. OMGUS, Monthly Report, No. 6, January 20, 1946, Denazification and Public Safety, p. 1.

2. Pollock, Meisel, and Bretton, *Germany Under Occupation*, pp. 173-74. Of the 13,098,100 registrants, 2,475,400 had been amnestied without trials and 310,900 had been amnestied as result of trials.

3. OMGH, Public Safety, OMGUS Denazification Field Inspection Unit, to OMGH: OMGUS Field Inspection Report (revised), with enclosure: Status of Denazification in SK and LK Marburg, March 24, 1948, OMGUS Papers. The total number of registrants for Marburg was 99,259. Of these, 20,005 (27 per cent) and 9,541 (30 per cent) came under amnesty in the Landkreis and the Stadtkreis, respectively. In all of Marburg 17,225 (18 per cent) and 12,321 (12 per cent) came under the youth amnesty and the Christmas amnesty, respectively.

4. OMGUS, AG 383 (CA): Expediting Completion of Denazification Trials in the U.S. Zone, March 27, 1948, OMGUS Papers.

5. A complete statistical breakdown is found in OMGH, Public Safety, OMGUS Denazification Field Inspection Unit, to OMGH, March 24, 1948, OMGUS Papers. General Clay estimated that under the Law about one-fourth of the total population would be judged by the other three-fourths. Clay, *Decision in Germany*, p. 259. A Hessian State Secretary estimated, in 1947, that 28 per cent of the registrants (above eighteen years of age) were affected by the Law. Karl H. Knappstein, "Die versäumte Revolution," *Die Wandlung* (Heidelberg), II (November 1947), 666.

6. Herz, p. 570, stated that "what Military Government was expected to achieve was a revolution by legal means." See also John D. Montgomery, *Forced to Be Free, The Artificial Revolution in Germany and Japan* (Chicago: University of Chicago Press, 1957); *Marburger Presse* (guest editorial by Dr. Gumbel), September 27, 1947, p. 2; Knappstein, pp. 663-77; Griffith, pp. 560-73; and Moses Moskowitz, "The Political Re-education of the Germans: The Emergence of Parties and Politics in Württemberg-Baden (May 1945-June 1946)," *Political Science Quarterly*, LXI (December 1946), 535, quoting a "middle-aged" German that denazification "if carried to its logical conclusion, will destroy a political, economic, social and cultural system much older than Nazism."

7. We have noted the conservative character of the political leaders who formed the political committee early in the occupation, and that American officers thought Marburg was an especially conservative, nationalistic community and a "hotbed of Nazism." See also James K. Pollock's review of *The Solution of the German Problem*, by Wilhelm

Röpke, *The Journal of Modern History,* XIX (September 1948), 276, for the statement that Marburg was a "nest of reactionary nationalism."
8. *Marburger Presse,* July 23, 1946, p. 7; Hermann Bauer to author, October 14, 1958.
9. SPA, Minutes, October 5, 1945; Paul J. Pohnke, "Inflation der Gutachten und Reden," *Marburger Presse,* June 18, 1946, p. 4.
10. *Marburger Presse,* August 2, 1946, p. 7.
11. *Marburger Presse,* August 6, 1946, p. 5.
12. OMGH, ICD, to OMGH: A Summary of SPRUCHKAMMER Decisions in MARBURG, July 9, 1946. OMGH, ICD, Intelligence Branch, to OMGH, Public Safety: Marburg Spruchkammer, with enclosures, September 28, 1946, OMGUS Papers. *Marburger Presse,* August 2, 1946, p. 7; August 6, 1946, p. 5.
13. *Marburger Presse,* 1946–48, *passim,* especially May 3, 1946, p. 7, and "Vom Unmenschlichen zum Allzumenschlichen" (editorial), May 3, 1948, p. 2; Hermann Bauer, interviews, June 14 and 16, 1954.
14. In this particular case he had the support of at least two conservatives, one of whom wanted to succeed the Oberbürgermeister. Hermann Bauer to Regierungspräsident Dr. Hoch, Kassel, September 19, 1946, Bauer Papers.
15. OMG, L and S Marburg, to OMGH: Estimate of the Situation of SK and LK Marburg, December 13, 1946. OMG, Marburg, to OMGUS: Weekly Intelligence Report, September 20, 1946, HICOG Papers. Hermann Bauer to Regierungspräsident Dr. Hoch, Kassel, September 19, 1946, Bauer Papers. *Marburger Presse,* September 17, 1946, p. 1.
16. OMG, Marburg, to OMGH: Report No. 85, Denazification, August 7, 1947, HICOG Papers.
17. Interview with subject secretary, June 20, 1954.
18. OMGH, Denazification Division, to OMGH: Field Adviser's Report of Special Branch Marburg, March 21, 1947. OMGH, Inspector G. M. Gert: Annex to Denazification Field Inspection Report L and S Marburg, March 6, 1947, OMGUS Papers. For a provocative discussion of military government officers' private views on denazification see Carl Dreher, "Close-Up of Democracy," *The Virginia Quarterly Review,* XXII (Winter, 1947), 89–107. Dreher argues that American officers were a good cross section of middle-class America and that as such they felt much closer to their German counterparts, the professional and business classes, many of whom were Nazis, than to the former inmates of the concentration camps or the politically organized workers who had opposed Hitler's regime.
19. OMG, Marburg, to OMGUS: Weekly Intelligence Report, October 11, 1946, HICOG Papers.
20. OMGH, ICD, Marburg Outpost, to OMGH: The Denazification Trial of Dr. Hitzeroth, August 19, 1948, OMGUS Papers.
21. *Marburger Presse,* February 14, 1947, p. 3. OMG, Marburg, to OMGH, Attention: Chief of Intelligence Division, April 2, 1948, HICOG Papers. LDP Ortsgemeinschaft, Nordeck, to Geschäftsstelle der LDP,

Marburg, November 28, 1947, Free Democratic party, Marburg Office, Papers, 1945–48.

22. OMGH, Inspector G. M. Gert: Annex to Denazification Field Inspection Report L & S Marburg, March 6, 1947, OMGUS Papers.

23. Hans Frese, interview, July 3, 1954; Gerhard Jahn, interview, May 12, 1954, said, "Some Gemeinden lost 50 per cent of their membership in 1948." A few of the losses in membership may have been caused by the deflation that accompanied the currency reform in 1948, making it difficult to pay the party dues.

24. OMGH, ICD, Marburg Outpost, to OMGH: Quotations from the Speech by Maria Sevenich, CDU, July 1, 1946, OMGUS Papers. *Marburger Presse,* May 17, 1946, p. 6; July 26, 1948, p. 3; April 30, 1948, p. 2; August 5, 1949, p. 2. OMG, Marburg, to OMGH: Information Report No. 62—Political, February 18, 1949. OMG, Marburg, to OMGH: Information Report No. 85—Political, March 9, 1949, HICOG Papers.

25. OMG, Marburg, to OMGH: Monthly Political Activity Report, June 3, 1948. OMGH to Nationaldemokratische Partei, Marburg: Issuance of Permanent License, July 23, 1948, OMGUS Papers.

26. OMG, Marburg, to OMGH: Information Report No. 360—Political. Denazification or Renazification in LK-SK Marburg, December 14, 1948. OMGH, Denazification Division, to OMGH, Executive Officer: Office Memorandum, April 27, 1948, OMGUS Papers. Oberbürgermeister Bleek to Militärregierung, July 20, 1948; December 3, 1948, Stadtkreis Marburg Papers. Landrat to Militärregierung, July 30, 1948; August 3, 1948, Landkreis Marburg Papers. The practice of dismissing incumbents to make room for former dismissed officials became so widespread in Hessen that in October 1947 the detachments were ordered to report to higher headquarters each instance in which a capable, qualified person was dismissed to make room for a former removal. OMGH, Denazification Division: Dismissal of Politically Clear Individuals, October 28, 1947, OMGUS Papers.

Chapter 11

1. Pollock, Meisel, and Bretton, *Germany Under Occupation,* p. 17, quoting from the Potsdam Agreement; pp. 78–79, quoting from JCS 1067; p. 92, quoting from JCS 1779.

2. OMGH, Historical Report, 1948, I, Narrative, 266.

3. OMGUS, Standing Operating Procedure, HICOG Papers.

4. Daily Journal, May 29 to May 30, 1945, OMGUS Papers.

5. OMGH, ICD, Marburg Area Surveys Unit, to OMGH: Students Discussion Group, July 18, 1946, OMGUS Papers; OMGUS, Monthly Report, No. 22, April 1947, Education and Religious Affairs (Cumulative Review) 1 May 1946–30 April 1947, p. 31; OMG, Marburg, to OMGH: Periodic Report for Week Ending 2400 hours, 22 January 1947, January 23, 1947, HICOG Papers.

6. Joseph Franckenstein to author, November 20, 1954; Carl Dreher,

"Close-Up of Democracy." Every Marburger whom I interviewed said there was never an American in his social circle. Of those interviewed, some said they entertained Americans and were entertained by them, but almost invariably the Marburgers in question were higher civil servants, well-to-do businessmen, university professors, teachers, clergymen, and others of high social and economic standing. Most Marburgers believe that the language barrier was the primary reason.

7. C. J. Friedrich, "Military Government as a Step Toward Self-Rule," *The Public Opinion Quarterly*, VII (Winter, 1943), 539. See also Ernst Fraenkel, *The Dual State, A Contribution to the Theory of Dictatorship*, trans. E. A. Shills, in collaboration with Edith Loewenstein and Klaus Knorr (New York: Oxford University Press, 1941).

8. C. J. Friedrich, "Military Government and Democratization: A Central Issue of American Foreign Policy," in Friedrich and others, *American Experiences in Military Government*, p. 14; OMGUS, Monthly Report, No. 6, January 20, 1946, Political Activity, p. 3.

9. Landrat to Mayors, December 28, 1945, Landkreis Marburg Papers; *Marburger Presse*, January 18, 1946, p. 5.

10. OMGUS, Monthly Report, No. 17, December 20, 1946, German Governmental Organization and Civil Administration, p. 1. OMG, Marburg, to addressees: Monthly Political Activity Report, July 25, 1946, OMGUS Papers. OMG, Marburg, to addressees: Politische Parteien in Marburg Land- und Stadtkreis, November 19, 1945 (trans. by Landrat's staff), Landkreis Marburg Papers.

11. OMGUS, Monthly Report, No. 8, March 20, 1946, German Governmental Organization and Civil Administration, p. 1; Litchfield, "Political Objectives and Legal Bases of Occupation Government," in Litchfield and associates, *Governing Postwar Germany*, p. 10; Joseph Franckenstein to author, November 20, 1954.

12. Hermann Bauer to Schulrat Tilgner, March 30, 1945, Bauer Papers.

13. Note Mütze's letter to Bauer regarding the formation of the political committee in April 1945, in which he cautioned Bauer that the committee should not give the impression that it was a continuation of the former Democratic party. Ludwig Mütze to Hermann Bauer, April 26, 1945, Bauer Papers.

14. *Marburger Presse*, December 21, 1945, p. 1; May 17, 1946, p. 6; April 23, 1948, p. 3; OMGUS, Monthly Report, No. 12, July 20, 1946, Political Activity, pp. 9–10.

15. The sources I have used in making this summary, and subsequent party summaries, are political activity reports made by the Marburg detachment to higher headquarters; political activity reports of the party to military government, the Oberbürgermeister, and the Landrat; reports of campaign speeches printed in the *Marburger Presse*; manuscripts and documents in party offices; and interviews with party members and leaders.

16. *Der Landkreis Marburg a. d. Lahn, von 1945 bis 1952*, with a

foreword by Landrat August Eckel (Marburg: Universitäts-Buchdruck-
erei John. Aug. Koch, 1952), p. 32.

17. The Democratic People's party, n.d. A statement of party principles, found in the FDP Papers. *Marburger Presse*, December 7, 1945,
p. 1.

18. *Marburger Presse*, May 17, 1946, p. 6.

19. *Marburger Presse*, August 5, 1949, p. 2.

20. *Marburger Presse*, November 18, 1950, p. 2.

21. "Hört Ihr Leut' und lasst Euch sagen, die Politik hat die Justiz
erschlagen," *Marburger Presse*, November 10, 1950, p. 5.

22. *Marburger Presse*, August 26, 1949, p. 1; November 10, 1950, p. 5.

23. *Marburger Presse*, May 17, 1946, p. 6; OMGUS, Monthly Report,
No. 12, July 20, 1946, Political Activity, pp. 8–9.

24. Professor A. Busemann to OMG, Marburg, July 7, 1946. OMGH,
ICD, Marburg Outpost, to OMGH: Political Activity Report, September
28, 1946, OMGUS Papers.

25. "Die grössten Schwierigkeiten und Hemmnisse kommen uns jetzt
von denen, die als Emigranten in alliierten Uniformen herumlaufen."
OMGH, ICD, Marburg Outpost, to OMGH: Quotations from the Speech
by Maria Sevenich, CDU, July 1, 1946, OMGUS Papers.

26. *Marburger Presse*, November 7, 1947, p. 1. OMG, Marburg, to
OMGH: Miscellaneous, Report No. 219, November 7, 1947, HICOG
Papers.

27. A military government investigator reported that the speech was
constantly interrupted by loud applause and calls of bravo. OMG, Marburg, to OMGH: Information Report Number 85—Political, March 9,
1949, HICOG Papers.

28. Statut der Kommunistischen Partei Stadtkreis Marburg, September 20, 1945, Police Reports and Papers. The Communist party file in
the police station is among the papers left there by Erich Kroll.

29. *Marburger Presse*, May 17, 1946, p. 5.

30. NDP to OMG, Marburg: Gründung einer Kreisgruppe der Na-
tionaldemokratischen Partei, March 1, 1947. OMGUS, Monthly Report,
No. 42, December 15, 1948, Report of the Military Governor, p. 15.
OMGUS Political Affairs Branch, to Civil Administration: The Mission
of the National Democratic Party as Viewed by Its Leader, Dr. Heinrich
Leuchtgens, January 6, 1949, OMGUS Papers.

31. *Oberhessische Presse* (Marburg), April 2, 1952, p. 4.

32. Demokratisches Gemeinwohl ohne Parteipolitik, Dropsheet, dated
April 25, 1948, Landkreis Marburg Papers; *Marburger Presse*, May 9,
1949, p. 3.

33. *Oberhessische Presse* (Marburg), May 6, 1952, p. 3. The Oberbürgermeister election of 1951 had caused a minor scandal, and the party
program was an attempt to correct abuses made public at that time.

34. Landrat to Regierungspräsident, Kassel, May 4, 1952, Landkreis
Marburg Papers.

35. "Es ist eine . . . grosse Selbsttäuschung der westlichen Demokratien, zu glauben, es genüge, das öffentliche Leben in Deutschland gewissen Spielregeln zu unterwerfen, um das Volk zu demokratisieren." "Schulungsbriefe für Demokraten," *Der Ruf, Unabhängige Blätter der Jungen Generation* (Munich), II (July 15, 1947), p. 3.

36. In the local elections of 1946, the Kreistag election of 1948, and the Bundestag election of 1949, 54, 64, and 67 per cent, respectively, of the eligible voters cast their ballots in the Stadtkreis. In the Landkreis 63, 82, and 76 per cent, respectively, cast their ballots. HSL, *Hessen Wählt zum Bundestag, Das Amtliche Ergebnis der Wahl zum ersten Bundestag in Hessen am 14. August 1949*, Beiträge zur Statistik Hessens, Nr. 29, p. 17.

37. The Marburgers whom I interviewed agreed almost unanimously on this point. To quote a few: "Der Untertanengeist wirkt noch," Franz Jahn, interview, May 24, 1954; "Only a few of the better-educated people and the Communist party members know their constitutional rights. Even the employees in the police station would not know that their home cannot be searched without a warrant," Alfred Klevinghaus, interview, May 22, 1954; "Only a small minority knows the rights of Germans under the constitutions," Hermann Bauer, interview, June 22, 1954.

38. OMGUS, Monthly Report, No. 42, December 1948, Report of the Military Governor, pp. 21–22; No. 44, February 1949, Report of the Military Governor, p. 17.

39. My sources for these statements are scattered, but include observations made in frequent visits to Kreistag sessions, Kreisausschuss sessions, city council meetings, and political party meetings and rallies. They are, in part, based upon interviews with political leaders and other Marburgers and upon manuscripts that I was permitted to read in the FDP, SPD, and CDU party headquarters in Marburg. See also Richard M. Scammon, "Political Parties" and "Postwar Elections and Electoral Processes," in Litchfield and associates, *Governing Postwar Germany*, pp. 471–99, 500–533.

40. OMG, Marburg, to OMGH: Estimate of the Situation of SK and LK Marburg, December 13, 1946, HICOG Papers. OMGUS, Monthly Report, No. 30, December 1947, German Governmental Organization and Civil Administration (Cumulative Review), 1 December 1946–31 December 1947, p. 19. Samuel R. Combs, "Our Reorientation Mission," a speech delivered at the opening session of the Hesse Reorientation Training Conference, Haus Schwalbach, on Monday, January 23, 1950 (mimeographed), HICOG Papers.

41. OMGH, Historical Report, 1948, I, Narrative, 266–98.

Chapter 12

1. OMGH, Historical Report, 1948, I, Narrative, 159; OMGH, Reorientation Committee, Minutes of the First Meeting, September 16, 1948, OMGUS Papers.

2. OMGH, Historical Report, 1948, I, Narrative, 158–59.

3. OMGUS, CAD: Functions of L and S Detachments, February 16, 1948, OMGUS Papers.

4. OMGH, ICD, to OMGH, Executive Officer: Reorientation Program, December 22, 1947. OMGH, ICD, to OMGUS: Reference material on establishment of public forums, December 24, 1947, OMGUS Papers.

5. OMGUS, Office of the Control Officer: Report on Field Trip, December 1–5, 1947, December 9, 1947. OMGUS, CAD: Functions of L and S Detachments, February 16, 1948, OMGUS Papers.

6. OMGH to All L and S Personnel: Reorientation Program in L and S Offices, July 24, 1948. OMGH, Education and Cultural Relations Division, Staff Meeting Minutes, August 1, 1949, OMGUS Papers.

7. OMGH, Historical Report, 1948, I, Narrative, 286. OMGH, Quarterly Historical Report, First Quarter, 1948, 1 January–31 March, I, Narrative, 58–59, OMGUS Papers.

8. Combs, "Our Reorientation Mission," HICOG Papers. OMGH, Historical Report, 1948, I, Narrative, 288–89. HICOG, U.S. Resident Officer's Handbook (Frankfurt: HICOG, 1951, lithographed). HICOG, *The Resident Officer—HICOG's Ambassador in the Field* (Frankfurt: HICOG, Office of Public Affairs, Public Relations Division, n.d.).

9. KRO, Marburg, to OLCH: Monthly Reorientation Statistical Report, December 2, 1949, HICOG Papers. OMGH to All L and S Personnel: Reorientation Program in L and S Offices, July 24, 1948, OMGUS Papers.

10. OMG, Marburg, to OMGH: Information Report Number 200—Sociological, July 28, 1948, HICOG Papers.

11. KRO, Marburg, to OLCH: Monthly Reorientation Report, October 4, 1950, HICOG Papers.

12. "An activity which must depend morally or materially for its continuation upon Military Government or any other agency of the occupation lacks this basic element of future success." OMGH to Addressees: Reorientation Program in Liaison and Security Offices, October 18, 1948, OMGUS Papers.

13. OLCH, FOD, Bulletin, Number 14, February 14, 1950, HICOG Papers.

14. OMGH to All L and S Personnel: Reorientation Program in Liaison and Security Offices, September 3, 1948. OMGH, Reorientation Committee, Minutes of the Third Meeting, September 29, 1948. Minutes of the Seventh Meeting, October 27, 1948, OMGUS Papers. Combs, "Our Reorientation Mission," HICOG Papers.

15. HICOG, Office of Public Affairs, Reactions Analysis Staff, U.S. Zone Germans View the Kreis Resident Officer, Report Number 78, Series No. 2, May 14, 1951, HICOG Papers.

16. *Kreisblatt,* January 6, 1949, p. 1; May 5, 1949, p. 3. OMG, Marburg, to OMGH: Commendation, Landrat and Bürgermeisters, Landkreis Marburg, May 27, 1949. OMGH to Landrat Eckel, June 24, 1949,

OMGUS Papers. KRO, Marburg, to OLCH: Monthly Reorientation Statistical Report, May 6, 1950, HICOG Papers.

17. OMGH, Historical Report, 1948, I, Narrative, 318.

18. KRO, Marburg, to OLCH: Monthly Reorientation Statistical Report, January 4, 1950, HICOG Papers.

19. *Marburger Presse*, August 3, 1950, p. 3; KRO, Marburg, to OLCH, Monthly Reorientation Statistical Reports, October 1949 to April 1951, *passim*, HICOG Papers.

20. KRO, Marburg, to OLCH, Monthly Reorientation Statistical Reports, October 1949 to April 1951, *passim*, HICOG Papers.

21. Landrat to Militärregierung: Town-Hall meetings in LK Marburg, May 25, 1949, OMGUS Papers. *Oberhessische Presse* (Marburg), July 13, 1951, p. 3; July 18, 1951, p. 4; August 3, 1951, p. 8; August 11, 1951, p. 7; August 13, 1951, p. 5 (editorial).

22. OMGH, Historical Report, 1948, I, Narrative, 298.

23. Interview, June 4, 1954, Marburg, Germany.

24. HICOG, Office of Public Affairs, Reactions Analysis Staff, Germans View the U.S. Reorientation Program, Report Number 11, Series 2, March 30, 1950. U.S. Zone Germans View the Kreis Resident Officer, Report Number 78, Series 2, May 14, 1951, HICOG Papers.

25. KRO, Marburg, to OLCH: Monthly Reorientation Statistical Report, December 2, 1949, HICOG Papers. Excerpts from the Report of Dr. Karl Loewenstein, Visiting Expert, August and September, 1949 (typewritten), OMGUS Papers. Interviews, June 4, 1954; June 7, 1954; June 12, 1954, Marburg, Germany.

26. Interviews, June 4, 1954; May 21, 1954, Marburg, Germany.

27. Ludwig Mütze to Hermann Bauer, July 5 and July 20, 1951. KRO, Marburg, to OLCH: Monthly Reorientation Statistical Report, May 6, 1950. KRO, Marburg, to OLCH: Special Report: New FDP Attitude Towards Reorientation Program, July 9, 1950. KRO, Marburg, to OLCH: Intelligence Report, No. 16: Attitude Toward the HICOG Reorientation Program, May 16, 1950; Interview, June 15, 1954, Marburg, Germany.

28. Landrat to Abteilung I, June 2, 1950, Landkreis Marburg Papers. OMG, Marburg, to OMGH: Reorientation Report Marburg District, May 2, 1949, OMGUS Papers.

29. Deutscher Städtetag to Magistrat, Marburg and others: Entsendung von Vertretern der Gemeinde zu den Sitzungen des öffentlichen Forums, September 23, 1949. Verwaltung und Forum—Aus einem Bericht vom 9. Mai 1949 des Landrats des Kreises Usingen an den Hessischen Minister des Innern (mimeographed), Stadtkreis Marburg Papers. Der Hessische Ministerpräsident to Francis E. Sheehan, Acting Director, OMGH, March 16, 1949, with enclosed letter from Minister of Interior Zinnkann to Ministerpräsident Stock: Arbeitsgemeinschaft der Foren Hessens, Giessen, February 16, 1949, OMGUS Papers. *Marburger Presse,* April 13, 1949, p. 1.

30. KRO, Marburg, to OLCH: Monthly Reorientation Statistical

Report, March 4, 1950, HICOG Papers. OMGH, Chief, L and S Control Division, to Director, OMGH: Evaluation of the Reorientation Program, August 3, 1949, OMGUS Papers.
31. *Oberhessische Presse* (Marburg), January 16, 1954, p. 6.

Chapter 13

1. See John D. Montgomery, *Forced to Be Free: The Artificial Revolution in Germany and Japan* (Chicago: University of Chicago Press, 1957).
2. Montgomery, *Forced to Be Free*, pp. 191–99.
3. See especially Harold Zink, *The United States in Germany*, pp. 10–18, 66–85, for a discussion of military government personnel.
4. *Der Landkreis Marburg a. d. Lahn*, p. 32. "Erst ein 1947 vom hessischen Landtag beschlossenes Gesetz und die Währungsreform brachten eine gewisse Ordnung und einen Schutz für den redlichen Gewerbetreibenden. Dem begonnenen Aufbau folgte durch die Proklamierung der uneingeschränkten Gewerbefreiheit im Jahre 1948 durch die amerikanische Besatzungsmacht ein erheblicher Rückfall. Durch zähes Bemühen der zuständigen gesetzgebenden Körperschaften und durch umfangreiche Kleinarbeit der Verwaltungsbehörden wird das Gewerberecht planmässig wieder in geordnete Bahnen gelenkt. . . . Die ungewöhnliche Zunahme von Gewerbebetrieben hat zu einer Uebersetzung in fast allen Gewerbezweigen und zu Absatzschwierigkeiten geführt."
5. "In der Stadt mag mancher untergehen und vergessen werden; hier auf dem Lande vergisst man nicht." Bürgermeister, Wetter, to Landrat, March 25, 1946, Landkreis Marburg Papers.

Bibliographical Note

The American and German manuscript sources for the study of military government at the local level are both extensive and scattered. The major sources in the English language are in the Kansas City Army Records Center, the location of the retired military government files, and in the State Department files, which were in the Office of the United States High Commissioner for Germany at Mehlem in 1954.

The military government manuscript materials in Kansas City contain correspondence, reports, files, and miscellaneous papers of detachments, liaison and security offices, resident offices, Land headquarters, and the Office of Military Government for Germany. Most of the papers are for the years 1945 through 1949. Their use presents certain difficulties. The files are not catalogued, except for a list of file-folder titles. The records are, in fact, collections of file folders taken from the office files of military government units in Germany and placed in army footlockers. Furthermore, local detachment records were destroyed, except for certain materials that were placed in the lockers containing Land headquarters materials.

The State Department files contain records for the period 1949 through 1953, except for activities that were continuous from military to civilian control. For those activities military government files are also found in the State Department records. There are reports, correspondence, and miscellanea of the Land Commissioners' Offices and the Office of the High Commissioner for Germany.

Both the Army and the State Department manuscripts contain classified materials that are not open to the private researcher. They include the denazification questionnaires as well as reports and correspondence that bear classifications of confidential or higher. As declassification appears impossible in the near future—the originating agencies no longer exist—the private researcher must be accompanied by a staff member of the agencies involved. He removes the classified materials from the files before they are turned over to the researcher. Although the agencies provide most efficient and adequate assistance, the procedure itself presents uncommon difficulties.

For Marburg there is an excellent collection of correspondence, troop-incident reports, and papers which E. Y. Hartshorne collected while he was University Officer in Marburg in 1945 and 1946. The papers were in the Marburg America House when I used them.

The German-language manuscript sources for the study of Marburg are found in the files of the Landkreis administration, the Stadtkreis administration, the police department, the three major political party offices in Marburg, and in the possession of certain private individuals who permitted me to use their papers.

The Landkreis and Stadtkreis papers cover the entire period of the occupation and include reports, correspondence, and files relating to the municipal and Landkreis administrations and military government, political parties, finance, military government requisitions, property control, denazification, elections, refugees, housing, industry, the tobacco factory, the Allendorf industries, and other topics. The Stadtkreis papers also contain the minutes and the files of the Staatspolitischer Ausschuss and the papers collected by the Sonderabteilung U of the police department.

The police department manuscripts, for the years 1945–52, include reports and correspondence relating to military government liaison activities, reports on police activities during the occupation, police registration lists, a complete file on the organization, structure, and early activities of the Marburg Communist party (left there by the Communist police chief during 1945 and 1946), and miscellaneous papers.

The political party offices of the Social Democratic, Free Democratic, and Christian Democratic parties have collections of correspondence, political activity reports, party programs, newspaper clippings, drop sheets, reports of meetings, membership lists, and many other papers.

The personal papers of Hermann Bauer are an excellent source. Bauer was editor of the *Marburger Presse,* the third military government–licensed newspaper in Germany, which began publication on September 1, 1945. He was a member of the political committee, a charter member of the Liberal Democratic party, a city councilman, and a denazification tribunal official. His papers include materials relating to all his activities, plus many other things he collected as editor of the newspaper.

The personal papers of Ludwig Mütze and Eugen Siebecke are less extensive, but no less valuable. Mütze was a political committee member and its chairman for a short time. As *Kreisschulrat* he collected manuscript materials on denazification, school reform, and education. He was a Liberal Democratic party member and a city councilman. Siebecke was the first Oberbürgermeister of Marburg after the capitulation and remained in that office until he was arrested for falsification of his denazification questionnaire early in 1946. His papers are especially useful for 1945 and early 1946. Their use is somewhat difficult, however, because Siebecke has collected virtually reams of evidence, most of it since 1949, to prove his contention that military government officers framed him because he knew too much about American corruption in Marburg.

Interviews and correspondence with Germans and Americans who participated in the occupation are helpful. Although the information gathered this way is often unreliable, there appears to be sufficient record material available to test the accuracy of statements made in interviews and letters. In part to guard against unreliable information, the procedure adopted for this study was not to interview any subject until there was sufficient record material at hand to prepare in advance the questions that would be asked of the subject. The interviews did provide background information and helped to set the tone for a better understanding of issues and incidents. Finding the people who participated in military government is facilitated by use of German police registration lists and by the cooperation of the Army Personnel Records Center in St. Louis, Missouri. The latter supplied last known addresses of military personnel—active and discharged—whom I wanted to contact.

Official publications that are the source for documents, statistics, descriptive summaries, and the like are *Germany, 1947–1949: The Story in Documents* (Washington, 1950) and *Occupation of Germany: Policy and Progress, 1945–1946* (Washington, 1947), both prepared by the Office of Public Affairs, U.S. Department of State; *Beiträge zur Statistik Hessens* (Wiesbaden, 1948–52), "Fünf Jahre Land Hessen 1945/46–1949/50" (Wiesbaden, 1951), *Hessische Beiträge zur Schulreform* (Wiesbaden, 1951), prepared and published by the Hessisches Statistisches Landesamt. Especially useful for Marburg are the weekly *Kreisblatt für den Landkreis Marburg an der Lahn* (Marburg, 1946–1953) and the summary *Der Landkreis Marburg a. d. Lahn, von 1945 bis 1952* (Marburg, 1952) prepared and published by the Landkreis administration.

Of the numerous U.S. Army, Office of Military Government for Germany, and Office of the U.S. High Commissioner for Germany reports and summaries published, the most complete and useful are the series of *Monthly Reports of the Military Governor* (Berlin, 1945–49) and the High Commissioner's *Report on Germany* [a quarterly] (Frankfurt and Mehlem, 1949–52). Both are general summaries, but include sections prepared by the divisions of military government and the High Commission describing their current activities and occasionally providing a historical sketch of their activities. The foregoing reports are supplemented by the more journalistic *Weekly Information Bulletin* (Frankfurt, 1945–49) published by the Office of Military Government for Germany and the *Information Bulletin, Monthly Magazine of the Office of the U.S. High Commissioner for Germany* (Frankfurt and Mehlem, 1949–53). The two agencies, and some of their divisions and field offices, also published numerous special reports, studies, and histories, some of which are printed but most of which are lithographed or mimeographed. There are files of these in the manuscript materials consulted for this study.

The most complete and recent accounts of the occupation are Eugene Davidson, *The Death and Life of Germany* (New York, 1959) and Harold Zink, *The United States in Germany, 1944–1955* (Princeton, 1957). Davidson's is chronological, Zink's topical. Earlier accounts are Julian Bach's very readable *America's Germany* (New York, 1946) and Harold Zink, *American Military Government in Germany* (New York, 1947), which is not superseded by his more recent book. Much more analytical than the other earlier accounts is Wolfgang Friedmann, *The Allied Military Government of Germany* (London, 1947). Hajo Holborn, *American Military Government* (Washington, 1947) is an excellent description of the organization and policy of American military government before 1947. John D. Montgomery, *Forced to Be Free* (Chicago, 1957) is a significant recent analysis of the "artificial" revolutionary nature of the occupation in Germany.

Important for their descriptions, but more for their essays and interpretive articles on the occupation by experts and participants, are Gabriel A. Almond, ed., *The Struggle for Democracy in Germany* (Chapel Hill, 1949); Carl J. Friedrich and others, *American Experiences in Military Government in World War II* (New York, 1948); Edward H. Litchfield and associates, *Governing Postwar Germany* (Ithaca, 1953); Hans J. Morgenthau, ed., *Germany and the Future of Europe* (Chicago, 1951); James K. Pollock *et al.*, *Germany in Power and Eclipse* (New York, 1952); and Arthur Settel, ed., *This Is Germany* (New York, 1950).

Especially noteworthy for their accounts or analysis of specific phases of the occupation are Karl Jaspers, *Die Schuldfrage* (Heidelberg, 1946), on the question of collective guilt; Louis Lochner, *Tycoons and Tyrant* (Chicago, 1954), on the role of German industry; Milton Mayer, *They Thought They Were Free* (Chicago, 1955), on the little Nazis, their attitude toward Nazism and their lot under the occupation; David Rodnick, *Postwar Germans* (New Haven, 1948), a study of the German character; B. U. Ratchford and William A. Ross, *Berlin Reparations Assignment* (Chapel Hill, 1947), a study of the reparations problem by two participants; and John L. Snell, *Wartime Origins of the East-West Dilemma over Germany* (New Orleans, 1959), a study emphasizing postponement as the major feature of Allied policy toward Germany.

Among the many eye-witness accounts by participants, journalists, and other observers, Lucius D. Clay, *Decision in Germany* (Garden City, 1950) and *Germany and the Fight for Freedom* (Cambridge, 1950) are important sources as well as descriptions. Drew Middleton, *The Struggle for Germany* (Indianapolis, 1949), emphasizes Germany's importance to the cold war. James P. Warburg, *Germany—Bridge or Battleground* (New York, 1946) and *Germany, Key to Peace* (Cambridge, 1953) argue for a policy leading to a stronger German economy. Lewis H. Brown, *A Report on Germany* (New York, 1947), and Russell Hill, *Struggle for Germany* (New York, 1947), in their own way argue for a change in American policy to permit more rapid recovery. Extremely critical of the occupation and its effects are Montgomery Belgion, *Victor's Justice* (Hinsdale, Illinois, 1949); Delbert Clark, *Again the Goose Step* (Indianapolis, 1949); Victor Gollanz, *In Darkest Germany* (Hinsdale, 1947); Hans Habe [pseud.], *Our Love Affair with Germany* (New York, 1953); Marshall Knappen, *And Call It Peace* (Chicago, 1947); Norbert Muhlen, *The Return of Germany* (Chicago, 1953); Hans Rümelin, ed., *So Lebten Wir* (Willsbach, Württemberg, 1947); Gustav Stolper, *German Realities* (New York, 1948); and Freda Utley, *The High Cost of Vengeance* (Chicago, 1949).

The student who would understand the occupation must look to the periodical literature, which contains some of the only published materials on certain phases of the occupation. A few of the articles that seem to be essential are F. R. Allemann, "Das Deutsche Parteisystem, Eine Politische Analyse," *Der Monat* (Munich), V

(January 1953), 365-88; Ernest Anspach, "The Nemesis of Creativity, Observations on Our Occupation of Germany," *Social Research*, XIX (December 1952), 403-29; Seymour Bolton, "Military Government and the German Political Parties," *The Annals*, CCLXVII (January 1950), 55-67; "Denazification," with a foreword by Alvin Johnson, trans. by Beate Salz, *Social Research*, XIV (March 1947), 59-74; Walter Dorn, "Debate Over American Occupation Policy in Germany in 1944-1945," *Political Science Quarterly*, LXXII (December 1957), 481-501; Carl Dreher, "Close-Up of Democracy," *The Virginia Quarterly Review*, XXIII (Winter, 1947), 89-107; Lewis J. Edinger, "Post-Totalitarian Leadership: Elites in the German Federal Republic," *The American Political Science Review*, LIV (March 1960), 58-82; Carl J. Friedrich, "Military Government as a Step Toward Self-Rule," *The Public Opinion Quarterly*, VII (Winter, 1943), 527-41; John H. Herz, "The Fiasco of Denazification in Germany," *Political Science Quarterly*, LXIII (December 1948), 569-94; Karl H. Knappstein, "Die versäumte Revolution," *Die Wandlung* (Heidelberg), II (November 1947), 663-77; Donald F. Lach, "What *They* Would Do about Germany," *The Journal of Modern History*, XVII (September 1945), 227-43; Hans Meyerhoff, "Parties and Classes in Postwar Germany," *The South Atlantic Quarterly*, XLVI (January 1947), 12-26; Moses Moskowitz, "The Political Re-education of the Germans: The Emergence of Parties and Politics in Württemberg-Baden (May 1945-June 1946)," *Political Science Quarterly*, LXI (December 1946), 535-61; Joseph F. Napoli, "Denazification from an American's Viewpoint," *The Annals*, CCLXIV (July 1949), 115-23; Hans Steinmetz, "The Problems of the Landrat: A Study of County Government in the U.S. Zone of Germany," trans. and annotated by Roger H. Wells, *The Journal of Politics*, XI (May 1949), 318-34; and "Die versäumte Evolution," *Der Ruf* (Munich), II (January 15, 1947), 1-2.

Index

Index

Aachen, 140
Absenteeism, 146
Adult education committee, 189
Air raids, 28–29
Allendorf, 16, 21, 177, 189, 211
Allendorf munitions industry, 28, 43–44, 120–25, 128, 130, 206
America House, 183, 194, 206, 211
American policy: assumptions, 208–9; changes, 3–4, 118–19, 129–30, 205–6; contradictions, 207–10; creates liberal and moderate dilemma, 8; German reaction to, 211–12; motivated by passion for democracy, 3
Amnesties, 154
Amöneburger Basin, 20
Anti-Nazis, 67, 81, 90
Anti-Semitism, 23, 177
Antifas, 52–53, 102–3
Apathy, 170–71, 182
Artificial revolution, 5, 11, 201
Arrests, 85; MG program of, 47–49; of Oberbürgermeister, 64, 112, 149
Atlantic Charter, 67
Attitude of Germans, 51, 132; anti-American, 1-2; reports and surveys on, 66, 75–84, 86–87
Aufsichtsbehörden, 22
Autobahn, serving Marburg, 21

Bach, Julian, quoted, 107
Barter economy, 146–47
Bauer, Herman, 43, 68, 95; and political committee, 90–91; collects Nazi literature, 61; critique of denazification tribunals, 158, 159–61; differences with Mütze, 161; early political activity, 172; editor of *Marburger Presse*, 50; favors reorientation, 195; loses *Marburger Presse*, 161; named Communist by MG, 160; no discharge from *Volkssturm*, 51–52; on destruction of Allendorf industries, 130; on fraternization, 50; on leftists in civil administration, 108; on plans for revolution, 53; quoted on denazification, 148; quoted on Oberbürgermeister's view of political committee, 103–4; report on early occupation, 79–80, 85; resigns from denazification tribunal, 160; resigns from FDP, 91, 161
Becker, Howard, quoted, 30
Behringwerke, 119–20
Berlin blockade, 130
Bi-Zone, 3
Black market, 36, 85, 203; and denazified persons, 146–47
Bleek, Karl T., 43, 127, 137. *See also* Oberbürgermeister
Bloc of Expellees and Victims of Injustice (BHE), 179
Bürgermeister, position description, 22
Bürgerrat, 99, 112–13
Byrnes, James F., 117–18, 131

Parent-Teacher Association, 189, 198

Patton, George S., 109, 212

Persilscheine, 157

Personnel of military government: characteristics of, 202; experience and training, 7–8, 37–41; lack of, 198; personal impact, 210; problems, 203–4; replacements, 39; turnover, 8, 64–65, 80, 86, 159

Police chief, 48, 69, 96, 150

Police Department, 150; Communists in, 107; leftists dominate, 92; organization, 48; special investigation section, 75, 88, 96–98

Political activity: apathy, 170–71, 182; detachment's use of reports, 42–43; reports to civil agencies, 136–37

Political committee, 67, 69, 71, 74, 80–112 *passim*; conflicts with MG, 104–5; conservative nature, 94–95; duties and functions, 98–100; leftist orientation, 91–92; origins, 88–91; political affiliation of members, 80–81, 89–90, 91, 94, 99–100; refugee policy, 105–6; report on early occupation, 80–84; views on denazification, 147–48

Political parties, 22–24, 49, 206; agents of democratization, 171; as special interest groups, 204–5; denazification and, 154, 155–57, 161–63; grass-roots activity encouraged, 169; oppose MG policies, 180–81; origins, 172; reorientation and, 195; reports to MG, 42, 171; require MG licenses, 170

Population, growth and density, 26–27, 29

Potsdam Agreement, 2, 56, 59, 105, 117

Press conferences, 211

Presumptive guilt, 203, 209

Prisoners of war, 51–52, 77–78, 83

Privileges of occupation forces, 36, 84, 202–3

Property control, 62, 119, 121

Proportional representation, 22, 100

Public forums, 134, 189, 192–93, 199

Public prosecutors, 154, 155, 157

Radio information programs, 211

Reconstruction, efforts at, 57–59, 99

Refugees, 36, 43, 56; affected by industrial dismantlement, 124, 127–28; assimilation, 29, 30; in Marburg, 26, 29; political committee policies, 105–6; political parties and, 162, 174, 175, 179

Regierungspräsident, 22

Reichstag elections, 23

Reorientation, 185–99; American pressure for, 34, 189–92; assumptions of policy, 209; deindustrialization and, 131; effects of, 198–99, 211, 212; KRO and, 183, 197–98; need for, 185–86; purposes, 132, 188, 195; reaction to, 193–99; relation to denazification, 207. *See also* Democratization; Public forums; Town hall meetings

Resident Office/Officer: and reorientation, 34, 183, 189, 191–92, 197–98; duties and functions, 36–37, 189; HICOG opinion survey on influence of, 191; report on German-American club, 194

Requisitions, 51, 54–57, 202; criticisms of, 56–57; Mütze on, 76–77; political committee on, 82–83, 98–99

Revised Level of Industry Plan, 117–18, 131–32

Rubble clearance, 33, 47, 58

School reform, *see* Educational reform

Security measures, 47–54, 83

Shop-steward elections, 85

Siebecke, Eugen: arrested, 64n, 112; attitude toward political committee, 90; criticizes investigators, 108; differences with MG, 106–7; dismisses Frese and Sonderabteilung U, 97; early political activity, 172; SPD, 173. *See also* Oberbürgermeister

Soap-box derbies, 189

Social Democratic party, Social Democrats, 6; advocates industrialization,